Dr. S. Fritz Forkel
د. سليمان فريتس فوركل
ד״ר שלמה פריץ פורקל
Skén:nen Rón:nis

D1719138

The Civilization of the American Indian Series

SACRED LANGUAGE

SACRED LANGUAGE

THE NATURE OF SUPERNATURAL DISCOURSE IN LAKOTA

By **William K. Powers**

University of Oklahoma Press : Norman

By William K. Powers

Indians of the Northern Plains (New York, 1969)
Indians of the Southern Plains (New York, 1971)
Oglala Religion (Lincoln, Nebr., 1977)
Yuwipi: Vision and Experience in Oglala Ritual (Lincoln, Nebr., 1982)
Sacred Language: The Nature of Supernatural Discourse in Lakota (Norman, 1986)

Library of Congress Cataloging-in-Publication Data
Powers, William K.
  Sacred language.

  (The Civilization of the American Indian series ; #179)
  Bibliography: p. 233
  Includes index.
  1. Dakota language—Religious aspects.   2. Lakota
dialect.   3. Sacred songs.   4. Dakota Indians—Religion and
mythology.   I. Title.   II. Series: Civilization of the
American Indian series ; v. 179.
E99.D1P83   1986   497'.5   86—40079
ISBN: 0–8061–2009–6 (cloth)
ISBN: 0–8061–2458–x (paper)

6   7   8   9   10   11   12   13   14   15   16   17   18

To Marla

CONTENTS

ILLUSTRATIONS

TABLES

PREFACE

This book of essays on Lakota religion was completed at Pine Ridge, South Dakota, during the summer of 1982. I am particularly thankful to a number of people who made my stay there pleasurable and productive.

First, to my wife, Dr. Marla N. Powers, who read all of the manuscript and commented critically, much to the benefit of the finished work. Let me hastily add, however, that, in addition to her academic contributions, she gave me a spiritual and moral uplifting in the process that seems to me to be much more important. As always, she has been my collaborator in every sense of the word, and this work is dedicated to her.

To my adopted family, Mrs. Zona Fills the Pipe, Mr. and Mrs. Clarence and Sadie Janis, Mr. and Mrs. Pugh Youngman, and all the nephews, nieces, and *takoja*, I offer my sincerest thanks for their hospitality, warmth, and kindness. In addition, all of them are incomparable depositories of Lakota wisdom, and I thank them for sharing it with me.

Much of the substantive material was gleaned from a long-term relationship with the late Mr. and Mrs. George Plenty Wolf; Mr. and Mrs. William Horn Cloud; the late Mr. Owen Brings; Mr. and Mrs. Oliver Red Cloud; the late Mr. and Mrs. Charles Red Cloud; the late Mr. Edgar Red Cloud; Mr. and Mrs. Melvin Red Cloud; Mrs. Celeste Brings, and all of the people from the Red Cloud Community. I take full responsibility for any errors as well as any interpretations that may not correspond to Lakota thought, intentionally, or unintentionally.

Much of the time at Pine Ridge in 1982, unlike other years, was spent completing this book. The day-to-day tasks were accomplished easier through accommodations made available by the Jesuits at Holy Rosary Mission. I would like to thank personally Eugene Zimmerman, S.J., Superior, Holy Rosary Mission; E. J. Kurth, S.J., President of the Heritage Center and of the Red Cloud Indian School; and Leonard Fencl, S.J., for a quick but badly needed lesson in Latin.

I would like to offer my very special thanks to Brother C. M. Simon, S.J., who, in addition to being Curator of the Red Cloud Indian Art Show and Director of the Heritage Center, provided me with everything from rare books to rare moments. Without his constant help the completion of this book would have been seriously delayed. Without his sense of humor the tedium of writing might have been less bearable.

Finally, my thanks to the American Philosophical Society and the Rutgers Research Council, for support in 1966, 1967, and 1971; and to the Rutgers Research Council for support in 1981. Some of the initial work on song translation has been made possible by a grant from the National Endowment for the Humanities, which graciously funded my work on Oglala music and dance during 1980–82 and 1983.

WILLIAM K. POWERS

Holy Rosary Mission
Pine Ridge, South Dakota

SACRED LANGUAGE

INTRODUCTION

ANY study of sacred language must acknowledge previous research on the various special languages or argots spoken around the world. In particular, the field of sociolinguistics has opened our eyes to the relationships among language, speech, and social structure. The best explanation of the role of these special languages in the larger context of language and culture remains, in my opinion, Dell Hymes's seminal work on the ethnography of speaking. His insights into the nature and function of speech communities are integral to an understanding of the subject at hand.[1]

My major concern in this book is to isolate a body of speech and song texts that are used by a limited number of Lakota-speakers,[2] namely, medicine men and women, as a means of addressing supernatural beings and powers that inhabit and control the Lakota universe. Sacred language is also used to communicate philosophical ideas about the creation of the world, the nature of life and death, and the hereafter among medicine men. As such, medicine men form a speech community, or, rather, two: one with their fellow medicine men and the other with those supernatural beings and powers who serve as their spiritual helpers in time of need, generating, as we shall see, two different types of sacred language. Supernaturals in the context of this book are a category of deceased human beings, animals, birds, and, as is pointed out in several of the chapters, certain inanimate objects, such as stones, all of which have knowledge about life, death, sickness, and health. They also have the power to come to the aid of common people during times of duress and hardship and are capable of curing illnesses and diseases through the inter-cession of a medicine man.

These supernaturals may be propitiated by both common people and medicine men and women through the proper prayers and songs, but all rituals must be supervised by medi-cine men. Medicine men are "chosen," one might say, as a re-sult of recurring encounters with sickness, depression, mel-ancholy, or general malaise which most of them begin to experience in their adolescence.[3] Once propitiated, it is be-lieved that supernaturals travel from their homes in the West to the actual place in which the ritual is being held and in-struct the medicine man about that for which he seeks help.

These supernaturals are frequently encountered out of the ritual context, at which time they are generically regarded as "ghosts." However, in ritual context—on the Vision Quest, in the Sweat Lodge, during the Sun Dance, and in various other rituals—they may actually make their presence known to in-dividuals by appealing to their sensory modalities. For ex-ample, the supernaturals may be seen by common people, and they are *always* seen by medicine men even in the darkness of the Sweat Lodge and the Yuwipi. Their voices may be heard in the stillness of the Vision Quest, when even the smallest insects seem to be bellowing their mysteries into the ears of the supplicant. In the close confines of the Sweat Lodge or the Yuwipi they warn of their presence through the aroma of sage, as if a breeze has just entered the crowded ritual space carrying its sacred fragrance. Some supernaturals can be felt, touching the patient softly on the part of the body that is expe-riencing pain.

Supernaturals also comprise a pantheon of named per-sonae who are addressed in both prayer and song and are the subjects of mythologies related to the creation of the Lakota universe and humankind. These supernaturals are most fre-quently the subjects of philosophical discussions between medicine men or between medicine men and their followers. Through this kind of discourse between medicine men, com-mon people, and the supernaturals themselves, sacred lan-guage is born. In Lakota religion it is believed that the supernaturals talk to the medicine men and common people just as common people talk to them, thus creating an ongoing theosophical dialogue. In the process sacred language is created out of performance, sometimes public and sometimes private, and is always perceived to be mysterious, unfathomable, indecipherable, and unintelligible to the common people.[4]

I have chosen as the title of this book *Sacred Language* because it is the best translation of the Lakota *wakaniye* (from *wakan* 'sacred' and *iye* 'to speak'). Chapter 1, "Incomprehensible Terms," deals with the manner in which sacred language has been characterized by other investigators, first at a more general level and then as it applies to the Lakota. I broach the problem that has been posed by early ethnographers, namely, the peculiar, incomprehensible nature of sacred language and the exclusivity that serves as one of its diagnostic features. I am also concerned with the process whereby sacred language comes into being and the relationship between sacred and profane discourse, which is differentiated only through contextualization. I also examine the relationship between persistent forms of traditional Lakota culture and Lakota sacred language. For the Lakota sacred language, like other aspects of native language, is not static or archaic. Although many languages of the world employ archaisms for the purposes of underscoring the inexplicability of their gods, the Lakota do not.[5] Moreover, sacred language is strongly marked for its contemporaneity and the fact that it changes readily.

It is perhaps this vitality of Lakota sacred language that makes it so interesting, continuously being created in the Vision Quest and in philosophical discourse between medicine men and adepts. Older Lakota continue to be consulted to bestow names on newly introduced technologies and institutions that have encroached on the traditional way of life. Hence a new political campaign that promised people new houses, jobs, and social welfare was named *piya wiconi* 'rebirth' (to make life over), and a department of the tribal administration was named *wicayutecakiyapi* 'rehabilitation' (they make them new).

The creation of language, both sacred and secular, is an

ongoing process with the Lakota; they love their language and love to analyze it, play games with it, remember it, and create it. In my own studies time after time I was led from one home to the next looking for the man or woman who could give me the correct answer to a linguistic question. I remember one incident well. I wanted to learn the Lakota word for the notch in an arrow. My friend and host, Henry White Calf, did not know. He thought for a while. "That's an old word," he said. "Not many would remember that."

He suggested that William Spotted Crow might know, and we took off on a four-mile walk into town, where the old man lived. We waited several hours for him to come home. He finally arrived, and Henry put the question to him. The man thought for a while. But before he could answer, he interrupted his own train of thought to give a harangue about how bad the drinking problem was on the reservation. He went on and on about the *semni,* the teenagers, and how they *had* to have alcohol. He then moved on to problems with the upcoming Sun Dance and commented on why one of the medicine men wanted a lot of money. We listened to hours of talk and gossip and complaint. Then, finally—"*Ikpage,*" he said. With a sudden nodding of his head, Henry acknowledged the old man and looked at me with a great deal of satisfaction. We shook hands and left. We had gotten our word. *Ikpage,* the word for the notch in an arrow.

In chapter 2, "Oglala Song Terminology," I am interested in providing an alternate model for music based on the notion of natural versus cultural models. I put forth the notion that, although Western man sees music as part of his culture, not all people may classify it the same way. Borrowing an interesting idea of participation and "appurtenances" associated with Lucien Lévy-Bruhl, I try to show that the Oglala verbalize about music in a way that underscores their conceptualization of music as part of the natural world. In this world all things that emanate from the body—and this would include speech—are regarded equally with other physical and physiological functions. Song, therefore, is an extension of oneself much as are speech, sweat, blood, and tears.

Of course, for the Lakota as for all other peoples, song is one of the most important means of communing with the spirits. And this is a two-way discourse, for the very songs sung by the medicine men and their trained singers to propitiate the spirits are learned in visions from those very same spirits. In chapter 3, "Song Texts," I translate a number of songs sung in the Yuwipi ceremony and the Sweat Lodge. These songs represent a wide range of sentiments about Lakota cosmology, and each series of songs sung by a medicine man is believed to be exclusive to him. He learns these songs over several years, and after each new vision he instructs his singers on the appropriate songs to sing to bring about the required effect: curing, coaxing spirits to the meeting, giving them gifts, and bidding them farewell, all of which are accompanied by songs whose texts can be understood only by the medicine man and, of course, those spirits with whom he communes. For the common person to come to know about the sacred lore divulged to medicine men in their vision quests, the common person must be trained by the medicine man, go on a vigil to the hills, and wait for a vision that can later be interpreted by the medicine man who serves as his mediator.

It is important to note that these songs are not necessarily old songs, although a few may be. What is important about them is that they are viable. They are created each year, usually in the springtime, when the medicine men and others fulfill their vows taken over the winter, promising to seek seclusion in the hills such as Bear Butte, in the sacred Black Hills. The songs are learned in these visions; therefore, each year new songs are introduced into the inventory of Lakota sacred knowledge. The songs of the Vision Quest are the most dynamic. The spirits address themselves to matters relevant to the Lakota. They are not the songs dealing with warrior traditions and the thrill of the buffalo hunt. They are texts dealing with the problems of poverty, planning a large and healthy family, finding and holding a job, and trying to get along with one's kin and friends. They concern the realities of reservation life and the particular way in which Indians are supposed to live in peace and harmony with the white man. Yuwipi songs fit these functions because they are the songs of visions. Other songs, like those sung to the Sun Dance, are no less sacred, but they are regarded as old songs, part of a tradition that dangerously teeters on the brink of extinction. Yuwipi songs and others sung in the Sweat Lodge represent all that is new and meaningful to contemporary Lakota culture.

No study of sacred language can be complete without some consideration of the effect of Christian teachings, particularly the translation of bibles, psalms, and other liturgical texts into the native language. The problems of Bible translation have been dealt with by a number of scholars,[6] but in chapter 4, "Containing the Sacred," I emphasize that Lakota sacred terms change practically with each generation following missionary contacts and that each generation produces a somewhat different translation of the same word while at the same time insisting on its authenticity. In addition, I address the various ways in which the Lakota describe the concept of ritual in an attempt to clarify and unify some of the diverse ways in which the concept has been inadequately translated in the past. I also analyze *wakan* and Wakantanka, generic terms widely used in both anthropological and missionary writings. In doing so, I critically evaluate some of the works written by and about James R. Walker, a physician at Pine Ridge at the turn of the twentieth century who contributed a great deal to our understanding of Lakota religion, sometimes clearly, sometimes not.

Chapter 5, "Sacred Numbers," continues an argument put forth in my earlier *Oglala Religion* with respect to the utility of numerical systems as a means of classifying the social universe.[7] I employ theory and methodology from structural, semiotic, and symbolic studies to elucidate the structural relationships between Lakota concepts of time and space, particularly focusing on directions, color symbolism, and animal and bird metaphors. It is well known that the Lakota employ two systems, one based on the sacred number four and the other on the number seven. The two systems function in different ways, serving in a very general way to distinguish what Lévi-Strauss would regard as a polarization between nature and culture. At the same time, the two systems are interrelated.

Chapter 6, "Naming the Sacred," deals with the manner in which the Lakota classification system can be regarded as a logical and rational system. The theme developed here is that much of the Lakota world—like our own—is a linguistic universe and that the process of naming people, objects, and places gives them ontological status. I also examine what I call the paradox of Inktomi, the Lakota trickster who, in the process of naming all things in the world and thus fixing their identity in perpetuity, is himself amorphous and without a specific appellation.

Chapter 7, "Shamans and Priests," examines another logical process, that of the manner in which the Lakota classify their own ritual specialists. Medicine men and women are placed in the larger context of shamans and priests, and I argue that, from a functional point of view, there are no substantive differences between these two categorically different ritual specialists.

Appendix A provides an introductory phonological key for the pronunciation of Lakota. For a more sophisticated introduction to the pronunciation of Lakota, as well as rules of grammar as they apply to common Lakota, the works of Buechel and the Colorado University Lakhota (sic) Project should be consulted. Appendix B provides a glossary of all Lakota terms employed in this book as a convenience for the reader who is not a Lakota-speaker and as such serves as an introductory lexicon of Lakota sacred language. Like any other dictionary, this glossary should be seen as a tentative collection of terms which at the present time are distinguished by their use in rituals but which perhaps will someday be returned to the secular language from which they have been temporarily borrowed. It should be remembered that sacred language has an important function in all societies in which it is found. In Lakota culture sacred words increase the status of the medicine men. They serve as an emblem of superiority in a group of exclusive people who have no other material way of distinguishing themselves from the common people. Yet these common people are not inferior in a class sense—their status goes far beyond the simplistic notion of class distinctions. The common people require a group of individuals, the medicine men, to mediate on their behalf and treat with the supernatural spirits and powers, who themselves are regarded as superior.[8]

The superiority of medicine men also helps distinguish between Indian and white society in that in the former the commoners' agreement that sacred language is comprehensible only by and between the medicine men is partly an affirmation that native religion is viable and powerful. The medicine men and their special language and their ability to commune with the spirits and with each other are akin to the incomprehensibility of religion itself. Once the commoners understand the language, they understand the religion, and once religion becomes explicable, it is no longer sacred—or useful to those who require it to answer questions about belief, justice, and truth. The mysticism of sacred language is then directly analogous to the perceived mysticism of religion.

Sacred language as a category of words and phrases incomprehensible to the common people does not form an opposition to common language. Sacred language and common language are one and the same; only the contexts provide the sense of opposition. Just as sense gives rise to nonsense, incomprehensibility ultimately produces an understanding of one's religious culture.

CHAPTER 1

INCOMPREHENSIBLE TERMS

Magicians used Sanscrit in the India of the Prakrits, Egyptian and Hebrew in the Greek world, Greek in Latinspeaking countries and Latin with us. All over the world people value archaisms and strange incomprehensible terms. From the very beginnings, practitioners of magic . . . have mumbled their *abracadabras*.

—Mauss 1972, 57–58

UNLIKE most other peoples all over the world, the Oglala of the Pine Ridge Reservation in South Dakota, whose native language is Lakota, do not value archaisms in the sense that Mauss meant. However, many Oglala metaphysical concepts found in the language of myth, ritual, song, and prayer are couched in terms incomprehensible to most common people, or so the Lakota say. Adult speakers regard sacred language as something exclusive to sacred persons, and implicitly to the sacred beings and powers that reside in a place believed to be somewhere between the earth and the sky (Powers 1977, 1982).

When questioning native speakers about the differences between sacred and secular language, the Oglala assert that sacred language is simply not understood. They claim that the words are unknown, strange, even humorous. They believe that sacred language can be understood only by *wicaša wakan* 'sacred men': it is the language *they* use to talk to each other, and to pray and sing. However, if one turns for a moment from the *general* category 'sacred language' and questions native speakers about *specific* lexical items and grammatical features that are acknowledged to be the essential components of sacred language, many Lakota speakers are quite capable of interpreting the parts, despite their admitted incomprehension of the whole.

For the linguistic anthropologist this is indeed a perplexing problem, a paradox, incomprehensibility piled upon incomprehensibility. But if we begin to regard sacred language as a reformulation of secular language, and as a special language whose connotative significance depends partly on ritual contextualization, the paradox soon seems to vanish. We then begin to understand that the common people do not comprehend sacred language because their philosophical and religious canons decree that they are not supposed to comprehend it. Admitting incomprehensibility about sacred language is tantamount to declaring one's allegiance to all that is historically and culturally Lakota. Contrarily, to admit to comprehension is to deny one's sense of social identity, one's Indianness.

But even from this simple contextual analysis, new problems arise creating new paradoxes that cannot be understood within a simple synchronic framework of investigation. The new paradox is this: under closer scrutiny one soon finds that not all sacred persons understand the sacred language of their cohorts. This inability for even the initiated to comprehend the sacred language that is claimed to be exclusively theirs stems from two important facts: the particular manner in which the Lakota theorize about sacred language and classify it; and the manner in which, historically, sacred language is formulated and reformulated. As I shall demonstrate, sacred language emerges from a continuous process whereby secular words are transformed into sacred ones, and in time, sacred words are returned, if you will, to the domain of the common people.

The relationship between sacred and secular language is not unique to Lakota, and perhaps it is a universal feature of languages. Burke, who is interested in the relationship between "words" and "The Word" tells us:

> For whereas the words for the "supernatural" realm are necessarily borrowed from the realm of our everyday experiences, out of which our familiarity with language arises, once a terminology has been developed for special theological purposes the order can become reversed. We can borrow back the terms from the borrower, again secularizing to varying degrees the originally secular terms that had been given "supernatural" connotations. [Burke 1961, 7]

Perhaps the same can be said for all special languages including physical and social sciences jargon. Similarly, induction into these guilds requires that the initiates become fluent in their respective scientific argots, part of whose vocabularies are already known because in many cases they are only familiar words whose connotations have been changed.

The objective here is to examine just how the interaction of sacred and secular language actually operates. Obviously, the beginning point for the string of formulations and reformulations in this interaction can only be hypothetical. However, many sacred terms in Lakota are traceable to known historic periods, such as those employed to classify material culture and ideas associated with euro-american contact in the seventeenth and eighteenth centuries, as well as contact with other tribes. In particular, in labeling new cultural imports the Lakota tended to regard such objects as the horse, gun, and alcohol as inherently sacred, and accordingly, sacred terms were invented, presumably by medicine men, and applied to these new objects. Subsequently, however, these once-sacred terms became conventionalized and returned to the secular speech of the common people, thus transforming incomprehensible terms into comprehensible ones. Before examining the process, it is useful to review what anthropologists, linguists, and other scholars have had to say about sacred language.

WORDS AS WORDS

One of the most insightful statements regarding the ubiquity of sacred language can be attributed to the French sociologist, Lucien Lévy-Bruhl, who is perhaps best known for his theories of "primitive mentality" for which he has been criticized severely.[1] Nevertheless, because he was concerned with thought processes, Lévy-Bruhl was sensitive to the way people spoke and classified their universe. In speaking of sacred language, he writes:

> That which finally proves the mystic worth and power in words as words is the widespread custom, in magic ceremonies and even in ritual and religious ceremonies, of using songs and formulas which are unintelligible to those who hear them, and sometimes even to those who utter them. For these songs and these formulas to be effective, it is enough that they have been transmitted by tradition in a sacred language. [Lévy-Bruhl 1966, 156]

Lévy-Bruhl is one of the few scholars to call attention to the fact that even some ritual specialists are sometimes unaware of what some sacred terms signify. As I mentioned earlier, this *is* one of the peculiar features of sacred language in Lakota, and I shall elaborate on this later. The Oglala also agree that "it is enough" that the sacred words have been handed down over the generations as a means of allowing some individuals to distinguish themselves from others as is the case between the medicine men and common people at Pine Ridge and other reservations. Although anthropologists have aptly suggested that "the analysis of meaning, or, more exactly, with cultural symbols and how and what they signify, has come to occupy a prominent place within the (anthropological) discipline" (Basso and Selby 1976, 1), any systematic study of meaning will have to consider categories of nonmeaning as well. Here sacred language, with its emphasis on incomprehensibility, provides a major example.

Some would suggest—and there would be some agreement between both medicine man and scholar—that there is perhaps more significance in incomprehensibility than in comprehensibility. Further along, Lévy-Bruhl again tells us:

> What we call the meaning of the words or the form matters little. The people remain indefinably attracted by them, because their

mystic virtue and magic efficacy have been known for time im-
morial. The most accurate and intelligible translation could not
take the place of these incomprehensible songs, for they could
not fulfill the same office. [Lévy-Bruhl 1957, 157]

Despite the mystic connotations here, Lévy-Bruhl is correct
that meaningful translations could not effectively replace incomprehensibility for the same reason that William James sees
the function of sacred language as a means of providing "a
stable verbal support, so that the inexact, nebulous, and fluc-
tuating concepts may be recalled to the mind whenever required, without any prejudice to the elasticity of the concepts" (James 1961, cited in Ogden and Richards 1923, 41).
And it is not only in Lakota that we find a strong sentiment
for incomprehensibility. Witness the opposition if not outrage
among Catholics when the Latin Mass was to be offered in the
vernacular, as if the newly introduced secular language would
somehow profane the religious world.

Lévy-Bruhl's mystically based explanation of sacred language is later complemented by another French sociologist,
Van Gennep, who concludes that people around the world
used special languages, as he called them because

they are merely one of the innumerable methods by which col-
lectivities of every kind maintain their existence and resist external pressures. For those who employ them, they are simultaneously a means of achieving cohesion and protection against
outsiders. . . . Thus the special language plays the same role
within the society as a whole that each general language plays
in relation to other general language. It is one of the consciously
devised forms of differentiation that are necessary to the society's very existence. [Van Gennep 1908–14, 2:315–16, cited in
Belmont 1979, 107]

One may add to Van Gennep's position that sacred language
achieves differentiation *within* a society as well as providing
protection against outsiders. In the Lakota case, sacred language obviously is considered to be foreign to outsiders, but it
is also claimed to be incomprehensible to insiders. This internal differentiation serves two purposes: it helps to establish a

class of ritual specialists upon whom communication between the common people and the supernatural depends; and it reinforces the sense of differentiation between Lakota and non-Lakota to help maintain traditional values that are important to the Lakota.

Expectedly, Van Gennep is also interested in the relationship between special languages and rites of passage. His most significant contribution is understanding how individuals change their status through ritual. In his classic work, Van Gennep finds that:

> Especially during the transition periods, a special language is employed which in some cases includes an entire vocabulary unknown or unusual in the society as a whole, and in others consists simply of a prohibition against using certain words in the common tongue. . . . This phenomenon should be considered of the same order as the change of dress, mutilations, and special foods (dietary taboos) i.e., as a perfectly normal differentiating procedure. [Van Gennep 1960, 169][2]

These are indeed ideas worth considering, particularly Van Gennep's notion that there are analogical relationships between sacred language and other symbols of transition such as clothing and special foods. In Oglala society it is precisely during these transitional periods, particularly those rituals held in darkness, that incomprehensible language becomes the medium of discourse between the medicine men and supernaturals. Unfortunately, Van Gennep does not provide examples of societies whose special languages consist of an "entire vocabulary," or for that matter, ones in which there are interdictions against using "certain words." In Lakota and other American Indian languages there are many examples of, say, restrictions against speaking the name of the deceased. But it is difficult to constitute this particular reference as an example of special language. And it is also unlikely that any society would be able to formulate sacred language that was comprised exclusively of esoteric terms. Even when Latin was the sacred language of the Roman Catholic Mass, translations into the local language were available in the printed missals. It also seems unlikely that a sacred language could exist if it relied exclusively on unspeakable words! Nevertheless, Van Gennep does provide a methodological framework within which special languages potentially may be examined. And there certainly seems to be a consensus among these writers that sacred or special languages are part of a universal human phenomenon, even though we rarely find examples of these special linguistic categories. Even Franz Boas, recognized as the father of American anthropology, was concerned with "the connotation of meaningless syllables that occur in songs, the frequent use of distorted words in poetry, and the fondness for secret language, including obsolete, symbolic, or arbitrary terms, [which] deserve the most careful attention" (Boas 1940, 209).

Boas does not provide any empirical data for a now-magnified field of possible candidates for sacred words. Boas writes with convincing and usual authority, and we intuit that he is correct. However, his choice of special linguistic categories is problematic. For example, no empirical evidence supports the claim that most "meaningless syllables" ever had any semantic range.[3] In fact, only rarely do we find archaisms, even though there has always been a great deal of speculation that vocables in song have somehow mystically emanated from archaic words. Similarly, "distorted words" are found in numerous types of linguistic expression: song, prayer, jokes, and poetry, a literary genre whose constituent members are continuously being invented, mainly by poets. Furthermore, when Boas subsumes under secret language "obsolete, symbolic, or arbitrary terms," he is being too general. Certainly, some secret languages exist in which ritual specialists employ obsolete or archaic terms, but one cannot make the same case for "symbolic" words given that language, sacred or secular, is regarded as a symbolic medium sui generis. And it is unlikely that any society permits its ritual specialists to speak in purely "arbitrary" terms. Any sacred language, despite its incomprehensibility to some, requires operative rules.

Short Bull, a famous Oglala medicine man and leader of the Ghost Dance. Photograph by Heyn and Matzen, Omaha, Nebraska, 1900.

One of Boas's most distinguished students, Edward Sapir, also mentions "esoteric language devices, such as passwords or technical terminologies for ceremonial attitudes or practices," pointing out that among the Eskimo "the medicine man has a peculiar vocabulary which is not understood by those who are not members of his guild" (1966, 37). Perhaps this category appears to be so basic to Sapir that he feels a reference to empirical data is unnecessary, and provides us with none.

It becomes apparent from the above statements that any systematic anthropological or linguistic study of meaning must also include the study of those sacred languages in which meaning is couched in consciously or unconsciously constituted non-meaning. Despite our intensive interest in the past two decades in how humans may develop better ways to communicate clearly and effectively, a large part of the world's population, and this would include segments of our own society, prefers to participate in belief systems that are predicated on incomprehensible utterances.

It is also apparent that there has been no systematic means of classifying this elusive genre of speech—special language, sacred language, secret language, mystical language, ceremonial language. Also absent are empirical data, inventories of words and phrases understood to be incomprehensible. Rarely do we find any corpus of corrobative information in the quality and quantity of Malinowski's descriptive analysis of Trobriand Island spells and songs texts (Malinowski 1961, 428–63). Nevertheless, the conclusions drawn by our intellectual antecedents endure because they are theoretically interesting and because they offer an appetizing perspective on a universal linguistic phenomenon. In all of these writings there is an agreement—implicit if not explicit—that once religious ideas are explicable and comprehensible, religion as a means of organizing social relations is weakened. All societies are apparently willing to exchange incomprehensibility in the religious sphere for longevity and survival for both the individual and the social group, as Van Gennep has suggested.

FAMILIAR WORDS AND OCCULT MEANINGS

In the study of Lakota sacred language, we must begin with
the work of missionary Stephen Return Riggs, who is best
known for his lexicography among the eastern "Sioux,"[4] or
Dakota. Riggs published a number of works on language, but
in one volume, dedicated to a study of Siouan ethnography,
he provides information specific to sacred language. In it
he writes:

> The Dakota conjurer, the war prophet, and the dreamer, experi-
> ence the same need that is felt by more elaborate performers
> among other nations of a language which is unintelligible to the
> common people, for the purpose of impressing upon them the
> idea of their superiority. Their dreams, according to their own
> account, are revelations made from the spirit world, and their
> prophetic visions are what they saw and knew in a former state
> of existence. It is, then, only natural that their dreams and vi-
> sions should be clothed in words, many of which the multitude
> do not understand. This sacred language is not very extensive,
> since the use of a few unintelligible words suffices to make a
> whole speech incomprehensible. It may be said to consist, first,
> in employing words as the names of thing(s) which seemed to
> have been introduced from other Indian languages; as, nide,
> *water;* paza *wood,* etc. In the second place, it consists of employ-
> ing descriptive expressions, instead of the ordinary names of
> things; as in calling a man a *bird,* and the wolf a *quadruped.* And
> thirdly, words which are common in the language are used far
> out of their ordinary signification; as, hepan, *the second child, if a
> boy,* is used to designate *the otter.* When the Dakota braves ask a
> white man for an ox or cow, they generally call it *a dog;* and
> when a sachem begs a horse from a white chief, he does it
> under the designation of *moccasins.* This is the source of many
> of the figures of speech in Indian oratory; but they are some-
> times too obscure to be beautiful. [Riggs 1893, 166; italics in the
> original]

If one can ignore the condescending attitude common to
the period, Riggs makes some important observations on sacred language, namely, that there are various ways of for-
mulating sacred words from common, everyday language. He
is probably also correct when he writes that the conjurers and

dreamers who communicate with each other in this particular form of language do so to establish their superiority over the common people. But here "superiority" should be read to mean superior knowledge of the sacred lore.

Riggs is also correct when he states that much of what the dreamers tell the common people originates in dreams, and the medium through which the content of the dreams is reported is like the visions themselves in the realm of the supernaturals. Unfortunately, Riggs does not give us more information about such terms as "otter," "dog," and "moccasins," and perhaps these terms are strictly a conceit of the Dakota with whom he worked. However, the terms for "biped" and "quadruped" continue to serve as metaphors for humans and animals, respectively, in Lakota.[5]

Writing somewhat later, Frances Densmore, who worked with the Hunkpapa of the Standing Rock Reservation and who is generally regarded as an excellent ethnographer, particularly in the collection of Lakota music, states that:

> A full and complete expression is not in accordance with Indian customs. The unspoken element may be a matter of mutual understanding, no indication of which appears in words, or it may be something which is indicated in such a manner as to be intelligible only to those for whom it is intended. Thus there is a "sacred language" used by medicine men in which familiar words take on occult meaning. [Densmore 1918, 85]

As to the function of this language, she speculates that "A [sacred] language of this kind was said to be necessary in order that persons intimate with supernatural things could communicate without being understood by the common people" (Densmore 1918, 120).

Again, if we pass over the sometimes supercilious attitudes of early investigators, Densmore acknowledges that "familiar words take on an occult meaning." She also alludes to the fact that shamans require a special language so as not to be understood by the common people. At this point both Riggs and Densmore agree that the common Lakota cannot understand the sacred language, and that the function of sacred language enables medicine men to maintain a position of superiority over common people.

A contemporary of Densmore, although not academically trained, was the physician James R. Walker, who, as the consensus of Siouan scholars clearly reveals, makes significant contributions to our understanding of Oglala religion.[6] In his now famous monograph on the Oglala Sun Dance, Walker, who underwent an apprenticeship with Oglala medicine men, discusses secret instructions that medicine men receive. He writes:

> When the Mentor is satisfied that the Candidate understands the social customs of the Oglala sufficiently well to know when a Shaman may, or may not, interfere with them, he should then instruct him relative to the doctrines and ceremonials pertaining to the Gods. Some of these are known to the people, but most of them are known only by the Shamans and they hide these in a ceremonial language known only by them. This language is made up of common words to which an esoteric meaning is given and of strange words that are known only by the Shamans. The sacred mysteries are thus hidden from the people because they are unfitted to know them. [Walker 1917, 78–79]

Walker reiterates two important themes found in Riggs and Densmore: first, sacred language consists of common words with esoteric meanings, and strange words known only by the medicine men; and second, common people are somehow "unfitted" to comprehend these terms and thus remain oblivious to the real significance of the sacred terms. To some extent, this idea of exclusivity is acknowledged even by the Lakota themselves. While interviewing Oglala medicine men, Walker discovers a number of interesting points of view about sacred language from the medicine men, and he is careful to record their views in their own words. The Oglalas—Sword, Finger, One Star, and Tyon—provide a number of accounts of the significance of sacred concepts and sacred terms such as *wakan*, Wakantanka, Škan, and *šicun*, terms that are critical to understanding Lakota religious thought.

In the interviews Sword admits that sacred ideas are difficult to understand, but he appears to have little trouble in explaining even some of the most abstract ones. For example, he tells us that there is consensus among the medicine men that sacred terms make reference to all that is inexplicable. The term *wakan* denotes a state of sacrality or incomprehensibility of any being or object that has been invested with a spirit. This spirit is called *tun,* a term which I have elsewhere translated as 'potentiality' (Powers 1977, 52). The relationship between *tun* and *wakan* then is one between the potentiality of being transformed into a sacred state (*tun*) and the sacred state itself (*wakan*). The ability for the transformation to be realized comes from the supernatural beings and powers who are good or evil.

The most incomprehensible characteristic of *wakan* is that neither it nor its potentiality are visible. However, both manifest themselves through changes in behavior, either in the medicine man, the common person, or an object through which the transformation is perceived to occur. Belief validates the fact that a sacred object or being is *wakan,* and people's behavior toward that which has been transformed changes accordingly. Thus in the Catholic belief system, if it were to be explained by an Oglala medicine man, common water has a *tun,* i.e., the potentiality to be transformed through the proper ritual into sacred water. Once the transformation has taken place, one validated through the belief system, i.e., that the priest has the power to make such a transformation, the water then achieves the state of being *wakan,* and people's behavior toward it changes in such a way that it is used to extend its sacred qualities through the administration of the water to the body and other objects in the practice of "blessing." Blessing then would be explained as the process whereby the *wakan* of one object or being is transferred to the *tun* of another through the proper ritual, thus rendering each successive object invested with *tun* into the state of *wakan.*

In a posthumous publication Walker provides more insights into the manner in which Oglala medicine men classify sacred language. This enables us to see more clearly why *certain* sacred terms are incomprehensible, while others are understood.

The Oglala, Sword, elaborates. He tells us that a message

from Wakantanka may be communicated to medicine men and common people either in everyday Lakota or "*hanbloglaka* (language of the spirits). . . . If the communication is in Lakota he will understand it, but if it is in the language of the spirits a shaman should interpret it" (Walker 1980, 79). "The language of the vision," Sword continues, "is *hanblogagia* (*habloglagia*) [*sic*]. Only the shamans understand this language" (Walker 1980, 85). He then concludes that "The shamans speak this speech in all their ceremonies and songs so that the people may not learn those things that only the shamans should know" (Walker 1980, 94).

In the same volume, Ringing Shield states that "The shaman should know the word[s] of a shaman. He talks in the spirit language" (p. 114). Another, Lone Bear, says that the term "*Hunonp* (*hununpa*) is of the language of the shamans. It is the Spirit Bear who is of the *Tobtob*. He taught the shamans all their secrets. No one can talk with *Hunonp* without understanding the language of the shamans" (p. 128).

Red Hawk presents his credentials by stating "I am a *wicaša wakan* and . . . I know the *Wakan Iya, Econpi,* and *Lowanpi* (sacred speech, ceremonies, and songs)" (p. 136). And Thomas Tyon confirms that the medicine men "speak in the spirit language (*he hanploklakapi* [sic] *eciyapelo*)" and then proceeds to provide examples of sacred language employed by the medicine men in the Sweat Lodge (p. 154). DeMallie and Jahner, who edited Walker's book, provide the following translation of Tyon's Sweat Lodge prayer:

"Sweat Lodge stones (*tonkan yatapika*), pity me! Sun, pity me! Moon, pity me! Darkness of night (*hanokpaza kin*), pity me! Water, standing in a *wakan* manner (*mni wakanta najin kin*), pity me! Grass, standing in the morning (*pejihinyanpa najin kin*), pity me! Whatever pitiful one is scarcely able to crawl into the tipi and lie down for the night (*takuxika teriya tiyoslohanhan hinyunke*), see him and pity him. Unhappiness causes coldness within the body so that even the place of eating and the place for lying down and the place for seeing become as nothing (*cuwita tanmahel taku iyokipi xni na owate na oyunka na owakita kin lena ekayex koye ecetu xni kin*). This way the sweat lodge stones frantically persuade the Spirit of the Sky (*heun tonkan yatapika Ite Peto knax-*

kinya ciyelo). The holy man makes this kind of speech. He tells these things from his vision. [Walker 1980, 154][7]

It is important to recognize that the Oglala medicine man's exegeses make reference to more than one type of sacred language, distinguishing the generic *wakan iye* 'sacred language' from the more specific *hanbloglaka* 'vision talk'. From an analytic standpoint we can view the first, *wakan iye*, as the form of language used *between* medicine men, a language of philosophical commentary on the nature of religious things; and the second, *hanbloglaka*, that employed in sacred discourse *between individual medicine men and their spirit helpers*. Both types are incomprehensible to the common people when they are used in their ritual context—in the Vision Quest, the prayers at the foot of the hill, in the Sweat Lodge, and during the Yuwipi meeting. But outside the ritual context, the first type of sacred language termed *wakan iye* is translatable by the uninitiated. The second type is not. It is incomprehensible to common people, and to other medicine men as well. It represents a personal reenactment of a discourse between a single medicine man and his sacred helpers who communicate with him, and instruct him, during the course of one or more visions. Even the privileged medicine man who has received a vision may have to wait for subsequent visions to understand the significance of his previous one(s). *Wakan iye* is sacred language whose meaning is always public; the meaning of *hanbloglaka* is always private.

Being a private discourse between medicine man and spirit helper, the *hanbloglaka* is found in a rather restricted ritual context. The speech generally serves as a prelude to a Yuwipi ritual,[8] and as such provides a means for the medicine man to present his credentials to the spirits and the adepts before he begins the ceremony. Since spirit helpers prefer to visit and instruct the medicine man in the dark, the *hanbloglaka* is most frequently spoken in the Sweat Lodge, on the Vision Quest, and in the Yuwipi. However, the other form of sacred language, *wakan iye*, is likely to be spoken not only in these contexts, but others as well, including the following rituals:

1. Naming ceremonies. In the old days it was considered propitious to have a child named (*caštun* 'to give birth to a name') by a berdache (*winkte*). Often the source of names were visions and the names frequently took on esoteric meanings. One of the reasons there is controversy over the "real" meaning of family names today is because originally the names were esoteric and required exegesis from the person who performed the naming ritual.

2. Heyoka Kaga. The well-known "contraries" of the Great Plains exhibited a much peculiar behavior not the least of which was speaking in an unnatural manner. The person who dreamed of lightning or thunder, or symbols associated with these phenomena, were required to forever behave in a backward manner lest they be struck by lightning. Well-known examples of this unusual behavior include improper dress, manners, attitudes, and emotions. The speech of the Heyoka was also "incomprehensible" because it was spoken in distorted ways. Although the language was not intelligible, it was understood to the extent that observers could describe the fact that Heyoka spoke too fast or too slow, or backwards. Unfortunately we do not have any examples of this most unusual form of speech play, but certainly it was considered *wakan*.

3. Nonhuman language. It is believed that a number of animals and birds can communicate with common people and medicine men and that frequently these nonhuman species speak in Lakota. The communication between humans and nonhumans occurs most frequently during the Vision Quest. Under ritual conditions, virtually every species is capable of speaking to the medicine man in Lakota—buffalo, deer, elk, coyotes, wolves, snakes, and so forth. Sometimes the animal or bird is capable of signaling the medicine men in the species's natural utterances, for example, the howl of a wolf, the bark of a coyote, the hoot of an owl, and the crowing of a cock, all of which are interpreted as omens of death particularly if the sounds are heard during what is considered to be an inappropriate time of day or night for the animal or bird to be active. Most often, communication between people and animals occurs in the Vision Quest, Sweat Lodge, or in the Yuwipi.

Henry Standing Bear praying with the pipe. Photograph taken ca. 1945. Courtesy Heritage Center, Inc., Holy Rosary Mission, Pine Ridge, South Dakota.

However, on occasion various nonhuman species may communicate with common people in a secular context. For example, it is believed that the meadowlark has a rich inventory of meaningful sentences in Lakota, and often the bird was questioned by war party leaders as to the potential outcome of their forays against the enemy. The meadowlark also has a large vocabulary related to food and kinship (Buechel 1970, 483).[9] Except for ominous sounds heralding the imminent death of someone, most animal and bird communications had to be interpreted by medicine men.

4. Prayers and songs. Prayers and songs in and out of ritual context provide the largest and most fluid forms of both *wakan iye* and *hanbloglaka*. Hence some parts of both songs and prayers are comprehensible to the common people, while others are not. Because of the generative nature of sacred language, and because it is derived from familiar terms to which esoteric meanings are applied, songs and prayers cannot be analyzed exclusively in terms of categories. To understand the meaning of sacred language in songs and prayers it is necessary to examine the structural features of sacred language and particularly the process whereby secular language is transformed into sacred language.

PROCESSES OF TRANSFORMATION

The processes by which common language is transformed into sacred language are accomplished not only by assigning esoteric connotations to familiar terms, e.g., *witunšni* 'liar' in common language, 'white man' in sacred language, but by modifying morphological, lexical, syntactic, and stylistic features of Lakota. For purposes of analysis, I have labeled these processes (1) attenuation, (2) affixation, (3) reduplication (which apply to phonemic, morphemic, and lexemic transformations), (4) inversion (which applies to syntax), and (5) stylistics, which can apply to all of the preceding categories. Below are some examples of each category.

1. Attenuation. Abbreviation of common words is one of

the most prevalent means whereby secular terms are transformed into sacred ones. There are a number of structural ways in which this attenuation occurs. For example, when words are comprised of radical elements plus affixes, either the radical element, the affix, or both may be modified. Additionally, phonemic and morphemic modifications often are made by reduction or complete elimination. The secular and sacred terms for the Four Winds provide good examples of each of these attenuative possibilities.

Direction	Common Term	Sacred Term
West	Wiyohp̌eyata	Eya
North	Waziyata	Yata
East	Wiyohiyanpata	Yanpa
South	Itokagata	Okaga

The authority for this form of attenuation is Walker (1917, 1980; Red Cloud Indian School n.d.) who provides a large inventory of mythological personae who are also referred to by abbreviated names (Ink or Unk for Inktomi 'Spider', the culture hero; *gnaš* for *tatang gnaškiyan,* normally translated 'crazy buffalo [bull]' but more at 'enraged buffalo', which figures prominently in sacred and secular lore.

Here, in West Wind, the attenuation takes place by combining the final phoneme /e/ of the radical element *ȟpe* 'to fall off' with the initial morpheme *ya* in the locational suffix *yata* 'toward'. In the term for the North Wind, however, the radical element *wazi* 'pine' is eliminated, and only the locational *yata* is retained.

The attenuation of the East Wind is more complicated. First the secular term derives from a corruption of *wi* 'sun' + *o* 'in' + *hinanpa* 'to enter' and *yata* 'toward'. *Hinanpa* is corrupted into *hiyanpa.* In the abbreviation the first morpheme of the radical element, as well as the locational suffix, are dropped.

The term for the South Wind is equally complex. The common term itself is an attenuated form of *ite* 'face' (here having the connotation of 'facing') and *okaga* (it is not certain whether the *o* is a nominalizing prefix or the preposition 'in'); but *kaga* means 'to make, create,' hence 'facing creation' or facing the place of creation, a reference to the belief that people's ghosts (*wanagi*) travel south along the *Wanagi Tacanku* 'Ghost Road' [Milky Way], thus completing a cyclical "visit" on earth during their lifetime.[10] The suffix *ta* is also an abbreviated form of the locational *yata*. The sacred term then is formed by dropping all but the radical *okaga*.

Other examples of attenuation include Škan, an abbreviation of Takuškanškan 'something that moves', a term which approximates the notion of a creative life force, the energy behind things that move, such as the force that causes the wind to blow. This term is best understood as that aspect of Wakantanka that is creative, original. Another term is Yumni, the name designating the little brother of the Four Winds who never grows up and who is never assigned a direction. The little brother most frequently lives and travels with the South Wind who is kind to him. *Yumini* is an unusual form of attenuation; it is short for *wamniomini* 'whirlwind', usually referring to the small dust devil that skips about on the prairie. It is inordinate in that a new prefix *yu* replaces *wa* and the reduplicated part is eliminated.[11]

Although there is a great penchant for attenuating words in transforming them from secular to sacred, there appear to be no hard and fast rules for the attenuation process. I have simply tried to give as many variations as possible.

2. Affixation. Walker (1917, 1980) provides still another type of sacred term that apparently has become obsolete, with very little exception. These sacred terms are formed by affixing the radical element *kan* to common words. About *kan* the Oglala, Sword, says:

> *Kan* means anything that is old or that has existed for a long time or that should be accepted because it has been so in former times, or it may mean a strange or wonderful thing or that which cannot be comprehended, or that which should not be questioned or it may mean a sacred or supernatural thing. [Walker 1980, 96–98]

A full inventory of *kan* words appears in Walker (1917, 1980). The following examples demonstrate how secular ideas are transformed into sacred ones by the addition of *kan:*

English Gloss	Common Term	Sacred Term
Mother Earth	Maka Ina	Makakan
Sun	(Anpetu) Wi	Wikan
Moon	(Hanhepi) Wi	Hanwikan
Rock	Inyan	Inyankan
Wind	Tate	Tatekan

Words that have been transformed by another process such as attenuation may also take the *kan* suffix. For example, Sword refers to Yumnikan (from *wamniomni* abbreviated to Yumni) when speaking of the mythological younger brother to the Four Winds. Similarly, *hununpa* 'two-legged', which I treat below under "Stylistics," is referred to as Hunonpakan 'Human Beings'. Sword's explanation is that "*Wakan Tanka* is like sixteen different persons; but each person is *kan*. Therefore they are all only the same as one" (Walker 1917, 153).

Kan also gives us the root for *wakan* 'sacred'. Although there are no agreements on glosses for *wakan*, it appears to be an important word in sacred language whose significance is often vague, but perhaps vaguer to most anthropologists than to native Lakota speakers. As Sword states: "*Wakan* means many things. The Lakota understands what it means from the things that are considered *wakan*" (Walker 1917, 152). From an analytical point of view, that which is sacred is irrevocably linked to that which is old, and *kan* is an element that underscores this relationship.[12]

3. Reduplication. Reduplication is a common feature of Lakota; the process serves to underscore plurality or frequency of occurrence. A few sacred terms are formed by reduplicating common words. For example Takuškanškan (referred to above) is derived from *taku* 'something' and *škan* 'to move'; *škanškan* connotes 'continuously moving'. In this case both Takuškanškan and its attenuated form *škan* are regarded as sacred language, but the former is understandable by common people and is used frequently in prayers.

Another term ubiquitous in Lakota prayer and song is *tobtob* formed from the word for 'four' *topa* which under certain circumstances is abbreviated to *tob* in common language. *Tobtob* may be glossed as 'four times four' and refers to what the Lakota believe to be the constituent members of Wakantanka, a term frequently glossed as Great Spirit, Great Mystery, and by the missionaries as God. Unfortunately, none of these glosses do justice to the complexity of the significance of Wakantanka; translators suggest that it refers to a unified whole and is thus suggestive of monotheism; but clearly the sacred term *tobtob* underscores its parts, all of which are related to each other in a significant way.

The term I have glossed as 'potentiality' *tun* as a common Lakota word means 'birth' and can apply to childbirth and metaphorically to 'sound' i.e., *hotun* 'the birth of a voice'. In sacred language it appears as *tuntun* and *tuntun šni*, roughly referring to positive and negative potentiality, respectively.

These terms are the only ones recorded as examples of reduplication.

4. Inversion. With little exception, modifiers follow the words that they modify in everyday Lakota. A number of sacred terms are formed by reversing the word order. Among the most common are the following:

  a. *wakan iye* 'sacred speech' instead of *iye wakan*.
  b. Šawicaša 'red man' instead of *wicaša ša*.
  c. Skawicaša 'white man' instead of *wicaša ska*.
  d. *wašicun tunkan* 'sacred stones' instead of *tunkan wašicun*.
  e. *wakan oyate* 'sacred nation' instead of *oyate wakan*.
  f. *wakan wicoȟ'an* 'sacred rituals' instead of *wicoȟ'an wakan*.
  g. *wakan wacipi* 'sacred dance' instead of *wacipi wakan*.

Here it should be noted that in examples b and c above we see a form of what might be called (in the language of rhetorical analysis) periphrasis. Both terms are proper nouns, 'Red Man', or 'Indian', and 'White Man'; therefore, two operations are required to form sacred terms; (1) substitution of a descriptive word for a proper name and (2) inversion of the normal grammatical order.

5. Stylistics. In addition to the above types of sacred language and the linguistic processes employed to form them, there are a number of stylistic features, linguistic and paralinguistic, that demarcate sacred language and the manner in which sacred persons speak and sing.

Hanbloglaka, which is spoken in a ritual context and in the dark, is marked by certain paralinguistic features as well as various kinds of figures of speech.

The darkness of the ritual space undoubtedly contributes to this particular style of speaking. The medicine man prays in a subdued, sometimes muffled voice; his utterances are part of an intimate discourse between him and the spirits that are believed to have entered the darkened room. Often the prayers are formulaic, each line beginning in a vocal register somewhat lower than in normal speech, occasionally rising in microtonic steps reaching perhaps an octave or more above. The voice then abruptly drops to the beginning tones of the register, and sometimes below, in many ways paralleling the traditional cascading patterns of singing, but in a softer voice. The last few words of each line of prayer are almost inaudible.

The Lakota believe that the spirits commune with the medicine man in the Sweat Lodge and in the Yuwipi meetings. Frequently, those in attendance can hear a "dialogue" between the medicine man and these spirit helpers, that is, participants hear the medicine man addressing and responding to spirit voices whom only he can hear. This one-sided conversation provides an unusual quality to the tone of the medicine man's voice, one that is similar to listening to someone in the same room speaking on the telephone and trying to determine the nature of the conversation by analyzing only the part actually heard.

From the standpoint of verbal stylistics, however, most terms employed in sacred language are generated out of familiar words to which occult meanings have been assigned, as well as other kinds of verbal ornamentations. As one form of trope, metaphor plays an important part in the creation of sacred language.

For example, *hununpa* 'two-legged' is the sacred term for human beings, while *hutopa* 'four-legged' signifies all animals. The terms *wahununpa* 'those who are two-legged' and *wahutopa* 'those that are four-legged' are also employed. Interestingly the specific terms for man and woman, and young and old, frequently are generalized in sacred language so that words for humans, and some animals such as buffalo, elk,

Pete Catches, a well-known medicine man on the Pine Ridge Reservation and Sun Dance leader. Photograph taken in 1983 by Lisa Clifford. Powers Collection.

and deer, are not marked with respect to gender or generation as they are in common Lakota. Similarly, the common
word *oyate* 'people, nation' is employed in sacred language
and song texts to refer to nonhuman species as well. Thus all
buffalo, for example, are called in sacred language *pte oyate*
'buffalo nation'. Here, the term for buffalo cow becomes the
generic marker for all buffalo, in part, a linguistic means
for underscoring the particular relationship between Lakota
women of child-bearing age and the buffalo as the prime
source of nurture in the old days (M. Powers 1980, Powers
1977).

Let a few other examples of metaphor suffice. A certain ar-
tifact called *cangleška wakan* 'sacred hoop' refers to many representations of a circle inscribed by a cross. These sacred
wheels are frequently used as hair ornaments, or hat bands,
or carried as a dance ornament. The design may also be found
on beadwork and quillwork, and in various forms of traditional and modern painting. At one level of explanation, the
material representation of the sacred wheel or hoop (it is referred to by both glosses) symbolizes the Lakota universe: the
intersecting cross stands for the Four Winds or directions,
and the circle itself is the totality of the world and everything
in it. At a higher level of explanation, however, the *cangleška
wakan* symbolizes the unity of the Lakota people, and thus is
employed by medicine men as a metaphor for 'camp circle'.

Similarly the term *hocoka* 'inside the camp circle' (as opposed to *hokawinħ* 'outside the camp circle') signifies the periphery of the camp demarcated by a circle of tipis. *Hocoka* in
common language is a metaphor meaning all that is safe, unified, Lakota, as opposed to its opposite which signifies danger, disorganization, enemies. In sacred language, however,
hocoka signifies ritual space, the place within which all rituals
are conducted, and which is socially and culturally Lakota. In
song (see next chapter) this term generates the figure *hocoka
wanji ogna iyotake cin* 'the one sitting in the camp circle' and
signifies the medicine man himself who sits in the center of
the ritual space when conducting the ceremonies (cf. Powers
1982 and here chapter 3, song 1). The person seated in the

center of the camp circle is called *iyeska*, the common word for
either a person who is of mixed ancestry (usually Lakota and
white) or a person who acts as an interpreter. From the middle
of the nineteenth century on, the two were identical: interpreters were essentially recruited from the children of mar-
riages between Lakota and whites. In sacred language however, *iyeska* means 'medium', a term employed to classify
those medicine men whose function it is to relay messages
from the spirits to the common people, and vice versa.

Finally, there is no other aspect of language, common and
sacred, that is as rich as the Lakota expressions about weather.
Although most sacred language is used to discuss cosmological characters and events, and propitiate the supernaturals in
speech and song, medicine men also use sacred language to
talk about climatological phenomena, and it is common to refer to empirical events in nature in the same language employed to discuss the same events in cosmology. Given the
richness of expressions regarding the weather, particularly
the metaphors used in everyday speech, there is no question that in some earlier period the terms used to discuss
the weather in common Lakota were originally composed of
sacred terms and expressions (for a summary of common
speech see Colorado University Lakhota Language Project
1976, 10:16–19). Many of these common terms (as well as sacred ones) are again metaphors in their own right. For example *wakinyan agli* 'thunder beings are coming home' and
wakinyan ukiye 'thunder beings are coming' both mean "there
is a storm brewing." In sacred language the same expression
becomes Tunkašila *ukiye* 'the Grandfathers are coming', because medicine men address all supernatural beings as Tunkašila 'Grandfather'.

The Lakota believe that winds normally blow from west to
east. Whenever the wind direction shifts the medicine men
say *catkatanhan ukiye* 'they (thunder beings) are coming from
the left,' an expression which delights structuralists and sym-
bolists, but which is incomprehensible to the common people.

Even the distinction between lightning and thunder probably originated in sacred language. Lightning, for example is

commonly called *wakinyan etunwanpi* 'thunder beings are glaring'; and thunder is called *wakinyan hotunpi* 'thunder beings are rumbling (making a noise).' Both terms originate from the cosmology in which the cause of lightning and thunder are attributed to a large eaglelike bird that is believed to live atop Mount Harney in the Black Hills. When it flashes its eyes there is lightning, and when it flaps its wings there is thunder. Other myths attribute thunder to the sound of the young thunder beings hatching out of their shells.

ARCHAISMS

Since so many writers have assigned great importance to the role of archaic terms in sacred language, it is necessary to examine this relationship between sacred terms and archaic terms in Lakota.

Many early researchers have suggested that sacred language is archaic. Although one cannot dispute that the Lakota place a great deal of emphasis on the relationship between sacrality and oldness, there are a number of methodological problems that arise if sacred language is partly defined on the basis that it is unintelligible to everyday speakers. The major problem with archaic language then is that it is impossible to determine whether or not certain terms are incomprehensible because they are sacred, or because they are archaic, that is, words simply not in vogue anymore.

Lakota people are habitually recalling words and phrases that they remember from their grandparents' days. Archaic speech as such is usually looked upon with fondness. "A long time ago," they begin, "the old people used to have this word. . . ." Then follows a recitation of an old word or expression that somehow has been remembered, followed by a lengthy exegesis about circumstances under which the words were used, and how they have been lost today to slang and the younger generation. But not all of the speech that is recalled is necessarily sacred language; it is simply *forgotten* language.

For example, eastern Dakota speakers still use the term

hoišta 'fish eye' for the English word 'match'. To some old Dakota the sulphur tip of a wooden match resembled the eye of
a fish, hence the name. The Lakota speakers however regard
hoišta as an archaic word, a term they used long ago, and now
use the term *yuilepi* meaning literally 'to make something
blaze', 'to light something'. There are many examples of this
kind of archaism, with even phrases or complete sentences
regarded as archaic. For example, in the spring when the
grass has begun to grow and there a sudden, late snowfall,
the old Lakota used to comment "*pejito aicamna,*" 'it is snowing on the green grass'. This phrase is no longer in common
use and is therefore archaic. The point here is that both the
single word and the phrase are regarded by Lakota speakers
as archaic, but neither of them is sacred.

Methodologically it is more reasonable to assume that archaic language may be of two types, one common, one sacred, and examples of both types are found. But categorically
one cannot assume that sacred language is archaic language
per se. For the Lakota most archaic words and phrases belong
to everyday speech that has fallen into disuse.

FROM SACRED TO SECULAR

I will conclude by making some references to the mutually in-
teractive process of transforming initially constituted sacred
terms into secular ones, Burke's "borrowing back from the
borrower." The term *wašicun* 'white man' is a good example.

It is an established fact that *wašicun*, the term applied to Europeans, is etymologically related to *šicun*, a term that may be
conveniently glossed as an aspect of one's being that is immortal (Powers 1977, 52). Of course there are other terms such as
witunšni 'bearer of falsehoods' mentioned earlier, but this is
rightly a sacred term not understood by common people. It
should be emphasized that despite the sacred nature of *šicun,*
wašicun should be regarded as a common term. A number of
stories have circulated widely on the Lakota reservations that
explain the origin of *wašicun* differently (for example, *wašin*

icu 'person who steals bacon'), but all of them are specious.

Perhaps it was the first glimpse of the white man's skin that gave rise to the notion that he was really dead. The association between white man and some aspect of death is not uncommon in Native North America. No matter what the original reaction to the white man was, something about his physical characteristics likened him to what the Lakota could only describe as a kind of *šicun*, an ethereal quality of a person that persisted after death to become invested in another human.

According to all historical accounts, the first white men thus described were French. Later British and Americans were described by the particular features of their dress and weapons. The British became known as Šaglaša, perhaps some reference to 'red coats' although the etymology is puzzling; and the Americans were known as Mila Hanska 'Long Knives', a reference to their swords.

We must assume that originally the term *wašicun* was a sacred term, one derived from another sacred term referring to an aspect of "soul." This term again at the beginning was applied to the French, the only white people in Lakota country. But as more and different whites came into Lakota country, the term *wašicun* was employed as a generic term for all whites.

According to some Oglala, the sacred term Skawicaša 'white man' and its counterpart Šawicaša 'red man' came into use when many different kinds of whites and Indians began to live as neighbors. So at some time, perhaps around the turn of the twentieth century, we see the sacred term *wašicun* being transformed into a secular term, and at the same time a new sacred term Skawicaša now in the exclusive domain of the medicine men in referring to the white man.

In almost a pendulous way, in recent times the terms Ska- and Šawicaša, once a part of the sacred language, are being employed in strictly secular speeches—at powwows and in political speeches. At the same time, the validity of the term *wašicun* is being challenged by younger Lakota. Here the current choice of Skawicaša over *wašicun* is ideological, and has been motivated by a renewed interest in native religion by the young people. With this renewal there is a reluctance by some to associate the term *wašicun* with the sacred term *šicun* from which the word for white man is derived. It is almost as if the use of a sacred term to denote a white man is sacrilegious if not blasphemous from a theological point of view, since it was the white man who in the latter part of the nineteenth century tried to terminate native beliefs and rituals.

Some of the young generation Lakota are even opting for making a distinction between *wašicun* and *wašicu* (the only difference in pronunciation being the final nasalized consonant), insisting that the first term is a sacred one and that the second is not, even though there is no historical or linguistic evidence for this kind of change. The rationale for this distinction harks back to the false etymology of *wašicun* based on the stealing-the-bacon (*wašin icu*) myth in which the last word in the phrase (*icu*) is not nasalized.

However erroneous and specious this reasoning is, it is nevertheless interesting from the point of view of linguistic change, and how much sacred language means to the people who speak it. In this particular example, a whole religious and political ideology, and the expression of what is perceived to be a status relationship between Indian and white is ultimately reducible to the presence or absence of a nasalized phoneme—*wasicun* or *wasicu*.

It can be speculated further that at the time of European contact other once-sacred words became incorporated into everyday speech. For example, the terms for horse (*šunka wakan*), gun (*maza wakan*), and alcohol (*mni wakan*) were predicated on the idea that these foreign elements were somehow originally incomprehensible. Today, of course, these terms and others like them are part of the common Lakota language. But earlier perhaps they were understandable only to a select few medicine men who were responsible for the actual naming of these newly introduced items. Today some medicine men refer to all white technology as *wakasote šni* which may be glossed roughly as 'indestructible things' (from *wa* noun marker; *kasote* 'to deplete or use up, waste by striking'; and *šni* negative enclitic). That a category of foreign technology is classified by a sacred term suggests that perhaps all foreign material things and ideas that were strange and awesome were originally termed 'sacred'.

Unquestionably, some terms commonly used today (but not in reference to foreign objects) were once sacred. For example, the generic term for animal is a metaphor *wamakaškan* from *wa* noun marker, *maka* 'earth'; and *škan* 'to move'. Hence animals are things that move about the earth. Even the common term for 'children' *wakanheja* is based on the term *wakan*, underscoring the popular saying *wakanheja kin wakanpelo* 'children are sacred'.

And so the creation of sacred from secular, and the return of the secular to sacred provides a never-ending means for establishing a communication between supernatural and natural categories. Similarly, comprehensibility is transformed into incomprehensibility so that the perceived nature of the supernatural may be understood.

Since much of sacred language appears in song, it is useful to understand just how Lakota conceptualize the idea of song and singing. To do so, it is necessary to review the traditional way in which anthropologists and ethnomusicologists have treated and analyzed American Indian song, particularly their frequent inability to distinguish between song structure, vocables and texts, and song performance. Again I conjure up some of the ideas of Lévy-Bruhl, who is too frequently seen as the black sheep of French sociology but who has given us many insights into the way people view their world. The ways sacred texts are borne out of visions may be discussed in both sacred and secular terms, but even the secular terms are special in that they are used by a relatively few singers and song makers.

CHAPTER 2

OGLALA SONG TERMINOLOGY

> Everyone of us believes that he knows exactly what consti-
> tutes his personal individuality, and where he would con-
> sider that it ended. My feelings, thought, recollections, are
> myself. My head, arms, legs, internal organs, etc., are still
> myself. All the rest that I perceive is not I. Thus my indi-
> viduality is grasped by my consciousness and circum-
> scribed by my bodily exterior, and I believe that my neigh-
> bour's is precisely so too.
>
> —Lucien Lévy-Bruhl 1966, 114

ADEQUATE exegeses, if not apologia, for Lévy-Bruhl, the
eminent French sociologist, have appeared in all recent references to his works (notably, Cazeneuve 1972, Douglas 1970,
Evans-Pritchard 1965, Needham 1972) and readers interested
in the argument over the significance of the terms 'prelogical',
'mystical', 'law of participation', etc., all terms associated
with perceived constructs of the "primitive" mind, should
consult these authors.[1] Once stripped of the evolutionistic
parlance of the turn of the century, the substance of Lévy-
Bruhl's thesis is enlightening without being demeaning to
non-Western peoples. He provides, sometimes obscurely, an
interesting theoretical frame within which one can interpret
how people structure their perception of reality, in this case,
music, and the manner in which they verbalize about it.

Historically, ethnomusicologists have expressed interest in
the same problem. Merriam, in speaking generally about how
songs are acquired, states that:

> Some standards must be held by all people if there is to be a
> music style or even a music system at all, and . . . enough ex-

amples are available to indicate that some, at least, of these standards are verbalized. It is also to be expected that cultures differ in the extent of such verbalization, but at the same time it is very doubtful that any people have nothing whatsoever to say about their musical style. [Merriam 1964, 169–70][2]

Recognizing that people do in fact have something to say about their musical styles and standards, we are not so much led to the inevitable question: what do they say? Rather, given that ethnomusicology, like anthropology, is still primarily a product of Euro-American tradition whose theories and methods are essentially proffered for Euro-American consumption, we are more properly concerned with asking: do people verbalize about their music in a manner similar to or different from our own? This is a frustrating question to answer.

For example, in discussing the techniques of conscious composition among American Indians, Nettl has written that "it is difficult to do research . . . because the natives do not ordinarily discuss such matters among themselves. Consequently native informants have trouble explaining techniques" (1956, 16). But the "trouble" here has nothing necessarily to do with native informants. Since the 1960s it has been well established in anthropology that ethnographies, in this case musical ethnographies, are largely sets of questions and answers which are collected by an investigator and ultimately described, analyzed, and published. But as Frake has succinctly pointed out, "The problem is not simply to find answers to questions the ethnographer brings to the field, but also to find the questions that go with the responses he observes after his arrival" (1964, 132).

I single out these statements because I think they are relevant to this chapter which deals with how the Oglala verbalize about their music style and standards. I would agree with Merriam that verbalizations about music differ because cultures differ, but I am more concerned with the *manner* in which people verbalize rather than the *extent* to which they do so. As I shall demonstrate, there is an important analytical difference between these two perspectives. I also agree with

Nettl that it is difficult to elicit explanations for some types of musical behavior, but I feel that it is not so much a problem with the respondent's inability as it is with the methods traditionally employed by ethnomusicologists to elicit such verbalizations.

These methods are in turn influenced by the Euro-American musical tradition, which seeks to compartmentalize vocabularies employed to analyze corresponding cultural domains. Although the terms used in these vocabularies are ultimately derived from the folk idiom, the process of compartmentalization renders them, in Western tradition, technical language. This technical language then becomes exclusively associated with the domain, in this case music, and is perceived to be isolable from other cultural domains which are in part defined in terms of the vocabularies themselves.

Euro-American technical language is very much analogous to culture itself in the evolutionary sense. As incipient *Homo sapiens* we sought to create culture, but, once created, we became forever subservient to our creation. As ethnomusicologists we spend most of our academic evolution creating and refining means of analyzing and comparing musics of the world. But once our theories, methods, techniques, and terminologies are established, we are forever chained to the products of our scholarly energies. Like culture, we are flexible: when our means of technical musical communication require change, we can alter our earlier constructs. But rarely do we change our general conceptual model of music.

The technical language of the Euro-American tradition is indeed complex, but I would simply characterize it as analytical in the linguistic sense, i.e., displaying a tendency to divide into component parts. I would then follow by characterizing the model of the musical universe as seen through the eyes of Euro-American ethnomusicologists as an analytical model of music. One of the most significant diagnostic features of this model is that it is presumed that all music is a cultural phenomenon which should be analyzed and described in purely cultural terms. One of my objectives is to demonstrate that it is more often the nature of the model rather than the competency of the native that renders cross-cultural interpretations of musical behavior difficult. Using our own analytical model as a basis for investigating the music of small societies, or even for segments of Euro-American cultures, presupposes that the native's model is somewhat akin to our own. Methodologically, we attempt to elicit glosses for what we perceive to be meaningful components of the native's musical domain, but which, cross culturally, may not be meaningful. It is in this spirit that I seek an alternate means of interpreting Oglala song terminology.

TOWARD AN ALTERNATE MUSICAL MODEL

All models begin somewhere, and I agree with Lévi-Strauss's notion that an anthropologist's model must be built from what the native tells him (Lévi-Strauss 1962, 322 and passim). New models are constructed from raw ethnographic data, not from old models an anthropologist brings to the field. I suggest an alternate model for music, in this case built from ethnographic data I have collected from the Oglala over the past thirty-five years. I require a different kind of model for two important reasons.

First, in the past, one of the initial problems that has confronted Western musicologists and anthropologists investigating music verbalization was that our own preconceptions about technical languages presuppose that these vocabularies are exclusive. We fully recognize that the technical language of music in Western society is in the purview of specialists. In small societies, however, what musicians or others say about their music is not necessarily a part of any exclusive domain. Not only the specialists, but people at large understand what is being said about their musical culture, and all may freely participate in musical discourse despite their lack of specialization. But this in itself does not demonstrate that what they have to say about their music is any less "technical" or meaningful. In the spirit of cultural relativism it is safe to say that all people speak of their music in its cultural context, and they maintain a vocabulary which enables them to communicate their musical culture freely, totally, and clearly, relative to the cultural matrix in which their music is created and performed. Technical language, in fact, is very much like the incest taboo: although it is universal, or nearly universal, the way it manifests itself is often unique.

The second reason for an alternate model is that in Western society, music is perceived to be an aspect of culture, as Herskovits would say, "the man made part of the environment" (1948, 17). However, there is no reason to believe that all peoples of the world, given that they distinguish at all between natural and cultural domains, consider music as a cultural category. Lévi-Strauss's illuminating idea that places humans in a dialectic relationship between nature and culture (Lévi-Strauss 1949) perhaps may be modified to suggest that at least some people, including the nonspecialist in our own society, may classify music as part of the *natural* order. If this is the case, then we would expect to find music, and what people have to say about it, analogically related to other domains likewise perceived to be natural rather than cultural. In fact, music may be represented as a "natural symbol" (Douglas 1970) expressed in the metaphors of human bodily functions. Here I am inspired by Lévy-Bruhl's idea of "appurtenances," first discussed in *The "Soul" of the Primitive*, in which he writes:

> First of all the primitive's idea of individuality comprises, in addition to his own body, all that grows upon it, all that comes from it, its secretions and its excretions: hair of the head and body, nails, tears, urine, excreta, seminal fluid, perspiration, etc. . . . The hair and secretions, etc., of the individual are his very self, just as his feet or his hands, his heart or his head, are. They "belong" to him in the fullest sense of the word. Henceforth I shall speak of them as his "appurtenances." [Lévy-Bruhl 1966, 115]

Lévy-Bruhl's notion of "appurtenances" is critical to his ideas of "pre–logical mentality" and forms a fundamental part of his "law of participation," i.e., "primitive" man considers his appurtenances as an integral part of himself, but nowhere does Lévy-Bruhl suggest that so-called primitive mentality is inferior to "civilized mentality" (on this point see Cazeneuve 1972, 1–23); it is simply a different kind of logic. That this logic is to be found among all peoples is demonstrable, and if we were to substitute, in the above quoted passage, the term "a person" for "primitive," it would not be difficult to show that all of us "participate" in our "appurtenances" or those of others to varying degrees. Each of us is aware of culturally relevant appurtenances which we may or may not share with other cultures, for example, our emotional or sentimental attachments to a lock of hair or baby shoes; our preoccupation with coiffures, deodorants, makeup, false eyelashes and nails; and our dedication to cleanliness complete with soaps, powders, oils, douches, and scented bathroom tissue. All demonstrate quite adequately that what once might have been the purview of "primitive" mentality and "pre–logical" thought are quite civilized. Thus Lévy-Bruhl's theories, taken out of their evolutionistic context, are appealing and applicable to contemporary peoples, Euro-American or otherwise.

Lévy-Bruhl's theories, particularly the law of participation, were intended to explain a wide range of phenomena otherwise treated under the more usual rubric of "primitive" religion: mana, taboo, magic, witchcraft, sorcery, and others. In further modifying his ideas, I wish to add to his list of appurtenances music itself or, perhaps more appropriately, *song*, because the latter would seem to have a wider degree of application to peoples of the world than the more limited (to Euro-American tradition) *music*. This addition, upon which I will elaborate, seems particularly appealing when attempting to analyze the music vocabulary of the Oglala, which, like that of other American Indians, is almost entirely vocal. As I shall demonstrate, song is consciously or unconsciously conceived to be an extension of the human body rather than something external to it.

I am suggesting the following contrast between Oglala conceptualization of music and more traditional Euro-American concepts: Where Euro-American music is conceived to be cul-

William Horn Cloud, a well-known singer on the reservation and song leader in Yuwipi rituals. Photograph taken in 1983 by Lisa Clifford. Powers Collection.

tural and employs an analytical model for purposes of description and analysis, the Oglala perceive their music to be natural and employ a synthetic model to describe and analyze it. I use *synthetic* in the linguist's sense, i.e., displaying a tendency to combine two or more elements to form a unit. The two models may not be mutually exclusive, as Lévy-Bruhl suggested for the distinction between prelogical and logical mentality. Thus we may find "specialists" among the Oglala, who are more analytical, and nonspecialists among Euro-Americans, who are more synthetic. The model is primarily intended to be useful in understanding how one group of people speak about their musical tradition.

METHODOLOGICAL CONSIDERATION

In viewing how the Oglala verbalize about song, my approach is essentially structuralist and linguistic; the essential unit of analysis is the morpheme. In the past, ethnomusicologists have attempted to elicit information about verbalization using as the basis of their analysis the lexeme. But this presupposes that the music terminology under investigation somehow corresponds with the native language of the investigator. The result is an accumulation of lexical items which do correspond, for example, song, drum, drum stick, and flageolet. But ideas which do not translate easily, or at all, are not elicitable at this level.

At the morphemic level, given that a synthetic model will produce a vocabulary that relates music to other natural order, and in this case bodily functions, I am concerned with identifying morphemes employed to discuss music, and comparing them with the same morphemes in other natural domains, i.e., functions of the human body. This approach requires sensitivity to Lakota, the native language of the Oglala, and my own competency led me to initial identification of morphemes.

In addition to native language competency, as a starting point for analysis I find Lévi-Strauss's analysis of myth inspiring, and perhaps some analogue may be drawn between Lévi-Strauss's minimal unit of myth, the "mytheme," and my minimal unit of analysis, the morpheme. The structuralist approach to myth requires rearranging the myth in terms of recurring themes. These "bundles of such relations" (Lévi-Strauss 1963a, 207) say something not always clear in the myths themselves. For Lévi-Strauss, all myths serve to work out fundamental contradictions in the social order, most of which deal with basic problems such as food, clothing, shelter, and sexual relations.

Regarding morphemes as bundles of constituent units (since, like mythemes, they are minimal units of meaning), I arrange the total number of morphemes found in Lakota lexemic units related to song and compare them with the same morphemes as they appear in other domains. Just as Lévi-Strauss regards much of mythical thought as being unconscious, I regard the formation of most words employed to discuss music (or any other domain) similarly, although this may not always be the case. The resultant model is then a logical one based on ethnographic data and the native language, but as is true of all models of social structure, it may not necessarily be identical to the native model of music (see particularly Lévi-Strauss 1962, 323–24, "Consciousness and Unconsciousness").

This synthetic model not only explains how and why certain lexical units are selected over other possibilities, but it also gives some indication of the history of such selections and offers a modicum of predictability.

To illustrate the nature of the synthetic model and how the Oglala verbalize about their musical culture, I will focus on four aspects of music: (1) the concept of song, (2) performance standards, (3) composition and learning, and (4) classification of musical instruments. Throughout I will demonstrate how the synthetic model reveals a persistence in employing "natural" terms for recent musical adaptations, for example, newly introduced musical instruments from Euro-American culture.

THE CONCEPT OF SONG

In Lakota, there are seven morphemes called by linguists "instrumental prefixes" (Buechel 1939, 1970; Swanton 1911) which, when prefixed to verb stems, modify the mode of action. One such morpheme, *ya*, when prefixed to verbs and adjectives, indicates that the action is performed by means of the mouth. Also, *ya* appears with two inseparable prepositions to form *iya* 'to speak' and *eya* 'to say'. This morpheme may refer to actions performed literally or figuratively, for example, *yaka* 'to tell, mean'; *yatkan* 'to drink'; *yata* 'to chew'; *yaȟtaka* 'to bite'; or *yaȟwa* 'to bore by speaking' (from *ya* + *ȟwa* 'sleepy'); *yaignuni* 'to confuse by interrupting the conversation' (from *ya* + *ignuni* 'to lose with'); *yaiȟa* 'to make laugh by talking' (from *ya* + *iȟa* 'to laugh'); *yainila* 'to silence one by speaking' (from *ya* + *inila* 'silent'); etc.

Given that *ya* always refers to actions performed by means of the mouth, it serves as the basis for describing and evaluating a wide range of musical events, sounds, and standards.[3] For example:

Yatun 'to sing out' (from *ya* + *tun* 'to give birth to'; the same radical also means 'to bear children', 'to be born').

Yaotanin 'to make public in song' (from *ya* + *otanin* 'public, manifest, visible').

Yabu 'to growl as one sings' (from *ya* + *bu*, a radical element which suggests a rapid succession of sounds, e.g., *nabubu* 'to tap one's feet in time,' *kabubu* 'to clap one's hands in time'; the latter is used to indicate a type of bread in which the dough is shaped by flattening it with the hands).

Yahogita 'to become hoarse from singing' (from *ya* + *hogita* 'hoarse').

Yaȟmun 'to hum' (from *ya* + *ȟmun* 'to buzz,' as bees buzz).

Yaiyowaza 'to trail the voice' (from *ya* + *iyowaza* 'echo').

Yašna 'to sing incorrectly, blunder in song' (from *ya* + *šna*, an enclitic which suggests that an action or state of being was somehow interrupted, or prevented from successful completion). Compare *wošna* 'to blow out a candle'; *yušna* 'to extinguish a light'.

Yaštan 'to finish singing, end the song' (from *ya* + *štan* 'corked, plugged up'). Compare with *wapoštan* 'hat', literally, "something into which the head is 'plugged'."

Yatokca 'to alter, modify, change the song' (from *ya* + *tokca* 'different, unusual').

Yajo 'to play a wind instrument' (from *ya* + *jo* 'to whistle, or to sing like birds').

Yawankicu 'to begin or lead a song' (from *ya* + *wank(a)* 'upwards' and *icu* 'to cause to, to take').

Yaptan 'to change the tune, song' (from *ya* + *ptan* 'change').

Yazilya 'to sing slowly, drawl' (from *ya* + *zica* 'to stretch like rubber').

Yaȟla 'to make the voice rattle' (from *ya* + *ȟla* 'rattle'). Compare with *sinteȟla* 'rattle snake', i.e., 'rattletail'; also metaphorically, a 'death rattle'.

Obviously the use of the morpheme *ya* enables the Oglala to criticize or otherwise evaluate songs and singers infinitely. What is important is that the modality of song is not distinguished from other oral functions of the body, *except by context*.

Another morpheme (also used as a lexeme), *ho*, means 'voice' or, by extension, 'sound'. It is used in a number of ways to verbalize musical concepts:

Hotanin 'to raise one's voice in song' (from *ho* + *otanin* 'public, manifest, visible').

Hotun 'to sing out' (from *ho* + *tun* 'to give birth to').

Olowan kin ho 'melody' (from *olowan* 'song', *kin*, definite article, and *ho*; literally, 'voice of the song').

Wicaho hukuciyela 'low tones, notes' (from *wica*, generic noun marker; *ho*, and *hukuciyela* 'down below').

Wicaho wankatuya 'high tones, notes' (from *wicaho* and *wankatuya* 'up above').

Wicaho oegnake 'scale' (from *wicaho* and *oegnake* 'to place in a container,' i.e., a voice that is delineated).

Wicaho oyuspe 'tape recorder' (from *wicaho* and *oyuspe* 'to catch'). Interestingly, to record is *nagoya* 'to scratch automatically', which refers to the making of a disc.

Hokapsanpsan 'to whine' (from *ho* + *psanpsan* 'swaying back and forth', as a swing).

Hoiyoȟpeya 'to tire the voice from singing' (from *ho* + *iyoȟpeya* 'to cast out', as a fisherman casts a line).

Hoyeya 'to sing, send a voice' (from *ho* + *yeya* 'to cause to go').

Houkiye 'to receive, learn a song' (from *ho* + *ukiye* 'to cause to come', said of songs learned in a vision).

Singers under the Sun Dance arbor at Pine Ridge, August, 1966. Photograph by Paul Steinmetz, S.J.

Hotanka 'loud-voiced' (from *ho* + *tanka* 'large, great', said of both the voice in singing and the sound of an instrument).

Still another term, *jo* 'to whistle', appears in *jolowan* 'to whistle a tune' (from *jo* + *olowan* 'song') and *johotun* 'to whistle up a tune' (from *jo* + *hotun* 'to give birth to a song'). Later I shall return to this term because it figures prominently in classifying native and modern musical instruments.

The generic term for song is *olowan*, which is formed from the noun marker *(w)o* and *lowan*. In the past *lowan* has been translated simply as 'to sing' (Buechel 1970), but given the infinite range of verbalizing about various modes of vocality using the prefix *ya*, it is more profitable to gloss *lowan* as 'to sing a song'. Actually, *lowan* delineates the parameters of "song." It is interesting to compare this idea with the ethnomusicologist's concept of song, particularly the notion of *in-*

complete repetition, which has been widely regarded as a diagnostic feature of Plains Indian music (Nettl 1956, 111). As I shall show, the analytic and synthetic models of "song" conflict to some degree, making this contrast instructive to future classifications of Native American music.

In the past "incomplete repetition" has been used as a technical term to identify a particular type of song structure which is only partly repeated. This structure is normally written *A B C B D. A* stands for the introduction, or nonrepeated portion of the song; *B,* for the theme; and *C,* for the cadential formula. Thus in songs of the "incomplete repetition" type, the theme and cadential formula are repeated in one rendition of a song, but the introduction is not; hence the name.

The Oglala concept *olowan* 'song', however, corresponds with the ethnomusicological statement *BB,* which is to say (and this can be tested empirically) that a song is "equal" to two renditions of the theme. Since the cadential formula *C* is conceived to be an integral part of the theme, the Oglala do not distinguish between theme and cadence. This contrasts with the ethnomusicological notion of incomplete repetition in an interesting way, for partial repetition does not, in fact, adequately describe the structure of song; rather it describes performance of the song. Just how concepts related to performance are discussed will be treated below, but first I would like to make some comments on the relationship between *olowan,* 'song', and other body functions, since the relationship is not obvious at the lexemic level.

The morpheme *lo* is found in very few Lakota words and is relatively easy to isolate. The use of *lo* in domains other than 'song' is instructive:

> *Lolo* 'soft, tender, moist, flabby, fleshy'.
> *Locin* 'to be hungry,' literally 'to want meat'.
> *Talo* 'meat of a hoofed animal' (e.g., *tatanka* 'buffalo bull'; *tăhca* 'deer').
> *Logute* 'hollow of the flank of man or animal'.
> *Loȟe* 'the flabby part of the cheeks or throat'.
> *Lote* 'throat proper'.
> *Lotku* 'flesh below the center of the mandibular region' (the "second chin").

All other forms of *lo* are found in words pertaining to food and cooking, for example:

Loigni 'to hunt food'.
Lolicupi 'rations'.
Loliȟ'an 'to prepare food'.
Lolobya 'to boil until tender'.
Lol'opetun 'to buy groceries'.
Lolopiye 'bag for storing meat'.
Lowitaya 'fresh, raw' (as meat).
Loyake 'fresh' (as opposed to dried meat, etc.).

What I am suggesting here (perhaps on less firm grounds than my case for the morpheme *ya*, and morpheme/lexeme *ho* and *jo*) is that the radical element (*lo*) found in the term for song (*olowan*) is the same radical element found in lexemes associated with human anatomy (the face and throat), and with food and methods of preparing food. In all cases it is the function of the human body that generates a synthetic model of Oglala musical verbalization with respect to concepts of song and singing. Stated another way, the manner in which the Oglala verbalize about song is analogous to the manner in which they verbalize about other bodily functions such as eating, as well as human anatomy involved in food ingestion.

PERFORMANCE

As stated earlier, analytical and synthetic models of music culture need not be mutually exclusive. Nowhere else is this clearer than in Lakota terms associated with the performance of music. When speaking of performance, at least part of the Oglala conceptual model coincides with the ethnomusicologist's notion of incomplete repetition. But again it should be reiterated that incomplete repetition is a function of performance and not an adequate description of song structure.

Elsewhere (Powers 1970, 358–69), I have suggested that the performance model for Plains music should be refined and represented by *A A¹ B C B C*. *A* corresponds with the introductory phrase by an individual or the entire chorus (known in English as the "second"); *B* corresponds with the theme

of the song; and *C*, with the cadential formula. In actual performance, as noted before, the Oglala do not distinguish *B*
and *C*; they are both regarded as the song proper (*olowan*).
However, for purposes of performance, the Oglala identify
both the introduction (*A*) and the second (*A*¹) in their native
language.

The introduction is called *yawankicu* 'to take the voice upwards'; while the second is referred to as *pawankiye* 'to push
the voice upwards' (from *pa*, instrumental prefix, 'to push or
press'; *wank(a)* 'upwards'; and *iye* 'to cause to'). Since approximately 1974, the Oglala have called this particular seconding
effect in English "push ups." The term is used to determine
the number of renditions of a war dance song each group will
sing, one "push up" being equivalent to one rendition. The
term *pawankiye* carries the connotation of raising the pitch. In
normal practice the leader starts the song on one tone and is
seconded by a singer who slightly raises the pitch. The conscious raising of pitch is considered good singing technique.

In addition to these "technical" terms for the parts of a performance, there are some idioms. Thus the proper way to sing
the introduction is *pan* 'to whine, cry'; the second should be
sung *akiš'a*, a general term relating to both human and animal
cries of a piercing nature, best translated into English as 'yelp-
ing'. Both the introduction and the second may also be sung
yuš'a, which is the squeaking sound produced by rubbing
one's finger around the rim of good crystal. Still another
idiom, *yupesto*, is used to indicate excellent attack in the introduction or second. It means 'to sharpen,' as one would
sharpen a pencil or stick. It is partially derived from *pa*, meaning an animal or human head.

The morpheme *ka*, when prefixed to verb stems, indicates
that action is accomplished by means of striking with the arm
and hand. Not surprisingly, this morpheme enables the Oglala
to describe or evaluate the act of drumming almost to the
same extent that *ya* can be employed to verbalize about singing. A partial list of words related to drumming is:

> *kabubu* 'to drum' (from *ka* + *bubu*, reduplication of *bu*, a radical
> element suggesting a succession of rapid sounds); it also means

'hand clapping,' although in all Oglala drumming a drumstick is used.

icabu 'drumstick' (from *i* 'by means of', *ca k* preceded by *i* changes to *c*, and *bu*).

kat'inze 'to drum in steady beats' (from *ka* + *t'inze* 'firm, tight').

kašna 'to miss a beat' (from *ka* + *šna*, an enclitic which indicates that an action or state of being was interrupted).

kaijena 'to drum out of time' (from *ka* + *ijena* 'to mix, to mix up', as apples with oranges).

The adverb *kpankpanyela*, when used with verbs meaning 'to drum', translates as "tremolo" or "thunder drumming." The word refers to anything "abundant" or "countless." The expression *sam iyeic'iye*, when used in conjunction with verbs signifying 'to drum' (and also 'to dance'), means that the singer has played too many beats, i.e., all the others have stopped drumming, but he continues. The expression means literally "to cause oneself to 'go over' or 'do more than required'."

During a performance of group singing, one song (*olowan*) is repeated anywhere from four to perhaps, nowadays, twenty-five times. The act of repeating a song is called *piyalowan* (from *piya* 'to renew' and *lowan* 'to sing a song'). Curiously, the Oglala regard repeating a song metaphorically the same as curing a patient, i.e., both are "renewed" (a medicine man is called *wapiye* 'someone who renews').

When the last complete song is finished, the singers pause and sing the *sinte* 'tail' (compare with *coda*). The *sinte* is comprised of *BC*, i.e., the theme and cadential formula without the introduction and lead.

Not all verbalization related to performance is necessarily constructed from instrumental prefixes and other morphemes. For example, tempo is classified into *ȟ'anhi* 'slow'; *oȟ'ankoya* 'fast'; and *iwaštegla* 'easy, casual', the latter identifying a preferred dance tempo intermediate between slow and fast. The pitch of the song may be classified as *wankata* 'high' or *kuta* 'low', a relatively higher pitch being preferred. The length of a song or performance of song may be classified as *hanska* 'long' or *ptecela* 'short', a higher value being placed on songs which are short (i.e., with fewer vocables or words to the strophe), than renditions which are long.

Often before beginning a series of songs in a normal voice
(*hotanka* 'loud-voiced'), a singer may practice a song to himself by whistling, *jolowan* 'to whistle a song'. If all the singers
are not sure of a new song, they may begin singing *jiyahan*
'lowly, softly' for one or two renditions until they become
confident. The Oglala also contrast the volume of the song in
terms of it being *iyonihan* 'just audible' or *iyoja* 'amplified'.

Finally, the members of the performance group are known
as *lowans'a wicaša* 'male singer' (from *lowan* 'to sing a song';
s'a, an enclitic indicating frequency, regularity, i.e., one who
normally does something; and *wicaša* 'man'). Female singers
are called *wicaglata* 'responders' (from *wica*, third person
plural, and *aglata* 'to answer, respond') because their voices
slightly trail behind the men's at the end of each song. The entire group of singers is called *ȟoka* (etymology unknown; it
may be a foreign word, possibly deriving from Omaha or
Ponca). When song groups perform, the verb *ahiyaya* 'to pass
around' (as a pipe in a council) is a metaphor for group singing. The term stems from the earlier custom of each man at
the drum taking turns beginning a new song, thus "passing
around the songs."

COMPOSITION AND LEARNING

With respect to the process of composition, Nettl has written
that "Among North American Indians there are two important ways in which new songs can be acquired: conscious
composition, a process akin to that of Western composers;
and learning songs in visions or dreams" (1956, 14). If by "acquire" Nettl means "compose," then his statement corresponds perhaps with all musical compositional processes
of the world. A synthetic model of music will not settle the
real or putative distinction between conscious versus unconscious composition because the process of composition is uni-
versally synthetic by definition, i.e., a bringing together of
parts whether they be musical, graphic, plastic, or otherwise.
If by "acquire," however, Nettl means to "obtain" or otherwise
"learn," the analytical model contrasts with the synthetic. It is

difficult to separate compositional from learning processes among the Oglala; they are bound conceptually by a model that serves to explain "how new songs are brought into being" (Merriam 1964, 165), as well as how old songs are retained in the tribal repertoire.

Given that music is part of the natural order, it is *there*, occupying a niche in the natural universe with a humanlike capacity to be born and to die, to undergo changes, to be renewed or "cured" if you will (as the language suggests). Music is not so much composed from whole cloth as it is, metaphorically, reincarnated, just as is true, so the Oglala believe, with humans. The term *yatun* 'to give birth to a song' is perhaps the closest gloss to 'to compose', but the connotation of *tun* is 'to give rise to something *that has already existed in another form*' (see Powers 1977).

Looking at how new songs are brought into being, it is impossible, given their reincarnative nature, to determine which are "consciously" composed and which have evolved through other means, such as visions or rearrangements of existing songs. These "compositional" processes are all aspects of the same phenomenon. For example, the noun *wounspe* means 'lesson' or 'teaching'. A song "learned" in a vision may be referred to as *olowan unspeic'iye*, while the process of "teaching" a song to another is *olowan unspekiya*. All these linguistic forms are derived from the verb *unspe*, which under different contexts means 'to know (have learned)'; 'to teach' (with the suffic *kiya* 'to cause to'); or 'to learn' (with the reflexive suffix *ic'iye* 'to cause oneself to'). Thus the Oglala consciously or unconsciously merge three concepts, which we as academics attempt to separate consciously or unconsciously, based on a simple axiom that that which is taught is learned, and that which is learned is known, that which is known is taught.

This is not to say that music is somehow an absolute form; once a song has been *unspe* (taught, learned, known), it may be altered, transmitted, studied, or casually "caught." The Oglala verbalize all of these operations. For example, what has been traditionally regarded as "conscious" composition by the analytical model is verbalized by the Oglala in the term

olowan kaga 'to make a song'. Songs which are made are by
definition those sung in a secular context, but the original
components of the song may have been sung in another context, for example religious, and thus ultimately were refash-
ioned from a song which was originally *unspeic'iye*, 'learned in
a vision'. The act of reshaping a song to fit a new context, i.e.,
transferred from a religious context to a secular one, is called
yatokca 'to change by means of the mouth'. Of course, in the
transformation the song structure is changed by the song-
maker, but the original song on which the alteration is based
remains in the tribal repertoire. The term *yatokca* may also be
used to indicate changing a song of one genre to fit the structure of another genre, for example, making a Rabbit Dance
song into an Omaha Dance song. But the term would never be
used to suggest a transformation of a song used in one religious context to another religious context, because this kind
of change would decrease the power of the song or perhaps
antagonize the supernaturals. This is not to say that such
transformations do not occur in practice. But they are regarded as inauspicious or in bad taste.

The process of learning songs in a secular context is called
olowan oyuspe 'to catch a song', and it would be improper to
speak of "catching" a song in, for example, a vision. The fundamental distinctions between sacred and secular contexts on
the one hand, and composing and learning on the other may
be illustrated:

	Yatun ('to give birth to a song')	
	Compose	*Learn*
Sacred	*Unspekiye* ('To teach')	*Unspeic'iye* ('To learn')
Secular	*Olowan kaga* ('To make a song')	*Olowan oyuspe* ('To catch a song')

Although in everyday usage one might hear *unspekiye* 'to
teach' employed in a secular sense, the proper word for
"teaching" another a song is *akiyapi* 'to practice, give mind to,
try, test'.

Whereas components of song performance are categorized (cf. *yawankicu, pawankiye*, etc., above), the components of the structure of a song are not. For example, there is no Lakota counterpart for the "vocable." I attribute this to the notion that the vocable is a structural feature of *olowan* 'song', i.e., of the theme and cadence, which are not distinguished from each other. Songs are made or learned with a set of vocables which remains intact, and unless the song is changed (in part by altering the vocables as well as thematic music), the vocables partly distinguish one song from another. Although there is no space to elucidate the problems of vocables in this paper, it should be stated that while vocables do not have meaning in a semantic sense, they do have a grammar which tends to render the range of song syllables finite.

It is probably safe to say that words in songs sung in a secular context are classifiable; such songs are said to be *wocaje* 'name' songs. Those songs with words sung in a religious context, however, are not so distinguished, and I speculate that the logic is that "supernatural" words are a structural feature of "supernatural" songs and cannot be further distinguished.

Finally, with reference to "the extent" to which the Oglala verbalize about musical composition as we try to understand it in Western tradition, it should be understood that questions like "Under what conditions did you compose (or learn) this song?" or "Where did this song come into being?" will elicit an infinite variety of responses that may not necessarily be further analyzed. Even if it were possible to categorize the "conditions" of composition, it is unlikely that there would be very much contrast cross-culturally. Densmore has pointed out that "the Indian isolated himself by going away from the camp, while the white musician or poet locks his door, but both realize the necessity of freedom from distraction" (1918, 59). While it is unlikely that all creative people require freedom from distraction, Densmore's statement does reflect that the creative condition is more properly the subject of psychophysical processes and is not necessarily restricted to the domain of musical inquiry.

Boys' band at Holy Rosary Mission, Pine Ridge, ca. 1920s. New music styles were readily classified in the native language according to the extant system.

My own inquiry as to the conditions under which songs come into being led to a number of standard responses which are not, or do not seem to be, unique to the Oglala. Among some of the responses about the composition of a song, singers told me: "I was just sitting there tapping two rocks together, when this song come to me"; "I was sitting in the back of the pick-up listening to the hum of the tires on the road, when . . ."; "I was standing there in the dance arbor and all of a sudden I began to sing this new song"; "All of a sudden I heard this song and began to sing it"; "I was taking my boy to the train station (to go to the army) when I sang this song"; "When he heard President Kennedy was dead, he began singing this song." Although the need to sing or compose a song under duress or in an emotional state may be more Oglala than not, the situations or conditions themselves reveal nothing unique.

As to a preference of composing one part of a new song prior to another part, for example, introduction before theme or vocables before words, there seems to be no standard practice. Most genres of songs are marked in part by strophic and final cadences; thus once the function of the song is determined, this part of the song remains standard. There is perhaps a logical argument that vocables hold primacy over texts (since there is no word for vocable), but this cannot be empirically verified. Texts may be added or dropped in the process of changing songs. In some genres,—Rabbit Dance Songs and Love songs—the introduction as well as the final cadences are standardized. In the Omaha Dance song, the introduction is derived from the theme, thus the theme is logically composed first. In songs emanating from supernatural origins, the texts are regarded as the most important; however, some songs sung in a religious context are comprised of vocables only.

The time required to compose a song also varies. Some songs are said to have been composed spontaneously at a dance or other kind of gathering, while others, partly completed, have, as one singer told me, been "carried around in my head for more than a year."

CLASSIFICATION OF MUSICAL INSTRUMENTS

Returning for a moment to Lévy-Bruhl's notion of "appurtenance," and regarding music as one of those qualities or states perceived to be part of human bodily functions rather than something exterior to it, it is quite simple to demonstrate that vocal music is a prime candidate for such "natural" considerations. In speaking of Oglala terminology specifically, although this would apply to all Native American music in varying degrees, their music is essentially and preeminently vocal. However, musical instruments are important as accompaniment and obviously must be considered with respect to what the Oglala have to say about their total musical system.

In discussing musical instruments, I want to focus on three considerations:

1. vocal music is logically an extension of the human body, and is expressed thus, as I have shown above, but musical instru-

ments are clearly *things* external to the human body; they are "manufactured."

2. given the limited number of musical instruments for the Oglala, namely, drum, rattle, flageolet, and minimal variations, is it really appropriate to talk about how the Oglala *classify* their instruments, or might we not merely investigate how they distinguish among instruments?

3. How do the Oglala incorporate Euro-American instruments into their own "natural" model of musical terminology, i.e., do newly introduced instruments become truly "classified" according to an existing scheme of musical instrument nomenclature?

In Western society it is assumed that music is a bounded domain, and the analytical model reflects this. In the past ethnosemanticists have had to focus their studies on similar bounded domains such as kinship, plants, disease, and color because these domains are perceived to be finite categories and thus subject to taxonomic classification. As I have demonstrated above, however, Oglala musical behavior and the means of verbalizing about it are theoretically infinite and thus are not readily subject to taxonomic considerations, except in those cases where the analytical and synthetic models coincide.

What may be regarded as the traditional inventory of Oglala musical instruments, one which existed prior to European contact and one which continues to be associated with the traditional music, includes the following:

Cancega 'drum' (from *can* 'wood' and *cega* 'earthern pot');
Wagmuha 'rattle' (from *wagmu* 'gourd' and *ha* 'skin, hide');
Šiyotanka 'flageolet,' 'flute,' 'whistle' (from *šiyo* 'prairie chicken' and *tanka* 'great, large').

The drum and rattle always serve as accompaniment to vocal music, while flageolet music is interchangeable with vocal music. Thus, in the case of the flageolet, used only in Love songs, a melody played on it may have been originally composed for vocal performance. In theory, every song played on a flageolet has a vocal counterpart with important song texts, but in practice this may not always be the case.[4]

The manner in which these respective instruments are played is described as:

Apa 'to strike with the hand', i.e., 'to drum';
Yucancan 'to shake with the hand', i.e., 'to rattle' (from *yu*, instrumental prefix signifying that an action is performed by means of the hands, and *cancan* 'to shake');
Yajo 'to whistle by means of the mouth'.

All native instruments are made from organic materials such as wood, clay, gourd, and skin. *Šiyotanka* 'big prairie chicken' is derived from the association between the mating ritual of the prairie chicken and human courting rituals. *Šiyo* is an onomatopoeic word perceived to be the sound of the prairie chicken during mating rituals. The analogy may not be obvious: both prairie chicken and humans inflate their cheeks to produce the appropriate mating sounds. The analogy is significant structurally on at least two levels, sound and performance.

The Oglala not only distinguish between the types of instrument based on structural features and analogies and the manner in which it is played based on the part of the body used to produce the sound, but they also distinguish between the method of producing the sound and the resultant effect of playing, thus:

Apa 'to drum', but *kabubu* 'the sound of drumming' (from *ka*, instrumental prefix signifying that the action was performed by striking with the arm, and *bubu*, reduplication of *bu*, a radical element suggesting a rapid succession of sounds).
Yucancan 'to rattle', but *yuhlahla* 'the sound of rattling' (from *yu*, instrumental prefix signifying that the action was performed by the hands, and *ȟlaȟla*, reduplicated form of *ȟla*, a radical element suggesting the sound of elements reverberating in a container', e.g., *sinteȟla* 'rattlesnake').
Yajo 'to whistle, play a flageolet,' but *yajoho* 'the sound of a flageolet, whistle' (from *ya*, instrumental prefix signifying that an action was performed by means of the mouth; *jo* 'to whistle,' as birds; and *ho* 'voice').

The idea of instrumental taxonomy is inappropriate here, given that each instrument is the sole member of its own class.

Although there are some minimal variations of drums (large bass types and smaller tambourine types), rattles (though even rawhide rattles are still called "gourd" rattles), and sizes of whistles, the native system regards all variations as simply drums, rattles, and flageolets. What is more interesting is the relationship between means of playing and resultant sounds of instruments (they are all derived from external bodily functions, i.e., actions performed by means of the hands, arms, and mouth, and thus cannot be isolated from other parts of the synthetic model).

Although musical instruments are manufactured and "exist" outside the human body, the way they are conceptualized integrates them into the synthetic model by emphasizing the manner in which an instrument is played and its resultant sound as analogues of human bodily functions. Although the names of the instruments themselves are "natural" categories—wood, clay, etc.—they can only be operationalized by means of bodily contact or manipulation, and this is what the native Oglala verbalize about modern Euro-American musical instruments. As is true in any kind of technological exchange, there are a number of ways that one society may linguistically incorporate new technologies of other societies. One way is simply to incorporate a loan word or corruption of the original word used to designate the technology. Another is to invent a new word in the native language, or conjure up an archaic word which has new-found relevance. Between borrowing in total and inventing anew, there are various permutations; although the Oglala deal with all of them easily (although there is a near absence of loan words from English) when speaking of song, the synthetic model persists.

Of particular note with respect to nonmusical domains is the Oglala tendency to describe the material out of which new technologies are made, as well as how new things function. As one example of the former, the Oglala were impressed upon seeing objects manufactured from metal and appropriately enunciated the sophisticated manufacturing process in a number of words: *mazawakan* 'gun' ("'holy' metal"); *mazacanku* 'railroad' ("iron road"); *masopiye* 'store' (i.e., "iron box, safe");

mazaska 'money' ("silver metal"), and so on. As an example of the latter, a boat was called *petawata* 'fire boat'; motorcycle, *napopela* ('an automatic explosion'); a side car was *patujela* ('a bending over,' indicating the manner in which the side car was pumped by two operators).

Despite the sophisticated manufacture of musical instruments, the technological features have never much impressed the Oglala, as the following examples will demonstrate.

Three categories of European musical instruments (which interestingly correspond with the ethnomusicological classification of musical instruments) are:

Waapapi 'things struck with the hands', i.e., "membranophones";

Wayuȟlaȟlapi 'things rattled with the hands', i.e., "idiophones" (*naȟlaȟla* 'to jingle one's bells' is derived from *na*, instrumental prefix signifying that the action takes place by means of the feet, and *ȟlaȟla* 'bells');

Wayajopi 'things played by blowing', i.e., "aerophones."

Chordophones were not known by the Oglala prior to European contact, but once introduced they were called generically *wayukize* 'things played on strings', literally "things which squeak by means of the hands"; *kiza* is an onomatopoeic word attributed to the sound of a mouse's voice. The Oglala further distinguish between two kinds of stringed instruments: those which are bowed and those which are strummed. The former is called *canyukize* 'to produce the sound of a squeak on wood'; the latter, *cankahotun* 'to strike wood and give birth to a voice'. The instrumental prefix *ka* is the same that we find in *kabubu* 'the sound of a drum'.[5]

While all modern brass and wind instruments are considered *wayajopi* 'things played by blowing', some brass instruments such as trombones and tubas are called *wayabupi* 'things that produce the sound of a growl.' Last, a mouth organ is regarded as being in a class of its own and is called *yapizapi*. *Piza* is an onomatopoeic word perceived to be the sound of a prairie dog which is called *pispiza*. Thus *yapizapi* means 'to produce the sound of a prairie dog by means of the mouth'.

Although a large inventory of Western instruments and their Lakota equivalents is yet to be collected, these examples demonstrate that the underlying means of classifying recently introduced instruments is consonant with the manner of verbalizing about native instruments and song, both of which are perceived to be "appurtenances" of the human body.

TAIL

The following points should be emphasized:

1. It is unlikely that part of any society's musical system does not include some means of verbalizing about it. And it is postulated that cultural differences are at least partly manifested in how such verbalizations are conceptualized and formulated, as Merriam has suggested.

2. Throughout the long history of music in the Western tradition, such means of verbalization have been codified and transformed from the folk idiom into a technical language which serves to describe and analyze music through what I have labeled an *analytical model,* one characterized by a tendency constantly to divide musical concepts into their component parts. I have suggested that the preconceptions of what music should be, based on the analytical model, have created problems in understanding not so much the extent to which non-Western peoples verbalize about their musical system, but the manner in which they do so.

3. Using data collected at Pine Ridge, I have suggested another model, here called the *synthetic model,* which provides another means of interpreting to an English-speaking audience how one non-Western society conceptualizes its music system. The synthetic model tends to combine units which are analogous to other cultural domains. I have referred to the seminal ideas of Lévy-Bruhl with hopes of demonstrating that among the Oglala the synthetic model of music is one consistent with what the Oglala perceive to be human bodily functions; vocal music is perceived to be an "appurtenance" of the human body classifiable along with other bodily functions, particularly speech. The analogies between music and other

particularly speech. The analogies between music and other functions, however, are not always obvious at the surface level, and my methodology requires that I compare morphemes rather than lexical units of speech.

4. The synthetic-analytic contrast is not intended to be an evolutionary model per se; however, it should be recognized that even the technical music of Western society is derived from a folk idiom. This is another way of saying categorically that the synthetic model does not go hand in hand with "primitive" society and the analytical model with "civilized" societies.

It is more profitable to view the two models as standing in a dialectical relationship with each other. I would also state unequivocally that I do not believe that the synthetic model as employed for the Oglala is necessarily the only other kind of model that may be contrasted with the analytical. In fact, I suggest that many other kinds of models await construction from raw ethnographic data from all parts of the world, including segments of Western societies. Perhaps our first step is to investigate more fully the phenomenon of synesthesia, which deals with the interpretation of one sensory modality in terms of another. Merriam has already introduced this idea and its potential usefulness to ethnomusicology (Merriam 1964, 85–101), but to date little has been done about it. Our own folk ideas about music suggest that within Western society as well as other societies of the world there are an infinite number of ways to verbalize about music—music which is hot, cool, blue, bouncy, funky, catchy; or music which jumps, moves, wails, rocks, or otherwise contorts itself, as if it were an "appurtenance" of our own "primitive" mentality.

CHAPTER 3

SONG TEXTS

Wakantanka unšimala ye.
Wani kta ca lecamun welo.

Wakantanka pity me.
I want to live; that's why I am doing this.
—Sun Dance song

THERE is no greater source of inspiration than those sacred words that are sung in the religious ceremonies of the Lakota. The above epigram is perhaps the most often repeated phrase in all songs and appears significantly in the opening song of the Sun Dance, the most important annual religious ceremony on Plains Indian reservations.

In all cultures of the world, it is as if exaltation of the supreme deity and propitiation of the supernaturals are somehow made stronger, clearer, more determined if sung rather than spoken in common prayer. Frequently, people feel more secure, more assured, somehow more satisfied if they can sing out their innermost feelings and sentiments rather than simply utter them in the monotonous register of prayer.

Like the spoken word, those texts that are sung are frequently done so in sacred language, words and phrases known only to the medicine men. These songs are sung at specific events: the Sun Dance, Yuwipi and other kinds of curing rituals, the Sweat Lodge, and the Vision Quest. Although they are learned by the medicine men in their visions, they are subsequently taught to other singers and common people. Thus most religious songs, despite their esoteric nature and frequent incomprehensibility, are most often sung by groups of people rather than by individuals.

In this chapter I focus on the classification of Yuwipi songs, and the meaning found in their sometimes puzzling texts. Here Yuwipi is the name of a curing ritual held in a darkened room and conducted by a medicine man known as a Yuwipi *wicaša* 'Yuwipi man.'[1] Elsewhere (Powers 1982) I have described an entire Yuwipi ceremony conducted by the late George Plenty Wolf from the Red Cloud Community at Pine Ridge. Most Yuwipis are performed to cure someone who is suffering from an illness deemed to be Indian, that is, not brought to the Indians by whites. Headache, backache, upset stomach, or sometimes a general feeling of malaise are the general symptoms. If one feels badly, he or she may approach a Yuwipi man with a pipe. If he is willing to conduct the ceremony, the two smoke the pipe together and preparations are then made. The ritual takes place in a house that has been cleared of all furniture. The windows and doors are covered with drapes, and the medicine man with his helper prepares the center of the floor as an altar. When it is dark, the patient and others take their places around the periphery of the room, and the designated singers usually sit at the west side of the room. Characteristically, the medicine man is wrapped in a quilt and tied and remains there while the lights are turned off. Most of the ritual takes place in the dark, and during this time spirits of humans and animals are believed to enter the room and commune with the Yuwipi man in the darkness. During their discourse the spirits tell the medicine man how to cure his patient. Frequently others attending may ask to be cured of minor ailments. When the spirits arrive, and when they leave, picking up offerings of tobacco that have been placed there for them, they emit a kind of blue spark visible to all in the blackness of the room.

When the lights are turned on, the medicine man has been untied by the spirits and sits calmly in the center of the floor. The altar which he assiduously built has been destroyed, and the patient has been cured. Following this part of the ritual all join in drinking water communally, feasting on traditional foods especially prepared for the ritual, and finally smoking the pipe together. The Yuwipi ends with each of the adepts repeating in succession the formulaic prayer *mitak oyas'in* 'all my relations', which underscores the unity of the people who have joined in the ceremony.

What is particularly important about the Yuwipi ritual is that all of the people present sing a series of special songs together. The Lakota classify these songs according to the ritual functions they accompany, and by understanding their classification one gets a better idea how the ceremony itself is divided into meaningful segments. After discussing the classification of Yuwipi songs, I analyze twenty-six songs which I have collected over the past fifteen years. The first seventeen of these songs appeared in their translated form only in an earlier work (Powers 1982). However, here I include the native Lakota texts with the free translations. These are followed by an explanation of what the sacred texts mean to the Lakota, and how they came into being through the visions of the medicine men.

All Yuwipi songs originate in the Vision Quest. They are taught to the Yuwipi man by various spirits of humans, animals, and birds. He in turn teaches them to the singers who perform for his particular ceremonies. As the songs are repeated during subsequent ceremonies, both men and women who help at the meetings learn them so that they may join in.

Most songs contain texts which describe what the Yuwipi man saw in his vision, or which repeat certain phrases used by spirits appearing in the vision. Occasionally one hears a song containing vocables only, usually a dance song.

Once the songs are learned, they are the property of the Yuwipi man who received them and should not be sung in ceremonies other than his. New songs that he learns through repeated Vision Quests may replace old ones. Thus Yuwipi songs are old only in form, but not necessarily in content.

CLASSIFICATION

Yuwipi *olowan*, 'Yuwipi song', is the generic classification for all songs sung in the Yuwipi ceremony. The same songs are used for the Sweat Lodge[2] and Vision Quest (including the placing of the supplicant on the hill and his removal). These songs may be subclassified according to their functions, e.g., *opagipi olowan*, 'filling the pipe song' (the first song sung in the Yuwipi ceremony). Translation labels are sometimes misleading, giving the notion that more classifications are used by the Oglala than actually exist. *Opagipi olowan*, for example, is sometimes translated 'opening song', but in this instance 'filling the pipe song' and 'opening song' are synonymous.

Theoretically, more than one song exists for each function depending on how quickly the spirits respond to the songs. If, for example, a song is sung to invite the spirits and they do not arrive, it may be necessary to sing another song of the same class. The selection of the appropriate song is made by the chief singer who is familiar with all of the Yuwipi man's personal songs. On one occasion the chief singer was uncertain what song to sing. After a silence, Plenty Wolf instructed him to sing *"wocekiye olowan!"* "prayer song!" The singer immediately began a prayer song of *his* (the singer's) choosing, although it could have been one of a number of songs of the prayer-song class.

ACCOMPANIMENT

Yuwipi songs may be sung with or without drum accompaniment. Two kinds of drum accompaniment are recognized by the Oglala: *yusupi*, or "tremolo" (literally, 'to make hail with the hands'), and *kat'inza*, "dance tempo" (literally, 'to strike firmly').

The drums (*cancega*) are small hand drums approximately 12 to 15 inches in diameter, covered on one side with deer or cow hide. They are struck with a small drum stick (*icabu*, 'to strike with'). Plenty Wolf normally requires two drums, each played by a separate man. One man leads the songs.

Although rattles (*wagmuha*) are heard, they are not regarded as accompaniment to the songs, but rather the sounds of the spirits. Plenty Wolf provides two rattles for the spirits to use. When not in use, Plenty Wolf keeps the drums, drumsticks, and rattles in his suitcase.

PERFORMANCE

All persons at the Yuwipi are encouraged to sing; the more singers, the better response from the spirits. One man leads the songs, but there is an absence of the traditional group format heard in dance songs: all join in as soon as they recognize the song.

One of the characteristic performance patterns of Yuwipi singing is the segueing from one song to another.[3] This kind of pattern is also found in the Sun Dance songs (of which there are currently seven), and Kettle Dance songs (of which there are five). A similar pattern is found in the performance of Rabbit Dance and Round Dance songs, both secular types, but usually no more than two songs are used in these two.

Apparently the act of sustaining a musical interlude by either repeating several renditions of the same song or segueing from one song to another serves to intensify the ritual event which the songs accompany. In the case of Sun Dance songs, it is necessary to sustain a musical accompaniment to the dance for as long as the Sun Dance director requires it. Only when a ritual event is performed (in this case the offering of a pipe to the singers) can the singers stop their performance to let the dancers rest. On the other hand, segueing may be part of a conscious attempt to routinize a ritual event, as in the case of the Kettle Dance, which, by Oglala standards, is highly choreographed. This is of recent origin however. In 1949 I participated in a Kettle Dance in which intervals occurred between major segments of the dance. Possibly the introduction of the Kettle Dance to non-Oglala audiences is partly responsible for the present performance pattern. The dance was traditionally performed at the Gallup Inter-tribal Ceremonials, and possibly there was a need to modify the normal performance pattern to comply with staging the dance of non-Oglala, and non-Indian spectators.

Although Yuwipi songs are always sung as complete songs (that is, without segueing into another) out of ritual context, during the actual performance of the songs they appear as clusters of songs interrupted by other spoken events such as declarations of intent, prayers by the medicine man, or conversations between the medicine man and spirits. For convenience, I have selected the term *set* to indicate a ritual segment in which one or more songs are sung. During each set, the ritual is intensified by sustaining the musical background, i.e., by segueing from one song into another. Some sets require only one song as accompaniment, as in the case of the opening song and the song sung while spirits leave the meeting. Other sets require two to four songs to complete the ritual segment.

Table 1 illustrates the distribution of songs during one ritual by sets and corresponding ritual segments. I have also included the name of the song class that relates to each set, and its corresponding translation label, number of renditions, and type of accompaniment. Again, song numbers are keyed to the numbers in the preceding ritual.

Most frequently, in the standard Plenty Wolf ritual, each song was sung twice through with the exception of Songs 2 and 3, which were rendered once. In comparing this distribution with two other rituals conducted by Plenty Wolf, it was discovered that the identical format of clusters was repeated in each ritual. The singing in each of the three rituals was led by the same singer. In another Plenty Wolf ritual which I observed, however, two songs were included in the first set. The songs in this latter ritual were led by a different singer, suggesting that the Yuwipi performance patterns are routinized as a result of repetitive use, and that song sequencing is directed by the chief singer.

In Table 1 the ritual segments can be synthesized:

Set I. One or more songs for filling the pipe.
Set II. Songs relate to calling the spirits and subsequent assertion that they have arrived.

Table 1. Distribution of Yuwipi Songs in Ritual Context

Set No.	Song No.	Ritual Event	Lakota Classification	Translation	Type of Accompaniment	No. Renditions
I	1	Recounting the vision	*Hanbloglaka* (spoken)	'Dream talk'	None	—
II		Filling the pipe (tying the shaman)	*Opagipi olowan* *Wicapahtepi*	'Filling the pipe song' 'They tie them'	Tremolo —	2 —
	2	Calling the spirits	*Tatetopakiya olowan* or *Wicakicopi olowan*	'Four winds song' or 'They call them song'	Tremolo	1
III	3	Calling the spirits	*Wocekiye olowan*	'Prayer song'	Rhythm	2
	4	Calling the spirits	*Wocekiye olowan*	'Prayer song'	Rhythm	2
	5	Spirits arrive	*Wocekiye olowan*	'Prayer song'	No drum	2
	6	Spirits report on supplicant	*Wocekiye olowan*	'Prayer song'	Tremolo	2

IV	7	Doctoring	*Wapiye olowan*	'Curing song'	No drum	2
	8	Doctoring	*Wapiye olowan*	'Curing song'	No drum	2
V	9	Kettle dance	*Wocekiye olowan*	'Prayer song'	Rhythm	2
	10	Kettle dance	*Ceȟohomni olowan*	'Dance around kettle song'	Rhythm	2
	11	Kettle dance	*Šunka pa aokawingapi olowan*	'They retreat from the dog head song'	Rhythm	2
VI	12	Untying the shaman	*Wicayujujupi olowan*	'They untie them song'	Rhythm	2
	13	The people dance	*Wacilowan*	'Dance song'	Rhythm	2
	14	Spirits dance	*Wicayujiupi olowan*	'Untying song'	Rhythm	2
	15	Spirits pick up tobacco offerings	*Wanaǧi kiǧlapi olowan*	'Spirits go home song'	Rhythm	2
VII	16	Spirits depart	*Wanaǧi kiǧlapi olowan*	'Spirits go home song'	Tremolo	2
	17	Spirits depart	*Wanaǧi kiǧlapi olowan, or Inakiyapi olowan*	'Spirits go home song' or 'quitting song'	No drum	1

Set III. Spirits perform tasks requested by the people in attendance.
Set IV. Doctoring of patients.
Set V. The Kettle Dance participated in by the spirits.
Set VI. Preparation for the conclusion of the ceremony.
Set VII. Departure of the spirits.

Even when Plenty Wolf was not tied, two of the songs sung in set VI referred to as "untying songs" were sung. This is possibly another case of routinization even when the function of the songs is absent. During an actual untying period, two events happen: the people are dancing while the spirits are untying the shaman. The dance song (no. 13) is called *wacilowan*.

Song 1
Filling the Pipe

LAKOTA:
1. Kola leci lecun ye.
2. Kola leci lecun ye.
3. Kola leci lecun ye.
4. Hecanun kin taku yacin k'un he hecetu kte.
5. Hocoka wanji ogna iyotake cin Wakantanka cekiya yo.
6. Hecanun kin taku yacin k'un he hecetu kte.

ENGLISH:
1. Friend, do this over here.
2. Friend, do this over here.
3. Friend, do this over here.
4. If you do it, whatever you want will be so.
5. You—the one sitting in the center, pray to Wakantanka!
6. If you do, whatever you want will be so.

This song was sung in the George Plenty Wolf Yuwipi as the *Opagipi*, or Filling the Pipe song. In this version, lines 1–6 are spoken by the spirits to the medicine man during the Vision Quest. The medicine man thus learns the song in his vision and teaches it to his lead singers. They in turn lead the song during the actual performance of the ritual. As is true in most sacred texts, one must first understand that the words are those of the spirits, not of the medicine man. As such, the rendition of each song constitutes a reenactment of the vision in which the song was learned originally.

In lines 1–3, "doing this" refers to the actual performance of the Yuwipi ritual. If the meeting is conducted appropriately, and the spirits who help the Yuwipi man cure the patient arrive, then whatever intentions the people offer will be fulfilled, as stated in line 4. In line 5 the spirit directs the "one sitting in the center," that is the *hocoka* or camp circle, to pray to Wakantanka. The medicine man is the only one at the meeting who can sit inside the center of the sacred space which he has partly created by building an altar delineated by a long string of minute tobacco offerings that circumscribe the sacred part of the room.

Some Yuwipi songs are interchangeable. William Horn Cloud, a well-known singer at Pine Ridge, used this song as the second song in the set. It was sung as the medicine man drew the face of the patient (*wicite* 'face') on a circular mound of mellowed earth located in the center of the *hocoka* called *makakagapi* 'mellowed (or fashioned) earth'.

Plenty Wolf sings this song for the opening song while he fills the pipe. The singers sing it twice, accompanying themselves on hand drums, striking them rapidly in tremolo style. During this part of the ritual the lights are still on.

Plenty Wolf renders line 4 somewhat differently on occasion, singing:

Hecanun kin nitunkašila waniyank u kte.
If you do it, your Tunkašila will come to see you.

Here Tunkašila 'Grandfather' is an honorific term employed to address all the spirit helpers. Interchangeability of texts is a common feature of various kinds of Lakota music including secular songs.

When this song is sung as a second song, the medicine man normally completes drawing the picture of the patient on the mellowed earth before the second rendition of the song has ended. He occupies the remaining time praying with the pipe until the song is completed. When the song ends, he calls for the lights to be turned out, and then begins a long recitation called the *hanbloglaka* 'vision talk,' which is a statement about his vision in which he is given power to cure.

Song 2
Four Directions Song

LAKOTA:
1. Kola hoyewayin kta ca namaȟ'un we.
2. Kola hoyewayin kta ca namaȟ'un we.
3. Kola hoyewayin kta ca namaȟ'un we.
4. Wiyoȟpeyata tunkan sapa wan kolatakuwayelo.
5. Kola hoyewayin kta ca namaȟ'un we.
6. Kola hoyewayin kta ca namaȟ'un we.
7. Waziyata tunkan luta wa kolatakuwayelo.
8. Kola hoyewayin kta ca namaȟ'un we.
9. Kola hoyewayin kta ca namaȟ'un we.
10. Wiyohiyanpota tunkan zizi wan kolatakuwayelo.
11. Kola hoyewayin kta ca namaȟ'un we.
12. Kola hoyewayin kta ca namaȟ'un we.
13. Itokagata tunkan ska wan kolatakuwayelo.
14. Kola hoyewayin kta ca namaȟ'un we.
15. Kola hoyewayin kta ca namaȟ'un we.
16. Maka akanl Inktomi wan kolatakuwayelo.
17. Kola hoyewayin kta ca namaȟ'un we.
18. Kola hoyewayin kta ca namaȟ'un we.
19. Wankatakiye Wanbli Gleška wan kolatakuwayelo.
20. Kola hoyewayin kta ca namaȟ'un we.
21. Kola hoyewayin kta ca namaȟ'un we.

ENGLISH:
1. Friend, I will send a voice, so hear me.
2. Friend, I will send a voice, so hear me.
3. Friend, I will send a voice, so hear me.
4. In the West, I call a black stone friend.
5. Friend, I will send a voice, so hear me.
6. Friend, I will send a voice, so hear me.
7. In the North, I call a red stone friend.
8. Friend, I will send a voice, so hear me.
9. Friend, I will send a voice, so hear me.
10. In the East, I call a yellow stone friend.
11. Friend, I will send a voice, so hear me.
12. Friend, I will send a voice, so hear me.
13. In the South, I call a white stone friend.
14. Friend, I will send a voice, so hear me.

15. Friend, I will send a voice, so hear me.
16. On Earth, I call a Spider friend.
17. Friend, I will send a voice, so hear me.
18. Friend, I will send a voice, so hear me.
19. Above, I call a Spotted Eagle friend.
20. Friend, I will send a voice, so hear me.
21. Friend, I will send a voice, so hear me.

After the lights have been turned off, this song is sung to in-
voke the powers from the whole universe. All respondents
agree that this is one of the most powerful of all Yuwipi songs,
and one of the most pleasing to the spirits.

The Four Directions song is unique among all Oglala songs
inasmuch as seven renditions (an unusually large number)
are sung, each rendition being sung to the same melody with
slight textual modifications specifying the directional sources
of power. While it is called the Four Directions song, actually
six directions are named; in order, West, North, East, South,
Earth, and Above. The first rendition does not specify any direction but is included to herald the whole universe.[4]

The order in which the powers are invoked is the same as in
offering the pipe. Walker ascribes this sequence to the order
in which the Four Winds were born in Oglala mythology
(Walker 1917, 171).[5]

Each direction is identified by name, its corresponding sacred object (in this case a sacred stone), and color (corresponding to the *wanunyanpi*, placed around the *hocoka* in the
meeting). The power of Inktomi, the spiderish culture hero, is
invoked from Mother Earth, and the Spotted Eagle, messenger of Wakantanka from above.

Each rendition is comprised of three lines: lines 1–3, and
the second and third lines of each rendition are identical.
Plenty Wolf has been directed by the spirits to address each
one of the directions by the term *kola*, friend. He tells the
spirits to hear his intentions.

Beginning with the second rendition, and the first line of
each following rendition, Plenty Wolf addresses each direction with the term *kolatakuwaye* which I have translated as "I
call a friend." The meaning however, is stronger than simply

"friend." The term literally means to consider one *related* by the term *kola*. While *kola* is the generic word for "friend" today, it is said to have meant a near-blood relationship in the olden days.

The Four Directions song is called *tatetopakiya olowan* 'toward the four winds song', and is accompanied by rapid tremolo drumming. It is rendered only once. Since it is the first song addressed to the spirits to entice them to come, Plenty Wolf also calls it *wicakicopi olowan*, 'They Call Them song'.

Song 3
Prayer Song

LAKOTA:
1. Maĥpiya kin taepiya cankuwaye.
2. Wanyankiye.
3. Wakan le tankikinyan najin ye.

ENGLISH:
1. I am building a road along the side of the clouds.
2. Behold it!
3. This sacred thing that I do is important.

This is a song describing a vision of Plenty Wolf. He was looking at the clouds and they appeared to open up revealing a sacred road.

The idea of the Wakinyan, or 'Thunder Beings', approaching the supplicant on the Vision Quest by means of a road built alongside the clouds is common among the Oglala. The supplicant is instructed to expect a phenomenon such as this. He is told that if he keeps looking at the clouds soon they will open up and he will see the Wakinyan Oyate 'Thunder People' coming toward him. He should not be afraid. There will be many of the thunder people each riding a horse and driving a slave before him. They will be coming toward the supplicant in great numbers, but all he has to do is point the sacred pipe at them and they will pass him by.

One cannot see the Wakinyan; they are behind the clouds. But they drive horses before them by means of a leash made from lightning. In front of the horses, again connected by lightning, are the Wakinyan *wayaka*, 'Thunder slaves', people

William Spotted Crow, Sun Dance leader during the 1940s. Courtesy Heritage Center, Inc.

who have been killed by lightning. They are there to test the bravery of the supplicant. As long as he holds the pipe, they cannot harm him. As they come toward the supplicant, they separate into two groups passing around him and eventually disappearing.

A vision similar to this has been described by Black Elk in Neihardt (1961, 20–47). The Horse Dance, discussed by Feraca (1963, 43) is a reenactment of this kind of vision. In the Horse Dance, people who have had this vision ride horses around the dance area. The horses seem to dance to the song. The dancers wear black hoods over their faces and paint their bodies and horses with lightning designs. The hoods are worn because the Wakinyan Oyate whom they represent are always faceless to the supplicant.

Plenty Wolf identifies this song as Wocekiye *olowan*, 'Prayer song'. He also calls it *hocoka wooglaka olowan* 'declaration of intent from the sacred place song'. It is sung twice through to a rhythmic accompaniment of the drum.

Song 4
Prayer Song

LAKOTA:
1. Tunkašila wanmayank u ye.
2. Tunkašila wanmayank u ye.
3. Tunkašila wanmayank u ye.
4. Ikce wicaša tacannunpe wan yuha hoyewaye lo.
5. "Mitakuye ob wani kte lo," eyaya hoyewaye lo.

ENGLISH:
1. My Tunkašila comes to see me.
2. My Tunkašila comes to see me.
3. My Tunkašila comes to see me.
4. Holding the old people's pipe, I send a voice.
5. Saying "I will live with my relatives," I send a voice.

Horn Cloud says that during this song the spirits enter and dance. The *wagmunha* strike the floor, walls and ceiling in time with the drum. Persons may also get up and dance in place. Sometimes, a dance song may be sung after this song and the spirits and people continue to dance.

This is another Wocekiye *olowan* 'prayer song', vigorously sung twice through to a rhythmic accompaniment.

Particularly significant in this song is line 5, "I want to live with my relatives." This is sometimes given as the basic explanation of why Yuwipi ceremonies are conducted. This concept is reiterated in an attenuated form after the ceremony has ended and the pipe is smoked and water drunk with the words "*mitakuye oyasin*" 'all my relations.' It is also repeated by each person after the feast.

Song 5
Prayer Song

LAKOTA:

1. Wankatakiya hoyewaye lo.
2. Cannunpa kin yuha hoyewaye lo.
3. "Mitakuye ob wani kta ca lecamun we,"
4. Eyaya Tunkašila cewakiye lo.

ENGLISH:

1. I send a voice upward.
2. With the pipe, I send a voice.
3. "I do this so that I will live with my relatives,"
4. Saying this I pray to Tunkašila.

This is Wocekiye *olowan* 'Prayer song', announcing the arrival of the spirits. It is rendered twice with no accompaniment.

Again the phrase "I want to live with my relatives" is sung. This particular song is heard frequently around the Red Cloud Community out of ritual context. It also was sung by Horn Cloud and Dick Elk Boy at the author's home when they were about to leave for Pine Ridge. It was sung for their own safety in traveling as well as my health and continued well-being.

After the conclusion of this song the medicine man communes with the spirits. The people then offer their intentions.

Song 6
Prayer Song

LAKOTA:

1. Tuwa tanyan kinyan hotanin yelo.
2. Tuwa tanyan kinyan hotanin yelo.
3. Tuwa cantewicakiya wancinmaye howakiye lo.

ENGLISH:
1. Someone who flies well is making a voice known.
2. Someone who flies well is making a voice known.
3. To whoever trusts in me to love them I send a voice.

Here, the medicine man has been instructed to pray to those spirit helpers to trust him to love people, and to pray on their behalf whenever they request it. The song is sung twice through to a tremolo accompaniment. While it is being sung, the spirits may actually be "flying" about the vicinity checking on people who are on a Vision Quest, or those lying sick in the hospital. Later, these spirits will return to the Yuwipi meeting and report through the mediumship of the medicine man on how the sick people are faring.

Song 7
Doctoring Song

LAKOTA:
1. Enana hoyewaye lo.
2. Enana hoyewaye lo.
3. Tuwe ca hoyewakiyin kta
4. Tunkašila toka hwo?
5. Enana hoyewaye lo.
6. Tuwe ca omakiyin kta
7. Tunkašila toka hwo?

ENGLISH:
1. I send a voice here and there.
2. I send a voice here and there.
3. To whom shall I send a voice?
4. Tunkašila, what do you say?
5. Who will help me?
6. Tunkašila, what do you say?

During this song and the next, any of those attending the Yuwipi who wish may request to be doctored. The medicine man instructs them to stand up and in the darkness reach out until they can touch and hold onto one of the seven offering flags that have been erected along the edge of the altar. They are also instructed to turn around so that their backs face the sacred space. As the song begins, the rattles begin to "dance"

around the sacred space, and soon they begin to gently touch
each of the persons standing up to be cured. The spirits, as
the medicine men say, touch that part of the body which is
ailing. Some of the spirits are also known to talk, and some
have short dialogues with the patients.

Songs 7 and 8 are sung in a lively dance tempo, and the
rattles move about the room in time with the drumming and
singing. The words of this song indicate that the medicine
man is asking aloud through the song which of his spirit helpers will come forth into the room and assist him in curing the
patients. Thus both songs are classified as *wapiye olowan* 'doctoring songs.' *Wapiye* is derived from *piya* 'to make over; to
renew', hence to doctor or cure. The medicine man is often
referred to as a *wapiye wicaša* 'man who renews'.

Song 8
Doctoring Song

LAKOTA:
1. Miye ca taninyan hoyewaye lo.
2. Tunkašila ecunmaši ye.
3. Miye ca taninyan hoyewaye lo.

ENGLISH:
1. It is me, I am sending a voice clearly.
2. Tunkašila told me to do so.
3. It is me, I am sending a voice clearly.

In this song, the medicine man is saying that he is doctoring
the patients because he has been instructed by the spirits to
do so.

Song 9
Kettle Dance Song

LAKOTA:
1. Wakantanka unšimala ye.
2. Wakantanka unšimala ye.
3. Unšimala ye.
4. Wani kta ca lecamun we.
5. Hanhepi kin le wakan yelo.
6. Unšimala ye.
7. Wani kta ca lecamun we.

ENGLISH:
1. Wakantanka pity me.
2. Wakantanka pity me.
3. Pity me.
4. I am doing this so that I may live.
5. This night is sacred.
6. Pity me.
7. I am doing this so that I may live.

Song 10
Kettle Dance Song

LAKOTA:
1. Maȟpiya mimemiya kinajinpelo.
2. Maȟpiya mimemiya kinajinpelo.
3. Henake wakinyan oyate ca kinajinpelo.
4. Maȟpiya mimemiya kinajinpelo.
5. Henake wakinyan oyate ca kinajinpelo.

ENGLISH:
1. They are standing at home around the clouds.
2. They are standing at home around the clouds.
3. Those thunder people are standing at home.
4. They are standing at home around the clouds.
5. Those thunder people are standing at home.

Song 11
Kettle Dance Song

LAKOTA:
1. Leciya šunka wan yutapelo.
2. Leciya šunka wan yutapelo.
3. Wiyoȟpeyata wakinyan oyate wan šunka wan yutapelo.
4. Sunka wan yutapelo.
5. Wakan yutapelo.

ENGLISH:
1. They are eating dog over here.
2. They are eating dog over here.
3. In the West, the Thunder People are eating dog.
4. They are eating dog.
5. Sacredly they are eating.

Songs 9, 10 and 11 constitute a unified segment of the Yuwipi ritual, and are sung whenever dog meat is prepared for the feast that follows. The *ceȟohomni wacipi* 'dance around the kettle dance', or simply, Kettle Dance,[7] was associated with two Plains Indian institutions, known among the Lakota as *pejimignaka wacipi* 'grass in the belt dance', or 'Grass Dance', and the Heyoka Kaga 'Clown Maker' or Clown Ceremony, the Lakota version of the well-known Contrary societies whose members behaved in an antinatural manner, speaking backwards, wearing inappropriate clothing for the season, and performing antics to make people laugh.

Among the Lakota the Kettle Dance was performed by both Heyoka and non-Heyoka at the popular Grass Dance. Hence the Kettle Dance, although performed up through the 1960s as a show dance on the Pine Ridge Reservation and at expositions such as the Gallup Indian Ceremonial and Sheridan All-American Indian days, it has always been regarded as an old-time dance. It is not unusual then, at the Yuwipi meetings when dog meat is served, that the songs are sung for the benefit of the spirits who arrive to aid the medicine man.

Although in the secular version of the Kettle Dance five or six songs are sung, during the Yuwipi only three are required. As the singers begin, the spirits, whom the medicine man is capable of seeing in the dark,[8] begin to dance portions of the Kettle Dance precisely the way it was performed when they were alive. The texts of the sacred versions do not correspond precisely with the secular ones. In Song 9, for example line 5 is normally a repetition of line 1. In this version line 5 is modified to the sacred meeting that is being held at night. During this first song of the Kettle Dance, the spirit dancers sit on their haunches around the kettle of dog meat that was placed in the sacred space before the ritual began. As the song progresses, the dancers raise their right hand, then left hand, then both hands in a movement saluting the kettle of meat. While only the medicine man can see the dancers performing, it is assumed by the remainder of participants that the little spirit helpers are dancing just the way the old-timers used to.

In Song 10 the spirits, who are referred to as the Thunder People, begin to dance clockwise around the kettle in a follow-the-leader style. As each passes the kettle of meat, he thrusts his hand into the boiling hot water exclaiming that it is cold. This movement is exactly the way the old Heyoka performed the Kettle Dance, often splashing the water on each other like frolicking children.

The third and final song in this sequence is sometimes called the *wicape wacipi*, literally 'fork dance' but more frequently glossed as "Spear Dance." During this segment of the dance, the spirits encircle the kettle and at certain points in the song rush toward it brandishing forked sticks that they use to try to skewer from the kettle choice portions of the meat. At the end of the dance, the dancers participate in a dog feast.

Song 12
Untying Song

LAKOTA:
1. Hotaninpe hotaninpe.
2. Wankatanhan hotaninpe.
3. Hotaninpe.
4. Wankatanhan hotaninpe.
5. Hotaninpe.
6. Wankatanhan hotaninpe.
7. Hotaninpe.
8. Wankatanhan hotaninpe.
9. Hotaninpe.

ENGLISH:
1. They make known a voice, they make known a voice.
2. They make known a voice from above.
3. They make known a voice.
4. They make known a voice from above.
5. They make known a voice.
6. They make known a voice from above.
7. They make known a voice.
8. They make known a voice from above.
9. They make known a voice.

This song is classified as a *wicayujujupi olowan* 'untying song' and is sung during that portion of the ritual when the spirit helpers untie and unwrap the medicine man who has been wrapped up since the lights were turned off. The texts signify that the spirits tell the medicine man how to cure his patient by making their voices known, that is, speaking to the medicine man.

The next four songs are each sung four times through to a strong dance rhythm on the drum. The spirits continue to untie the medicine man, and anyone who cares to may stand up in place and dance. The rattles hit the floor solidly, indicating that the spirits are dancing along with the people and are enjoying themselves. Persons who are not dancing are careful to draw in their legs close to their body lest they be stomped by enthusiastic spirit dancers.

Song 13
Dance Song

There are no words to this song, only vocables. It is a vigorous dance song like that sung in the Omaha or Grass Dance. During its rendition anyone may stand up in place and dance.

Song 14
Dance Song
(Untying Song)

LAKOTA:
1. Waci au we wanyankiye yo.
2. Waci au we wanyankiye yo.
3. Waci au we wanyankiye yo.
4. Inyan topakiya waci au welo.
5. Waci au we wanyankiye yo.

ENGLISH:
1. They come dancing. Behold!
2. They come dancing. Behold!
3. They come dancing. Behold!
4. From the Four Winds, the stones come dancing.
5. They come dancing. Behold!

Frequently during this song there is much confusion in the sacred space. Those who wish to are dancing, and at the same time the spirits are untying the medicine man. Some of the spirits are dancing along the string of tobacco offerings picking up tobacco for the journey home. Lines 1, 2, 3, and 5 refer to the spirits dancing. Line 4 makes reference to the sacred stones that also serve as spirit helpers to the medicine man.

Short Bull, famous medicine man and Ghost Dance leader. Photograph taken in August, 1933. Courtesy Heritage Center, Inc.

Song 15
Gathering Up the Tobacco

LAKOTA:
1. Kola lena kin cic'u we.
2. Hiyo u we.

ENGLISH:
1. Friend, I give these to you.
2. Come and get them!

In this song the medicine man is telling his spirit helpers that
he is giving them offerings of tobacco because they have helped
him cure his patients. In Lakota theory, the number of tobacco
offerings prepared for each Yuwipi corresponds to the number
of spirits actually attending the meeting. Occasionally one of
these spirits may be named in the above-mentioned song. For
example, Plenty Wolf might modify line 2:

Wanbli u welo.
The Eagle is coming.

Song 16
Song of the Departing Spirits

LAKOTA:
1. Tanyan kinapewaye.
2. Wanbli Gleška tacannunpe tanyan kinapewaye.

ENGLISH:
1. I have accomplished these things well.
2. With the pipe of the Spotted Eagle, I have accomplished
these things well.

Horn Cloud states that this song is sung to assert that the purpose of the Yuwipi has been fulfilled by means of praying
with the pipe, here referred to as the one belonging to the
Spotted Eagle who is the messenger of Wakantanka and who
carries the prayers above. The idea of accomplishment is expressed in the metaphor *tanyan kinapewaye* literally 'I send it
home well'.

This song and the next are both called *wanagi kiglapi olowan*
'spirits are going home song.' They are both accompanied by
tremolo drumming.

Song 17
Song of the Departing Spirits

LAKOTA:

1. Hotaniyan kinajinpelo.
2. Hotaniyan kinajinpelo.
3. Nitunkašila tawakunze ca hena cic'u we.

ENGLISH:

1. They stand at home and make a voice known.
2. They stand at home and make a voice known.
3. Because of your Tunkašila's influence, I give you these.

This final song of the Plenty Wolf rite is sung twice through with no drum accompaniment. While it is being sung, the spirits are gathering up their tobacco and leaving for home. In line 3 "I give you these" refers to the tobacco offerings which the medicine man is giving to the spirits as thanks for their help in the Yuwipi.

MISCELLANEOUS YUWIPI SONGS

The following songs were collected from George Plenty Wolf, and his lead singers Owen Brings and William Horn Cloud in the summers of 1966 and 1967. They represent songs that were not in current use during these years, but were, like the others, learned in visions and occasionally sung in Yuwipi meetings.

Song 18
Filling the Pipe Song

LAKOTA:

1. Kola leye na opagi yo.
2. Kola leye no opagi yo.
3. "Mitakuye ob wani kte lo," eyaya yo.
4. He e cin hecetu kte lo.

ENGLISH:

1. Friend, say this and fill the pipe.
2. Friend, say this and fill the pipe.
3. Say "I want to live with my relatives," over and over.
4. If you do, it will be so.

This song belongs to the class *opagipi olowan* 'filling the pipe song' and may be substituted for Song 1. It is sung at the beginning of the ceremony by the singers while the medicine man fills the sacred pipe with seven pinches of tobacco, each representing the Four Directions, the Above, the Earth, and the Spotted Eagle. As such, this ritual addresses in the same manner the same sources of supernatural aid as does the Four Directions Song (Song 2). The lights are on during this phase.

Lines 1 and 2 are spoken by the spirits to the medicine man, telling him to fill the pipe, and repeat over and over that he wants to live with his relatives (line 3). If he does, and if all the people pray in this manner, their wishes will be fulfilled.

Song 19
Declaration of Intent

LAKOTA:
1. Hokšila taku oyaka yo.
2. Nitunkašila wanicunzapelo.
3. Cannunpa wan nic'upi na oyagnišipelo.
4. Ikce wicaša nitunkašila wanicunzapelo.
5. Hocoka wan nic'upi na oyagnišipelo.

ENGLISH:
1. Boy, say something!
2. Your Tunkašila depend on you.
3. They gave you the pipe and told you to speak.
4. Old timer, your Tunkašila depend on you.
5. They gave you the camp circle and told you to speak.

Plenty Wolf calls this *hocoka wooglakapi olowan* 'declaration of intent from the sacred place song'. It immediately follows the spoken declaration which takes the form of a ritual prayer. The lights remain extinguished for the duration of the prayer and song.

The *hocoka wooglaka* (also called *hanbloglaka* 'vision talk') is an integral part of all Yuwipi meetings. In it, the shaman prays for all the people as he holds the pipe and faces west in the darkness, the place from which the spirits will arrive. Plenty Wolf specifies in the prayer those things which all the common people desire: health, success in business transactions (at the agency office), fecundity, and adequate money. He also offers up specific prayers for those he knows to be sick, in the armed services, or going off to school or on relocation.

In the song, the spirits address him first as "Boy" (line 1) and later as "old timer." *Ikce wicaša* means 'old time man', or 'original Indian'. This indication of generations (young and old) appears in many songs of the Yuwipi ritual. Not only are all aspects of the Lakota universe represented in the meeting in terms of ritual paraphernalia and altar decorations, but also all generations are represented. The generational aspects of Yuwipi are made more consistent by the fact that all Yuwipi spirits, human and animal, are actually spirits of those who once lived on the earth. Hence the Oglala feel the sense of continuity between the living and nonliving, and their belief that the spirit world is simply an extension of the earthly world is reenforced.

This song also points out the dual role played by the medicine man. Not only do the people depend on him to cure their illnesses and insure the welfare of the tribe, but the spirits depend on him to translate the needs of the people (lines 2 and 3). The fear and anxieties expressed by the common people are somewhat alleviated by knowing that at least one member of their group, the medicine man, has direct communication with the spirits, and to some extent they rely on him to serve as a medium. In lines 3 and 4, however, he is expected to recognize his obligations. He has been given the sacred duty of serving as *iyeska* 'medium' by virtue of the fact that the spirits gave him the sacred offices—the pipe (line 3) and the sacred place (line 5). They do not request him to speak in behalf of the common people, but rather command him to speak. Even the medicine man is not infallible, and he too may suffer the wrath of the spirits if he does not fulfill his obligations to the tribe.

At the conclusion of the prayer and song, the lights are turned on. Plenty Wolf hands the pipe to his wife, who plays an integral part in the ritual. He then removes his shoes and places them outside the sacred place and takes his seat on a bed of sage. He then calls for the lights to be turned out.

Song 20
Prayer Song

LAKOTA:
1. Wakantanka tokaheya cewakiye lo.
2. Wakantanka tokaheya cewakiye lo.
3. Mitakuye ob wani kta ca tokaheya cewakiye lo.

ENGLISH:
1. I pray first to Wakantanka.
2. I pray first to Wakantanka.
3. I pray first that I will live with all my relations.

This song belongs to the class *wocekiye olowan* 'prayer songs', of which there are many. The prayer song is offered at this ritual interlude to invite the spirits to enter the meeting place. According to Horn Cloud, sometimes they will not come immediately, and additional prayer songs may have to be sung to coax them in. Wakantanka represents the sum total of all supernatural powers, and is invoked first, lines 1 and 2. The Oglala when speaking English equate Wakantanka with God. This is at best a way of expeditiously translating the concept into English. There is no evidence that the Oglala believe in a Supreme Being, although they do recognize the embodiment of all powers in one term.

Line 3 reiterates the basic intention of all Yuwipi meetings—to "live with all my relatives."

Should the Yuwipi spirits arrive during the first prayer song, their appearance is heralded by the sound of the *wagmuha* rattling. Sometimes they arrive with a sudden crash of rattles.

Song 21
Prayer Song

LAKOTA:
1. Wamakaškan oyate ca wanniyank u welo.
2. Wanyankiye yo.

ENGLISH:
1. There is an animal nation coming to see you.
2. Behold them!

According to Horn Cloud, in the medicine man's vision he is told that his animal helpers will come in to join him during the meetings. They may include such animals as buffalo, deer, elk, or eagles, hawks—all animals that figure prominently in Lakota cosmology.[9]

In this text, the animals are telling the medicine man that they are about ready to arrive at the meeting and that he should look at them. The singing of this song is intended to call forth the animal helpers that are just outside the house waiting to be invited in.

Plenty Wolf frequently changes the first line of this song from *wamakaškan oyate* to *wakan oyate* 'sacred nation' referring to the sum total of animals, birds, and human helpers that come to assist him in curing the patients. This is another example of the interchangeability of textual materials sung to the same melodic line.

Song 22
Doctoring Song

LAKOTA:
  1. Inajin yo.
  2. He wanniyankin kte.
  3. Nitunkašila wanniyankin kte.
  4. Inajin yo.
  5. He wanniyankin kte.

ENGLISH:
  1. Stand up!
  2. He will see you.
  3. Your Tunkašila will see you.
  4. Stand up!
  5. He will see you.

Plenty Wolf calls this a *wapiyapi olowan* 'doctoring song' and it may be substituted for songs 7 and 8.

During the rendition of this song, those wishing to be doctored are told by the medicine man to stand up and reach out for the cloth flag closest to him, hold on to it, and face away from the *hocoka*. As the texts indicate, the patients stand up so that the spirit helpers, the Tunkašila, will see those who want to be doctored.

This is regarded as a lively song, and as soon as the singers begin it the *wagmuha*, the rattles, begin dancing. It is believed that the spirit helpers control the movement of the rattles, and during the course of the song each patient who is standing around the periphery of the *hocoka* are approached by the *wagmuha*. If a person, for example, suffers from a headache, the *wagmuha* will dance close by and touch him softly on the back and sides of the head. Sometimes they brush softly against the back of the neck and upper spine. Some medicine men employ spirit helpers who can be coaxed to speak at the meetings. And frequently during this part of the meeting, the spirits will speak with the patients in a high-pitched voice, asking them how they feel.

In this particular song, the word Nitunkašila in line 3 may be replaced by *tatanka wan* 'a buffalo' indicating a specific animal helper that has arrived at the meeting to help the medicine man. Frequently medicine men derive their greatest power from one or two specific animals that have appeared to them in visions.

Song 23
Declaration of Intent

LAKOTA:
1. Wankatanhan hotanin k'un le miye yelo.
2. Wanmayanka yo.
3. Iwaye cin wakan yelo.

ENGLISH:
1. The voice heard from above is me.
2. Look at me!
3. Whatever I speak is sacred.

The declaration of intent spoken by the medicine man is in many ways a recitation that validates his source of power. In the *hanbloglaka*, spoken from the center of the *hocoka*, the medicine man in effect presents a synopsis of his visions in which the spirits instruct him to walk with the pipe and cure people.

In this song, one which reflects the actual visionary experience, the spirits tell the medicine man that the voice that he hears is theirs, the spirits. Upon hearing their voice, he should not be afraid to look at them. Whatever they say, and subsequently whatever the medicine man speaks from the *hocoka*, is sacred and is to be reckoned with.

Song 24
Doctoring Song

LAKOTA:
1. Wankatanhan wau welo.
2. Wankatanhan wau welo.
3. Wankatanhan wau welo.
4. Wicanagi wan piya wakagin kta ca waun welo.
5. Wankatanhan wau welo.

ENGLISH:
1. I come from above.
2. I come from above.
3. I come from above.
4. I come to renew the spirit.
5. I come from above.

The Lakota believe that the spirit helpers live in the West somewhere between the earth and the clouds. Hence, references to coming from above and building a road alongside the clouds apply to the spiritual location of the helpers when they are at home.

In this song the spirits are telling the medicine man that they are coming from their homes above to join with him in the ritual to renew, literally 'make over,' the spirits of the patients who are to be cured. I have rendered the term *wicanagi* as 'spirit' here because I think that this translation is closer to what we understand as the psychological results of the curing process. *Wicanagi* is a generic term for 'ghost' but is frequently translated as 'soul'. For example the proper name for another ritual called Ghost-Keeping is *Wicanagi gluhapi*, literally 'they keep the souls of their own (kin).' *Nagi* is that aspect of the soul that lingers after death.

Song 25
Gathering up the Tobacco

LAKOTA:

1. Wakan oyate wan heyapelo.
2. Wakan oyate wan heyaya yau welo.
3. Iwaye cin wakanyan iyapelo.

ENGLISH:

1. A Sacred Nation is saying those things.
2. A Sacred Nation comes saying those things.
3. I speak what they have spoken sacredly.

Plenty Wolf calls this a prayer song, but states that it is to be sung during the Yuwipi when the spirits gather up the string of tobacco offerings that delineate the *hocoka*. The Sacred Nation refers to those spirits present at the meeting. They have arrived "saying those things," that is, telling the medicine man how to doctor the patients. The medicine man carefully points out in these texts that he is only a medium, an *iyeska*, a translator of sacred texts. He is only repeating those things that the spirits have rendered sacredly to him.

Song 26
Quitting Song

LAKOTA:

1. Miye yelo.
2. Miye yelo.
3. Miye yelo.
4. Miye yelo.
5. Tunkašila heya ca cewakiya ca namaȟ'un we.
6. Nitatunkašila tawakunze kin wakan yelo.
7. Tunkašila heya ca cewakiya ca namaȟ'un we.

ENGLISH:

1. It is me.
2. It is me.
3. It is me.
4. It is me.
5. Tunkašila said that and I pray so that he may hear me.
6. "Your Tunkašila's influence is sacred."
7. Tunkašila said that and I pray so that he may hear me.

Plenty Wolf calls this song *inakiyapi olowan* 'quitting song'. It is the last song sung while the spirits are still present at the meeting. In the text we find an individual spirit talking to the medicine man, identifying himself as the spirit and telling the medicine man that his Tunkašila's influence is sacred. This is another example of the spirit quoting the line that the medicine man is required to say when praying and singing.

These are the sacred Yuwipi songs of the George Plenty Wolf rite, some of which have found their way into the rituals of other practitioners. It is as if some of these songs, although learned through the personal experience of the Vision Quest, continue to be taught to fledgling medicine men by the same spirits. It is believed that they reoccur because they are taught to initiates by medicine men who are now living somewhere between the earth and the clouds in the West, and who join in those very meetings that they once conducted. Once they cured their patients through the mediation of the spirit helpers. Now they appear to those seeking visions as one of the spirit helpers themselves.

CHAPTER 4

CONTAINING THE SACRED

ONE of the greatest perplexities to be found in Lakota religion lies in the relationship between what is perceived to be their traditional religion and Christianity. When the first missionaries arrived in Lakota country, it was their mandate to begin teaching the Bible and other Christian doctrine. Some of the first missionaries at Pine Ridge were Roman Catholics and Episcopalians, and both denominations made great contributions to linguistics. Sometimes the only records of Lakota everyday speech are those in the grammars, dictionaries, and word books written by these dedicated and persevering people.[1]

In the creation of necessary analogies, certain Christian concepts such as the notion of one God, sin, Adam and Eve, the devil, and so forth required translation labels. In the process of translation, those missionaries who had managed to learn the language attempted simply to match a body of sacred language from one religion with a body of sacred language from another. This process is what many social scientists would call *explanation,* that is, the process of exchanging one set of symbols for another with the understanding that in the process some common relationship exists between the two sets of symbols that are being exchanged. In theory then, Christianity would be explained to the Lakota by selecting terms in Lakota sacred language that the translator deemed analogous to the significance of the Christian concepts.

This is no mean feat as other translators, particularly Bible translators, have pointed out (Nida 1964). For example, what does a translator do when confronted with a simple, but ubiquitous idea in Christianity, that of the Lamb of God, particularly when the formula "Lamb of God who taketh away the sins of the world have mercy on us" is put to the test of translation. In Lakota the translation of this idea is particularly difficult—some might say meaningless and futile—in a society where (1) there are no lambs, (2) God is not One, (3) sin does not exist, and (4) the world is a relatively small universe equal to one's own tribal territory. Fortunately for the missionaries, *mercy* does indeed have an analogue in Lakota.

In solving the problem of translation by analogies even when the analogies did not exist, the missionaries presumably relied on faith, and the knowledge that if one could provide a false analogy to begin the whole indoctrination process, that in another generation or two the analogies would themselves be transformed into a series of statements about Christianity based on raw belief. Thus the formula "Lamb of God who taketh away the sins of the world have mercy on us" (or in more contemporary translations "Lamb of God, you take away the sins of the world") was translated as Wakantanka Tahcašunkala Cincala, *maka etanhan wowaȟtani yutokanl iyeyaye, unšiunlapi ye*. A verbatim translation renders the following:

1. Wakantanka, a term that has been translated as God with the connotation of One God, but which among precontact Lakota designated sixteen sacred aspects.
2. Tahcašunkala Cincala, translated as Lamb, but which is a contrived word derived from *taȟca* 'deer', *šunka* 'dog', *la* 'diminutive suffix', and *cincala* 'baby'. The original significance for the Lakota was Mountain Sheep, since they had never seen a domestic sheep or used an animal as a sacrifice (except perhaps, a dog).
3. *maka* 'earth'.
4. *yutokanl* (from *yu* 'instrumental prefix' and *tokanl* 'another place, a place away from here') i.e., '(put) in another place'.
5. *etanhan* 'from'.
6. *wowaȟtani*, a term that has been translated conventionally as sin, but which is derived from *wo* 'noun marker'; *waȟta* a form of *waste* 'good'; e.g., *he waȟtelašni* 'that's no good'; *ni* negative suffix derived from the enclitic *šni* 'not'; hence, 'badness', things that are simply no good.
7. *iyeyaye*, an emphatic form of the auxiliary verb *iyeya*, indicating a suddenness of action.

8. *unšiunlapi,* from *unši* 'pitiable' and *la* 'to consider' plus the conjugation *un . . . pi* 'us'; hence, 'pity us.'

9. *ye,* enclitic designating that the sentence is an entreaty.

It is curious to speculate just what these words must have meant (if anything) to that generation of Lakota people who were potential candidates for conversion. It would have taken a great deal of faith, certainly not lacking among the good father, to believe that these most sacred Christian words and their sacred meanings could be conveyed through something like "Wakantanka's little mountain sheep suddenly puts badness in another place, pity us."

Not only is this translation ungrammatical in Lakota, despite the intrusive commas inserted to give the appearance of grammaticality, but it lacks any reference to a meaningful cultural experience. In retrospect, the translators might have been better served if they had at least chosen "dog" over "mountain sheep" since there is a notion of sacrifice present in the eating of dog (Powers and Powers, 1984, 1986).

What is ironic about the notion that there are analogous terms—Wakantanka = God, *wowaȟtani* = sin, and so forth— and that all that is necessary for salvation is to discover these correspondences is that today numerous books on Lakota religion are being published and read presumably by native Lakota many of whom were brought up in parochial schools. With renewed interest in native religion among the younger generation of Lakota, there is a need to reverse the process of translation: those who were brought up albeit nominally as Christian now must assign values learned in a missionary school to a newly discovered Lakota religion much of which is being learned from books. The process of analogizing is reversed. Whereas the missionaries looked for Lakota concepts to match what they believed to be Christian ideas, young nativists look for Christian concepts—often the only ones they know—to help them understand Lakota concepts.

To confound the issue even more, perhaps most of the young people who now want to understand more about the religion of their grandfathers do not speak Lakota. Most were not instructed by medicine men, and if they received any advice, it was in English and by analogy. Their great-grandfathers learned that "God is like Wakantanka," while they learn that "Wakantanka is like God."

RITUAL AND BELIEF

If there is irony in the relationship between Lakota and Christian religion, there is a confusion over the relationship between ritual and belief. Rather than compartmentalizing the two, it is more illuminating to see them as two aspects of the same phenomena, and as dynamic rather than static qualities of a person, place, or thing. This is not a new idea. It may be traced first to E. E. Evans-Pritchard's reassessment of Emile Durkheim's distinction of the sacred and profane. Durkheim saw these as separate and mutually exclusive qualities. On empirical grounds Evans-Pritchard saw sacredness and profaneness simply as states or stages of the same phenomena. Later another British anthropologist, Edmund Leach, was to apply the same kind of thinking to the dual concept of belief and ritual, stating that the former was stative while the latter was active but both referred to different aspects of the same phenomena.[2]

When the Oglala medicine man says that the meaning of the term "sacred" is understood by understanding the things that are considered sacred, he is making a theosophical statement quite similar to those mentioned above. He also demonstrates that inherent in Lakota religious concepts is an understanding of the relationship between ritual and belief. That is why belief in sacredness is partly contingent on rituals that transform profane things into sacred ones. Similarly, rituals are performed because of their inherent ability to sustain belief.

The Lakota have one term which corresponds to the English term belief. It is *wowicala* derived from *wo* noun marker; *wica* third person objective plural 'them'; and *la*, the root word, one which has a wide semantic range, conveying such ideas as "intention," "consideration," "regard," "demand," and "asking." For example, in some ceremonies when a person is expected to ask the supernaturals for help, as in the Yuwipi, the medicine man or his assistant will ask of the person *Yala hwo?* This can be translated as "Are you going to ask for things?" Belief then, among the Lakota, originally carried the connotation of asking for help: *Belief is an asking* and is therefore a stative aspect of religious behavior.

There are four terms in Lakota that may be translated as ceremony or ritual. In English, the distinction between these two terms (although there is perhaps no agreement) is that ceremony refers to a series of behaviors enacted in a secular context, whereas ritual always refers to a religious context. Modern social scientists are likely to view ritual more broadly and identify anything from shaking hands to high mass as examples of ritual behavior. In the sense that I use the terms here, ceremony refers to any secular context, and ritual always explicitly refers to an interaction between humans and what they perceive to be supernatural beings and powers.

The first term, *woecun*, corresponds to the English idea of 'celebration', and normally denotes any 'doings' or 'happening' in which a large number of people gather for some common purpose, usually secular.

Second, *wicoȟ'an* from *wica* third person objective plural and *oȟ'an* 'act, action, way,' corresponds to the idea of continuing behavior or ritual, but in a generic sense. Thus Lakol Wicoȟ'an means 'Indian Way' and as such constitutes a category of behavior seen to be different from non-Indian behavior. The seven rites brought to the Lakota by Ptehincalasanwin, the White Buffalo Calf Woman, are called the *wicoȟ'an wakan* 'sacred ceremonies'.

Third, the term *lowanpi* from *lowan* 'to sing' and *pi* third person plural may be translated as either 'a sing' or 'ritual', in particular a religious ceremony such as Yuwipi in which songs figure prominently.

Fourth, the term *kaga* which literally means 'to make' when it follows certain nouns (Heyoka Kaga "Clown Maker" or Oinikaga "Sweat Lodge" or 'life ceremony') also means ritual.

Although it is tempting to try to rank these different terms for ritual and ceremony, the Lakota do not. What all these

George Plenty Wolf, Yuwipi man and Sun Dance leader, consecrating the sacred pole at a Sun Dance in 1966. Photograph by Paul Steinmetz, S.J.

terms have in common, however, is their reference to various kinds of *actions*.

Very generally then, ritual and belief are seen to be related in Lakota, and are roughly translatable as *doing* and *asking*, respectively.

Understanding these distinctions between ritual and belief make it less cumbersome to offer some explication on perhaps the most unexplained word in Lakota sacred language, the term *wakan* which I gloss with confidence as 'sacred'.

WAKAN

A great deal has been written about the meaning of *wakan*. It was a keyword for the French sociological school under Durkheim, and almost all of his students remarked on the relationship between *wakan* and the more popular Melanesian term *mana*, the most common analogy being a quality exhibiting the characteristics of electricity—that is, a force or energy that is derived from essentially an invisible source.[3]

Because *wakan* is a foreign term to the languages employed to discuss it, and moreover because it is an American Indian language, *wakan* has normally been regarded as perhaps more mysterious than any of its possible translation labels. Most frequently *wakan* is translated as sacred or holy, and these terms are usually used interchangeably as they are in English. Less frequently, the term is described as roughly analogous to 'inexplicable', 'mysterious', even 'awesome'. These latter terms are sometimes heaped upon the more usual terms, sacred and holy, in an effort to make the point that *wakan* is simply a difficult concept to translate.

Walker's works, published posthumously, provide some of the most detailed discussions of *wakan* and related concepts ever published and are particularly useful because they are from the native's point of view. As such they complement his earlier work on Oglala rituals (Walker 1917) in which he interviewed a number of medicine men on religious concepts, including the meaning of *wakan*. These interviews have also been reprinted in an anthology of American Indian religions.[4]

Walker himself provides an interpretation that is rather typical. He says "When an Oglala is amazed by anything he may say that it is *wakan* meaning that it is *wakanla* (like *wakan*)." Walker then suggests that "'divine' is a proper interpretation of *wakan*" (Walker 1980, 74).

The above statement simply does not make sense, despite the fact that the editors of Walker's work regard it as the proper interpretation of *wakan*. In fact, the editors are reluctant to translate *wakan*, using the Lakota term throughout the book, on the grounds that "the English term *sacred* has too many limiting connotations to serve as an adequate equivalent for *wakan*" (Walker 1980, 147).

One wanting a translation of *wakan* might be amazed that this term somehow is so *wakan* that no translation label can possibly reveal its manifold connotations. We are left with the feeling that the Lakota speaker is somehow emerging from some arcane intellectual swamp, refusing to reveal his complicated ideas about the supernaturals to the more civilized exegetes of Lakota religion. It is as if we must simply be satisfied that *wakan* is untranslatable because we are not capable of interpreting in English a term that is the most important link between the mundane and supernatural worlds.

Walker also makes the analogy that "*wakan* is *wakanla*," introducing a second, related term for which there is no interpretation. What could be so complicated that we are forced to accept nonsense as the only explanation for sense?

Part of the problem here is that the editors refuse to tell us clearly that Walker's grasp of Lakota is wanting. For example, the difference between the term *wakan* and *wakanla* is not substantive; the affix *la* added to the second term is a grammatical operation that renders the term a compound verb 'to consider *wakan*'. If Walker really understood the significance of *la*, then his original statement about the meaning of *wakan* must read: "When an Oglala is amazed by anything he may say that it is *wakan* meaning that it is to be *regarded as wakan*." But of course this makes no sense either, and we still beg to know just what being "regarded as wakan" means.

What about a proper translation? First, I think that *wakan* is not any more difficult to translate into English than are *sacer* or *halig*. The first term is from the Latin, which later gives us the French *sacre*. *Sacer* means 'sacred' in English, and is also related to the Latin *sanus* 'sane' and the Greek *saos* 'safe'. The second term comes from Anglo-Saxon and in English is translated as "holy" (Webster's Second Edition). The two terms are interchangeable, and unfortunately Webster relies on one to explain the other, hence, something sacred is that which is holy, and something holy is that which is sacred. Despite these weaknesses, if we match the exegeses of Walker's Lakota respondents with Webster, we find that 'sacred" and 'holy' are respectable glosses for *wakan*. The only time at which these terms are not interchangeable is when they are used specifically according to say rules of the Catholic Church which dictate that the term 'sacred' is to be used for places, and 'holy' is to be used for persons.

Walker's editors do not have the same reluctance to translate *wicaša wakan* as 'holy man' which they inform us is their only exception in providing a gloss for *wakan*. They further refuse to translate still another variation *yuwakan* claiming that "the only way to translate this concept would have been "is made *wakan*," a translation they dislike because it suggests "non-Indian concepts of causation, not to mention the clumsiness of the English expression" (Walker 1980, 147).

Of course, many will not find the translation clumsy, and in the context in which *yuwakan* is employed in the texts, it is highly unlikely that any non-Indian concept of causation is being violated. In fact, if there were an adequate translation label for *wakan* we would find agreement between Indian and non-Indian concepts of causation, because in each case *yuwakan* refers to a transformation from a state of *not being wakan* to *being wakan*. The instrumental prefix *yu* when added to *wakan* does in fact mean 'to make *wakan*'. In English, if *wakan* is synonymous with sacred and holy, then to make sacred, or holy, is quite respectably rendered "to bless," the act of blessing being synonymous with the act of transforming the profane into the sacred. Given that even in English terms such as sacred, holy, and blessing have negative as well as positive connotations, one might conclude that *yuwakan* can also refer to a transformation from sacred to profane. It is quite unacceptable to suggest that the English term sacred is too limited in its connotations. It is no more or less limited than *wakan*, for both words describe precisely the same process of transformation.

The process of transformation is accomplished through the ritual of blessing, blessing here being understood as the investment of the quality of sacredness into a person, place, or thing.

Further complications in translation arise when we believe that there are empirical changes in the persons, places, and things that undergo transformation. But transformations do not *cause* physical changes; they simply cause changes in the behaviors of those who believe that such transformations have taken place. For example, let us look at the phenomenon of holy water (a contradiction of the rule sacred = things, holy = persons) in Roman Catholicism. Holy water comes into being when the ritual of blessing is enacted upon common water. The priest makes the sign of the cross over the vessel of water and repeats a prayer formula.

The enactment of the ritual and prayer over the water creates a transformation in the state of the water, but the water does not undergo any physical change. What changes is people's behavior toward the water. Subsequently, the water may be used to create further transformations in state, that is, once the water is blessed it can be used to bless other objects. For example, the holy water may be used to bless the house and bed of newlyweds. It is believed that the common water now transformed into holy water has the capacity to make the couple fecund by its association with the couple's nuptial bed. There are, so far, two ritual changes: transformation of the profane water into holy water, and the transformation of the profane bed into a sacred one, the combination of which is believed to potentiate childbirth. If the woman becomes pregnant—the final transformation in this series—then there is an obvious physical change in the woman's "natural" state which is believed to have been caused by the previous ritual transformations. In this example as well as other Lakota examples, the cause is always determined retroactively: the transformation of the holy water, and the transformation of the nuptial bed caused the woman to become pregnant. But the cause is only discerned after the fact, not before. Thus the possibility that there will be a confusion between English and Lakota concepts of causality is unfounded. They are the same: both are determined retrospectively.

A Lakota example should help clear up the problem of translating *wakan*. I turn to a personal experience that I had in 1966.

I had become particularly interested in Yuwipi during this year, and had the good fortune to work closely with George Plenty Wolf, who conducted most of the meetings in Red Cloud Community. During my stay that summer Plenty Wolf told me that he wanted to give me a stone, a tiny transparent stone that he had found near an ant hill in the Badlands. According to Lakota beliefs, ants and other underground creatures are sacred because they transverse between the surface of the earth and the underground and thus in a mundane way continually act out the subterranean emergence of the Lakota. The stones, roots, insects, and the earth itself that are located underground are considered purer than the surface because they have not been contaminated by people or animals that live above. Stones then that are pushed up by ants and other creatures are particularly sacred and are the ones selected for use in rituals.

So Plenty Wolf presented this stone to me. My wife made a small buckskin bag for it, the kind that most of the Lakota at Pine Ridge use. The old man also told me that for the stone to be effective, that is *wakan*, it had to be named. Naming ceremonies, whether they are conducted to invest a stone with a name or to name a person in the traditional way, are called *caštun* from *caš* an attenuated form of *caje* 'name', and *tun* which here means 'to give birth to', that is, create a name. Plenty Wolf's ceremony was called Inktomi *lowanpi* 'Spider sing', and although it resembled a Yuwipi, some elements of the ritual were quite different.

Normally in Yuwipis proper,[5] Plenty Wolf used a long string
of *canli wapaȟte* 'tobacco offerings' to delineate the *hocoka*, and
a smaller string which encircled the round *makakagapi*, mellowed earthen altar, located in the center of the *hocoka* toward
the western part of the sacred space. This smaller string contained thirty-three tobacco offerings, each of which symbolized a spirit named after some peculiar aspect of Inktomi, the
mischievous character prominent in Lakota morality stories.
Now Inktomi himself is attributed with having named all
things in the Lakota universe after it was created, so it is not
unusual that he should bear so many different names and
continue to be invoked to provide new names. Each of the tobacco offerings then were for such aspects of *Inktomi* as Inktomi *oholašni* 'Inktomi (who) respects nothing'; Inktomi *mni
akan mani* 'Inktomi (who) walks on the water'; and Inktomi
kinyan 'flying Inktomi'. Plenty Wolf said that each tobacco
offering was for a different Inktomi, and that if necessary he
could name all of them. These spirits were particularly powerful and they were his most entrusted helpers. They were
called upon during normal Yuwipis, but they were deemed to
be particularly efficacious in meetings that were called for
special purposes, so-called "emergency meetings" for the
purpose of making a quick decision about a life crisis situa-
tion; meetings called *okile lowanpi* 'hunting or search ceremonies' for the purpose of finding lost articles or persons;[6]
and meetings for the purpose of investing stones with what
the Lakota called a *šicun*. As some early medicine men tell us:

> A shaman must impart a *ton* (*tun*) with the right ceremony
> done in the right manner. . . . When a shaman imparts a *ton* to
> anything the thing is made a *sicun*. A *sicun* is like the God. . . .
> A shaman must put the container on a *sicun* and this makes it a
> *wasicun*. [Walker 1980, 95–96]

Here the act of performing the naming ceremony potenti-
ated the investment of the stone with a named spirit generically called a *šicun* but specifically named after one of Plenty
Wolf's Inktomi helpers. Once the medicine man has placed a
container around the *šicun*, in this case the container being a

Lakota funeral, September, 1955. Courtesy Heritage Center, Inc.

stone, the stone is then *wakan* and is afterwards called a
wašicun tunkan or what we may roughly gloss as a "*sicunized*
stone," that is, one invested with *wowakan* 'sacredness'.[7]

Like other Yuwipis, the Inktomi *lowanpi* was held in a darkened room from which all furniture had been removed, and
the windows and doors covered with blankets and tarps. But
the altar, or *hocoka*, consisted only of the small earthen altar
around which the thirty-three *canli wapahte* had been placed.
Instead of seven *wanunyanpi*, or flag offerings, each representing the Four Directions, the Above, the Earth, and the
Spotted Eagle, only two were used, a red *wanunyanpi* placed

on the south side of the *hocoka* and a white one placed on the north side. Between them was Plenty Wolf's personal altar containing a deer tail, a shell, a piece of root, a feather, and other symbols of the universe.

The only other item laid on the sacred space was my buckskin bag containing the stone, which upon advice from Plenty Wolf had been wrapped in a wad of sage before being placed inside the bag. One further instruction was that after the stone had been named, the buckskin bag could never be opened again because this would be offensive to the spirit.

Plenty Wolf drew the picture of a spider on the earthen altar and filled the pipe in the traditional manner. He then asked for the lights to be turned out. The singers began singing, and soon one could hear a great racket in the *hocoka*, thumping noises against the floor, ceiling, and walls around us. The rattles crashed about us, signaling that the powerful spirits had arrived. After perhaps less than twenty minutes, the lights were turned on, revealing a disheveled medicine man and a disorderly *hocoka*, the altar obviously having been trampled by the spirit helpers.

He handed the buckskin bag to me and told me that the *wašicun* now bore the name of Inktomi Kinyan 'Flying Spider', and if at any time I was in trouble or needed help for any reason, I could pray to the spirit of Inktomi Kinyan to help me. He told me that I should always keep the *wašicun tunkan* away from the presence of menstruating women. If for some reason it should be contaminated, I would have to take it into a Sweat Lodge for it to be purified. He told me to carry it with me when I went on long journeys or thought that I would confront any kind of personal troubles. We all smoked the pipe together and after a small feast of sandwiches and coffee, the Inktomi *lowanpi* was finished.

We can draw a direct analogy between the transformation of profane water into holy water, and the naming of the stone. In both cases, the ritual of transformation is *yuwakan* 'making sacred', and the final result, transforming a profane object into a sacred one, results in the object's achieving a state of being *wakan*. If we extend the analogy, we can see that the ritual transformation for both the medicine man and the priest follows the same process:

1. Potentiation. The process of performing the proper ritual so that the person, place, or object to be transformed is rendered worthy of the change of ritual status.[8] The priest may recite a prayer to exorcise impurity in water before investing it with potentiality to sacredness. The medicine man fills the pipe, prays, and sings the proper words to entice the spirits to enter the room, and one of them to enter the heretofore profane stone. Both water and stone are potential "containers" for the sacredness that will be invested in them by conducting the proper rituals.

2. Transformation. The result of performing the proper ritual is that profane water is transformed into holy water; the water is now sacred, that is, people's behavior to it is changed. It is believed to have powers not attributed to profane water. Similarly, a profane *tunkan* 'stone' is transformed into *wašicun tunkan*; the *tunkan* is now sacred, and likewise people's behavior toward it changes; it has powers that common stones do not have.

If there is a difference between the two processes it is not in the perceived causes of the transformations: they are always believed to be of supernatural origins. But there is a difference in the effects of these processes of transformation. For the priest, each transformation from profane to sacred is the same: the proper prayers are spoken and the anticipated transformation is achieved. But for the medicine man, according to Lakota belief, each time the proper ritual is performed and the *šicun* invested, the medicine man loses a little of his power because his power is the sum total of the *šicuns* he owns as a result of Vision Quests. He does not receive new *šicuns* for old; each *šicun* given away to another remains permanently with the *wašicun* into which it was invested. If a person dies, his *šicun* leaves its container, the *wašicun*, and in a sense returns to a "pool" of *šicun* waiting to become part of another medicine man's stock of *šicun* that he receives through Vision Quests.

WAKANTANKA

Wakantanka is most frequently glossed as Great Spirit or Great Mystery, both terms having a romantic quality which at the same time comes very close to the significance of the word. Missionaries adopted this term for God, and added a further qualification that Wakantanka originally meant Supreme God, carrying the further connotation that the Lakota too believed that there was only one God. Of course all of this is a most welcomed convention if one is in the business of converting by analogy.[9]

Some missionaries have gone so far as to see the sacred pipe of the Lakota as a "foreshadowing of Christ" (Steinmetz 1969, 83), a statement that is more about religious imperialism than empirical reality. Both the notion of a Supreme God and Son of God are foreign to original Lakota belief.

I have opted not to translate Wakantanka in my own work because normally the Lakota do not translate it when speaking English. Moreover I believe that retaining the Lakota term is a minimal courtesy which I think all religions are due. Although it is ludicrous to suggest that native Lakota religion could be called Wakantankanism, it is only so because we have never allowed native American Indian religions to be compared with the other "isms" of the world to which extreme importance is attached—Shintoism, Taoism, Buddhism, Judaism. Although "isms" can become tedious, the suffix does add a certain status to the belief to which it is attached, and American Indian religions have never been able to achieve that kind of religious status owing to the need of the Western (and Eastern intellectual tradition) to retain its sense of superiority.

However, Wakantanka can be broken down into smaller analyzable components. *Wakan* means sacred and *tanka* means great or big; its reduplicated form *tankinkinyan* means 'important'. No one knows why these two words have been combined to symbolize the sum total of all that is sacred in the universe. In fact, the term is most unusual grammatically because its two adjectives combine to form a noun, but without any of the conventional noun markers (such as *wa, wo, wica,* or *pi*). Perhaps sometime in the unenlightened past several ancient philosophers, antecedents of the modern Lakota, decided that not only was everything potentially *wakan,* but also that supernatural elements coalesced and gave rise to all things that are or are potentially *wakan.* In a single burst of inspiration they coined the neologism Wakantanka.[10]

Wakantanka is a complicated concept, not because it is Lakota but because figureheads of all religions are complex. It is unlikely that any two religions, unless they are derived from a common source, can be seen as objectively similar except in an analytical way, one which requires analogues and metaphors to make the point. It takes not analytical ability but raw faith to see the Sacred Pipe as a foreshadowing of Christ. The only thing the two concepts have in common is the analytical imposition of the notion of mediation between common people and the supernatural. From the perspective of raw faith there is always the possibility that Christ was a foreshadowing of the Sacred Pipe, but it is unlikely that any Lakota would *believe* that.

In 1977 two independent exegeses of Wakantanka were published (DeMallie and Lavenda 1977, and Powers 1977). Each is from a different perspective but both are complementary.

The two treatments are similar in that they focus on the structural components of the concept, called *tobtob* 'four times four'. This is based on the agreement that Wakantanka is a single term that refers to sixteen aspects, all of which are related to each other in a special way. DeMallie and Lavenda are interested in seeing Wakantanka as an extension of *wakan* but unfortunately entitle their piece "*Wakan:* Plains Siouan Concepts of Power." This article, which also treats the Omaha concept *wakonda,* supports an earlier claim by J. Owen Dorsey (1894, 365) that *wakan* is "not really a distinction between nature and supernature" but "between the human and the superhuman, the understandable and predictable as opposed to the incomprehensible" (DeMallie and Lavenda 1977, 153).

A better title, since the anthology in which the article appears deals with the anthropology of power, would have been "*Wowas'ake:* Plains Siouan Concepts of Power" since *wowas'ke* most clearly means 'power' in Lakota, not *wakan* which can only mean 'sacred'. The need to use a term that the Lakota do not use probably stems from the same kind of thinking that gave rise to the customary use of the English term "medicine" as an equivalent of *wakan*. This term gives rise to the reference to Indian ritual as "making medicine" which does not make sense among contemporary Lakota.

The article also contains errors which reduce the credibility of what is otherwise an adequate historical statement of what nearly everyone in anthropology has had to say about the meaning of Wakantanka.[11] These are essentially linguistic errors. For example, the relationship between the sixteen aspects of Wakantanka are seen to be metaphorically related to the human kinship system

> inasmuch as the various *wakan* beings were addressed by humans with kinship terms. For example, the buffalo were considered to be brothers of the Dakota, and what is important here were the moral obligations of mutual respect and support that this relationship automatically prescribed. Significantly, the term *cekiya* 'to pray', or 'to call out', also means 'to address by kinship term'. Thus the method of prayer was the invocation of relationship. [DeMallie and Lavenda 1977, 156]

Presumably, although it is not clear, the *wakan* beings are aspects of Wakantanka. If this is the case most of them were *not* addressed by kinship terms with the exception of the Sun sometimes addressed as 'father' and Earth sometimes addressed as 'mother'. Wakantanka is sometimes honorifically addressed as Tunkašila 'Grandfather'. If the buffalo were regarded as "brothers," they certainly are never ritually addressed as such. The relationship between buffalo and humans is always seen as a relationship between females of both species (Powers 1977, 1980). In ritual language, the Buffalo

Mass in an Oglala cabin, ca. 1900. Courtesy Heritage Center, Inc.

Nation is addressed as Pte Oyate, *pte* being the term for buffalo cow.

Therefore it is difficult to see what relationship between
the sixteen aspects of Wakantanka was "automatically pre-
scribed." Although the authors regard as "significant" the
term *cekiya* 'to pray', the term cannot be translated as 'to call
out' (which in Lakota is *kico*). The idea that it also means 'to
address by kinship term' is erroneous. Since the authors do
not cite a reference for this translation, presumably it is their
own. However, the verb 'to call by a kinship term' is *takuya*
from which *otakuye* 'relatives, relations' is derived. *Cekiya* is
derived from *ceya* 'to cry, to lament', and the inserted preposition *ki* meaning 'for', hence 'to cry for', are the terms commonly used as the translation for 'to pray'. Missionaries used
this form to translate *wocekiye* 'prayer'. The term *cekiya* simply
does not carry the connotation of kinship, and never has.

My analysis of Wakantanka (Powers 1977) generally focused
on the structural relationship between the sixteen aspects,

particularly the way they are hierarchically ranked, and other aspects of Oglala society, particularly social organization at various levels of organization. The source for both explanations is Walker (1917) who explains that Wakantanka is divided into two classes called *Wakan kin* 'the *wakan*' and Taku *wakan* 'something *wakan*'. Each of these classes is further divided into two subclasses *Wakan kin* being comprised of *wakan ankatu* 'superior *wakan*' and *wakan kolaya* 'kindred *wakan*' and Taku *wakan* being comprised of *wakan kuya* 'subordinate *wakan*' and *wakanlapi* '*wakan*like'. Each subclass is again divided into sets of four personae. The total picture looks like this:

Wakantanka [12]

Wakan kin		Taku wakan	
Wakan ankatu	*Wakan kolaya*	*Wakan kuya*	*Wakanlapi*
Wi	Hanwi	Tatanka	Nagi
Škan	Tate	Hununpa	Niya
Maka	Woȟpe	Tate tob	Nagila
Inyan	Wakinyan	Yumni	Šicun

My particular concern was to examine the internal structure of this paradigm making the point that other aspects of Oglala social structure were identical, that is, they were all constructed from the same template, one which placed a high priority on the uses of the sacred numbers four and seven. I was not concerned then with criticizing Walker's schema. Although I still believe that his ideas hold up well structurally, I now have some other thoughts on the components of his schema.

The major distinction (and this is in agreement with Walker) between the two classes Wakan *kin* and Taku *wakan* is that the former is believed to have existed prior to the creation of the world; the latter exists as a result of its creation. But these distinctions are not apparent in the Lakota terms for each. One would like to know where Walker learned these terms, as well as those for the next subclasses. If we compare the four components of *wakan ankatu* with those of *wakan kolaya*, the relationships are very asymmetrical, making one wonder what the basis for the classification is. One can say with certainty, however, that it is not kinship. For example, Wi is "married" to Hanwi in the early cosmology; but Škan is the force that makes Tate, the wind, blow. Woȟpe is the daughter of Wi and Hanwi and is later transformed into the White Buffalo Calf Woman, but there is no particular relationship between Woȟpe and Maka; Maka Ina is metaphorically the "Mother of us all," but there is no particular relationship between the two. Finally Inyan and Wakinyan are related in such a way that they are the parents of Inktomi, the culture hero, and *Iya*.

In the next set, Taku *wakan*, relationships do not exist between the classes either paradigmatically or syntagmatically. It makes no particular sense to match, say, Tatanka and Nagi because the *wakanlapi* paradigm contains properties found in both animals, represented by Tatanka, and human beings, represented by Hununpa. These properties, for the time being, can be considered aspects of "soul." The division of Wakantanka into sixteen parts or aspects is undeniably a Lakota concept, one reiterated today in prayer, song, and philosophical exegesis. But the problem of the classes and subclasses remains: Are they Lakota or are they Walker?

For example, if we systematically examine all the classes and subclasses into which the concept of Wakantanka is divided, we find the following alternate explanations:

1. *Wakan kin*. There is no evidence, other than Walker's interpretations of Oglala medicine men, that this term represents a class. *Wakan kin* means 'the sacred' and can be used generically to refer to anything sacred, not only those partial aspects of Wakantanka. However, there is a logical relationship between the constituent elements of the class, that is, the relationship between Wi, Škan, Maka, and Inyan. From a cosmological perspective, they belong together by virtue of their primordiality in Lakota myth. They are the oldest.

2. *Taku wakan*. In modern Lakota Taku *wakan* is a viable sacred expression but it does not refer to a class of sacred persons or objects. It simply is a convention for referring to all things sacred in a collective way. It can be translated as sacred thing(s), or "what is sacred," or "whatever is sacred," depend-

ing on the context. One could refer to all sixteen aspects of Wakantanka as Taku *wakan*, not only those indicated by Walker. Additionally, one could refer to any collection of animals, birds, people, or objects that are designated *wakan* as Taku *wakan*. The problem here is that it is a viable class of things in Lakota, but not the class assigned to it by Walker.

3. *Wakan akantu*. This term is probably an error. There is no word *akantu*. Walker probably is trying to say *wankatu* 'up above.' But *wankatu* refers to a location, not a status, which is *wankapaya* 'to be in a high position.' The error is a reasonable one given that the Lakota phoneme /w/ is pronounced with the lips apart, frequently sounding like /a/.

4. *Wakan kolaya*. This is a verbal form and literally means 'to consider (that which is) sacred as a friend.' Walker variously translates this class as "associate" or "companion" gods, and presumably refers to the relationship of each of these members to those in *wakan ankatu*. In contemporary Lakota prayer and song, the spirit helpers of the medicine man frequently are referred to as *kola* 'friend', as is the medicine man himself. However, *kola* implies male gender; a man does not call a woman *kola*, nor is the reverse true. Similarly, a woman calls another woman *maške* 'friend, chum.' *Kola* originally meant 'comrade', the relationship between two men who were willing to lay down their lives for each other on the warpath. It does not make sense in Lakota for, say, Wi to call his wife Hanwi *kola*, or for that matter any of the personae in these two subclasses. One must question the validity of this term.

5. *Wakan kuya*. *Kuya* means 'below'; but the idea of *wakan kuya* '*wakan* (that is) below' makes no sense. Walker translates this as 'subordinate', but it is clearly a reference to a location, not a status. One may probably see the relationship as indicative of a class of personae that "live below" the personae in the first two classes. Since the creation of the universe in Lakota mythology is partly caused by a rearrangement of time-space dimensions in which these members wind up on earth, i.e., below the others.

6. *Wakanlapi*. As a verbal form, this means 'they are regarded *wakan*'. Like the other terms, it seems to be specious

as a class marker. As I have mentioned, it is a grammatical construction.

Walker has been considered one of the greatest contributors to Oglala religion because he studied with medicine men himself and was for a short time an actual apprentice. However, he did not speak Lakota and one must wonder just how he pieced together such complex ideas without some benefit of linguistic competency. In his work published in 1980, a number of persons are interviewed in the forty-three narratives in a section called "Belief" (Walker 1980, 63–144). These narratives essentially form the foundation for Walker's classification of Wakantanka and other sacred concepts scattered throughout his works. Curiously, of the twenty-seven persons interviewed who are named, only one, Red Hawk, admits to being a medicine man (pp. 136–37). Most of the others clearly are not. For example Antoine Herman, Bruce Means, Bert (also, Burt) Means, Elmore Red Eyes, Thomas Tyon, and William Garnett are interpreters (although Tyon is also interviewed as a principal informant). Little Wound, American Horse, Bad Wound, No Flesh, Thunder Bear, Ringing Shield, Red Cloud, and Lone Bear all figure prominently in Oglala history, but not as medicine men. One interview is with "miscellaneous shamans," two are anonymous, and two are by Walker himself. Short Bull, one of the interviewees, was a medicine man, but one associated with the Ghost Dance of 1888–90.

Apparently, the fact that most of the Lakota people are not medicine men is of little consequence to the editors who make no mention of this controversial aspect of their research, one bearing directly on Walker's most important claims. Also, fully eleven of the narratives in the "Belief" section are based on interviews with George Sword, as well as two others in which he collaborates. One wonders why some of Sword's interviews seem to require an interpreter while others do not. This is of particular interest since George Sword's greatest claim to fame at Pine Ridge was that he was in charge of the Indian police, not that he was a medicine man.

Finally, although the editors suggest comparing the narratives in the "Belief" section with another, "Narratives by Thomas Tyon," as a valuable check on the validity of Walker they have not been so careful themselves. Whereas Walker's materials make constant reference to such concepts as *wakanpi, wakanlapi, wakan kuya,* and *kolaya,* Tyon's narratives, which were written in Lakota and translated by the editors, sound more like the philosophical statement about Lakota religion that one is likely to encounter today on the Pine Ridge Reservation. Where local people at Pine Ridge have a difficult time understanding Walker's concepts, or interpretations (of interpretations) of them, they have no trouble understanding Tyon's.

What can one make of all this? Is Walker to be chastized for inventing a theology that has been so well documented and so well enmeshed in the minds of younger generation Lakota that it is now taught as doctrine in bilingual and bicultural educational programs? I suppose one will never know for sure. One can say with a great deal of certainty that some parts of Walker still correspond with modern Lakota thought. A continuity of religion outside the Walker manuscripts and published literature can be traced, one that is the product of an oral tradition handed down by a dwindling number of tribal elders.

For these old people *wakan* means sacred, a state or quality waiting for medicine men to find the appropriate container for. And Wakantanka is the total of all possible investments and all possible containers—people, places, objects whose ritual status can be changed by people invested with the knowledge and power to do so.

CHAPTER 5

SACRED NUMBERS

UNDERSTANDING much of Lakota sacred lore is not simply a matter of defining and interpreting sacred words and phrases in song and speech. Sacrality is frequently achieved through patterning of common words, structuring them so that they form sacred language, codes that can be broken only if the total structure, not simply the constituent parts, is decoded.[1]

One of the most widely developed ways of structuring the parts of a whole is simply by counting them. Since this is such a fundamental way to classify important ideas and things, the process of numerical structuring must have been with humankind for most of its evolution.

Numbers not only have the capacity to connect important configurations of thought, but also frequently provide a frame within which these fundamental ideas continue for long periods of time. In addition to their digital qualities, numbers are perceived as having shapes such as circles to express unity, dyads such as the Chinese symbol for yin and yang, a triangle to express the trinity, or perhaps the dialectic, a box to symbolize fourness. It is as if shaping these numerical configurations in specific ways guarantees that they will become instantly embedded in the mind. As such not only will they serve as tools by which the meanings behind the shapes will become known but there will be an additional satisfaction that if the shapes themselves are somehow simple but meaningful they will be remembered much more easily.[2]

There is perhaps nothing sacred in numerical structures, even though all peoples of the world count their blessings arithmetically as well as with hope and sometimes relief. But the same holiness of the trinitarian representation of Chris-

tian faith can easily be reinterpreted to form a Marxist dialectic, and the reverse is true as well. If a dialectical relationship is one that expresses opposites mediated by the presence
of both oppositional qualities—plus as opposed to minus
with the mediation of plus-minus—then we can, with little
modification of the original Hegelian concept, talk about God
the Father, opposing God the Son, and the mediation between
the two by the Holy Ghost. This dialectic is based not on superiority or inferiority of each of the three parts but rather on
the belief that God's domain is heaven, while the Son's is on
earth. The Holy Ghost mediates between the two locationally;
it is capable of occupying both domains.

Three also has been a main unifying factor in the development of the Western intellectual tradition as any scholar, or
schoolboy, knows.[3] We are so accustomed to framing ideas
into threes that we rarely give it much thought. On the other
hand, we are quick to try to understand the same principles
as they apply in other cultures using other numerical devices.
This foreign unifying system often infatuates us and we expect somehow to learn more from exposure to yin and yang
than is readily available in our own trinitarian society, but
with less apparent mysteriousness.

No wonder then that we are struck by the systematic way in
which the Lakota classify their entire universe by fours and
sevens,[4] as if our own system cannot live up to the elegance of
a quadratic and heptadic system. Of course ours can, but we
are more inspired by the Lakota system because we expect
that there is knowledge there that we cannot discover in our
own less-than-natural society, one constrained by triplicity.

Perhaps what is appealing about Lakota numerical systems
is that rather than one system, there are two. One of these
systems is based on the number four, and generally relates to
what is perceptually all persons, places, and objects in nature—the four directions, the four seasons, the four stages of
life, four kinds of living things, four phases of a plant, and so
forth.[5] The other system is based on the number seven, generally a number related to divisions of what we may call, in a
Lévi-Straussian sense, culture. Empirically, the Lakota divide

Frank Fools Crow, well-known Sun Dance leader, leading a dancer to be pierced at the Sun Dance held in 1966. Photograph by Paul Steinmetz, S.J.

most of their social and political divisions into sevens, a fact well known in the Siouan literature. As examples, we may look only at the major political division, the Oceti Šakowin Seven Fireplaces; this social construct is further divided into what anthropologists would call "tribes" and "bands," and there is a rather predictable manner in which many of the

Lakota and Dakota subdivisions employ the number seven to organize themselves socially and politically.[6]

Both the number four and the number seven have the capacity to symbolize a sense of natural and cultural fulfillment. When one "reaches" the end of the ritual line so to speak, one gets off the ritual bus at either of these arithmetical stops. Both numbers not only establish a sense of fullness or completion, they are statements of denouement. They are also statements about the future as well as the past and present. In a sense there is a hope in numbers that have a definite stop point: the only thing that can happen after four or seven is reached in the natural and cultural counting system is that the series can start over again at *one*. There is a comfort that infinity can be controlled; it is cyclical, not ortholinear. In this system, and perhaps all systems which place a great deal of faith in numbers, the unpredictability of the future is controllable through repetition of the proper rituals and prayers, themselves divided into sets or parts that structure some numerical hope.

I think that these numerical systems, one based on four, the other on seven, should not be seen necessarily as mutually exclusive categories, one making reference to natural things, the other to cultural things. That would be too simple. The two systems are quite complementary, if not mutually dependent on each other. The basic number is four, and seven is partly derived from the basic numerical foundation to which other numbers have been added. I have already discussed this in an earlier work (Powers 1977) and have been taken to task by some of my colleagues who regard themselves as ethnohistorians, a discipline which apparently has little use for the idealistic and ideological manifestations of culture. For example, Fowler (1979), in a detailed review which must be lauded for the great amount of research that she did on a subject which is not generally in her field of expertise, tells us that some early explorers found that the "Sioux" were divided into ten (bands?) and then wonders why I did not use the number ten for my model of Lakota social organization instead of seven. The reason, of course, should be clear even to the novice student of Siouan culture: the number seven is one that the Lakota people employ, and not because they do not have access to the historical literature that Fowler has. The Lakota—all peoples of the world—are not as much interested in the way things are as the way things *should be*, and the way they should be is perceived as a structure organized into seven constituent parts in a very predictable way. It is the naïve anthropologist or historian who expects to find numerical systems that reflect reality, reality often being defined as something that can be stored in a library, museum, or archival bin. It is rather reality that is fitted into the numerical system, which preexists as an organizational principle.

Frequently these two numerical systems are imposed on each other in unusual ways; that is, four and seven coexist with a single ritual performance. In filling the pipe and in placing stones in the Sweat Lodge, a conceptual distinction is made between four, two, and one. In this system the quadratic structure symbolizes the four directions, the dyadic structure represents the opposition Above and Mother Earth, and the monadic structure symbolizes the Spotted Eagle. Of course, these structures are what Victor Turner would call multivocal (Turner 1967): they are capable of symbolizing a number of concepts independently and/or simultaneously. The quadratic structure can symbolize any natural category or metaphor for the constituent parts of these categories, such as colors, birds, animals, and seasons, all of which are paradigmatically related and as such stand as metaphors of the four directions. The dyadic structure can serve to symbolize any contrasting set that is significant in Lakota culture, good and evil, ancient and modern, left and right, and so forth. The monadic element also symbolizes not only the center of the earth but the place where the individual *is*, and as such is a metaphor for the individual himself.

The imposition of one numerical system on the other is not unique, and is certainly not limited to the Lakota or other American Indian belief systems. In Western thought we also find complementary numerical systems. For example, in baseball (as Dundes has pointed out) an ordering system prevails that is based on the number three, but frequently the number four serves as perhaps a secondary ordering system; we have three strikes, but four balls leading to different kinds of denouement, one negative and one positive. (You're "out" in the first; you "walk" in the second.) This series is repeated, as Dundes tells us in naming the bases as "first," "second," "and third" but the fourth is home "plate" (Dundes 1968).

Similarly in Christianity, where again the organizing principle is based in the tetradic structure, there is an accommodation in which the number four is imposed on the number three. In representational art (despite the inaccurate depiction of historical reality) the cross upon which Christ was crucified is depicted as an icon that is essentially divided into four parts. The attempt to depict the cross ritually and at the same time indicate its trinitarian importance results in the sign of the cross. Whether inscribed in the air, as when a priest applies a ritual blessing, or whether directed against oneself by placing the tips of the fingers of the right hand serially on the forehead, chest, left shoulder, right, there is an essential conflation of two numerical systems that coexist and emphasize the importance and dependence of the two systems. The process is not unlike a musician, say a West African drummer, who plays a time signature of 4/4 with his right hand on one drum, and at the same time plays "against" it in 3/4 time with the left hand on a second drum. The thrill of hearing such polyrhythm is probably analogous to the religious thrill one feels at the point of being exposed to the tension created by the imposition of four on three in the Christian system, or seven on four in the Lakota system.

There is another quality in these numerical systems, briefly alluded to above, and that is their capacity to express a dynamic. Although the symbols of these numerical systems are usually thought of as being static, for example, the *cangleška wakan* 'sacred circle or hoop',[7] or a circle inscribing a cross symbolic of the entire universe, they can also express movement and viability. Numbers that are sacred are generally those that somehow mark the end, the finality of a sacred process expressed in prayer, songs, and in ritual. It is the sacred

Julie Plenty Wolf, a medicine woman, participating in the 1966 Sun Dance at Pine Ridge. Photograph by Paul Steinmetz, S.J.

number that through its emphasis on the termination of a series implies the processes that lead to its termination. The sacred number four is important because of the implicit series that has created it 1,2,3. . . . The number seven is sacred because of the internal constructs and their respective serialization that has given them structure: 4,2,1. . . .

Since understanding this dynamic attribute of the numerical system is critical to understanding the very concept that is symbolized in the number, let me provide some Lakota examples.

In the most fundamental sense, all people in the world are animists, that is, they believe something gives rise to the living organism that contains it, and somehow survives this organism when it perishes. Animism, from the Latin *anima*, is in English the concept called soul. Despite the ubiquity of the ideas of soul, there is no agreement as to the nature of soul, or numerically speaking, just how many souls a living organism has. There is also no agreement about what kind of living organisms are supposed to contain the various numbers of souls, or aspects of one soul. Conventionally, based on a rigid interpretation of the word, animists are depicted as "primitive" people who believe that even rocks, trees, animals, and birds have "souls."[8]

Animism may be contrasted with another term, animalism, similarly derived from the Latin but which by convention identifies those who believe that humans are just another form of animal having *no* spiritual quality, that is, no *anima*. People who are animalists are usually defined as atheists, and sometimes scientists.

The Lakota, who are usually called animists (by both animalists and people who profess belief in Judeo-Christian religion), do not have the same kind of convention. In the Lakota tradition all animate beings (the redundancy is intentional) are born and die. In the process they pass through what might be called by analogy four states of individuation. Each individual comes into a being as the result of (1) having a potentiality for being (2), transforming this potentiality through birth into an essence that is independent of the body, (3) providing continuous evidence that this essence exists, and (4) finally providing evidence that the essence independent of the corporeal existence continues after death, therefore freeing its potentiality to inhere in another (potential) organism to begin the process all over, ad infinitum, in what we understand in English to be a system of reincarnation.

When old Lakota medicine men spoke of these four states, they named them (1) *šicun*, (2) *tun*, (3) *ni*, and (4) *nagi*, respectively.[9] These four states have been described as constituting a belief in four souls, or at least, four aspects of one soul. Most explanations have come from scholars whose own traditions require that each person have one soul and every other system is simply regarded as a variation on that theme. If a Lakota were writing a book on euro-american souls, he might conclude that we were somehow deficient because we thought in terms of "one" soul without any reference to process—unreasonable by Lakota standards.

Rather, if we regard these four states as parts of a process, parts that are named and stand as separate but related categories, then the Lakota concept of soul (which we may continue to call it for purposes of explanation) is much easier to understand. The terms are tied together as parts of a descriptive process that demark stages in the coming-into-being-and-dying process of each individual. I offer a crude, but perhaps telling analogy (recognizing the danger of analogy as well as its power). This is my own, and is not (except perhaps by coincidence) a Lakota concept. The analogy is that of the production of fire. The beginning assumption here is that the source of the production is finite. Assume that in the universe there is a limited but constant supply of *sparks* that will be called upon to begin the ignition process. Who or what calls upon the sparks to begin the process is really not important for this analogy, although subsequently we may want to assign this task to a Lakota concept Taku *škanškan* 'that which makes things move, creates energy'.

In addition to this finite amount of *sparks,* a variety of tinder is waiting to be ignited. To make the analogy seem more real, let us see this tinder as dry leaves, small twigs, and other natural, ignitable substances. We assume that once the spark ignites the tinder that there will be a *flame*, and after a certain period of time the flame will transform itself into *smoke*, an unequivocal symbol of fire. If we were to name these four stages, or more properly, the potentiality of the creation of three stages, by equating them with the Lakota terms, they would correspond like this:

Spark	*šicun*
Tinder	*tun*
Flame	*ni*
Smoke	*nagi*

Continuing the analogy, we might want to name the four separate but related parts of this process simply *fire*, just as we are inclined to name the four separate but related parts of the Lakota concept *soul*. But in reality, the Lakota have no general name for soul, except those conventions which have been translated by missionaries, usually, *woniya* from *wo* noun marker; *ni* 'life, breath'; and *ya* causal suffix 'to create, make', i.e., 'that which makes breath, or life'. In this case, the missionary convention corresponds with the English word 'spirit', whose Latin derivation gives us a wide semantic range, for example, 'breath, courage, vigor, the soul, life' itself derived from *spirare* 'to breathe, to blow'.

One usually struggles to interpret the parts of the whole independently: *šicun* is 'potentiality'; *tun* is 'giving birth'; *ni* means 'life' or 'breath'; and *nagi* means 'ghost'. These interpretations are only partly convincing when we think of them as static concepts, but when we look at their interrelationships and dynamic quality, the parts blend neatly into an interpretation which emphasizes the whole life process as one in which immortality is achieved through reincarnation.

But one need not turn only to metaphysical concepts to see how the number four implies the unfolding, the development, the evolution of important events. For example, take a more visible form or ritual, dance. In Lakota ritual a number of choreographic patterns are marked by the number four. In the

Raising the Sacred Pole at the Pine Ridge Sun Dance, August, 1966.
Photograph by Paul Steinmetz, S.J.

traditional *ceȟohomni wacipi* 'dance around the kettle, or Kettle
Dance', the dancers, after raising their hands in salutation to
the kettle filled with dog meat, dance around the kettle four
times. After completing this movement, they dance in place
while several of them, armed with forked sticks, charge the
kettle. Three times they charge the kettle, the fourth time
stabbing the choice morsels of meat with their spears.

In the *wiwanyang wacipi* 'gaze at the sun, or Sun Dance' we
find countless references to the number four as an organizing
principle for a longer and more complex ritual. When the sacred pole has been found, four virgins each strike the pole
four times with axes before it is felled. On the journey back to
the Sun Dance camp, the people carrying the pole stop four
times to rest. When the pole is to be erected, those men in
charge do so by resting three times as they raise the pole, the
fourth time heaving the pole into its proper position.

During the actual performance of the Sun Dance, the leader
directs all of the dancers to face each of the four directions

during the course of the daily ordeal. During one part of the dance, they dance up to the pole four times and finally grasp it to pray. At each rest period, a man or woman, or both, are selected to take a pipe and offer it to the head singer. If the singer accepts the pipe, it means that they will stop singing, and the dancers may rest in the shade. There is a peculiar way in which the dancers present the pipe to the head singer. The dancers dance up to the head singer holding their pipes in both hands in front of their chests. Three times they dance forward and present the pipe to the head singer who feigns at the pipe but refuses to accept it. At this point the dancers dance backward, then forward again to present the pipe. On this, the fourth time, it is accepted and the singers immediately stop singing, as soon as the head singer has taken the pipe from the dancers. The dancers then file off the dance ground to rest.

The number of ceremonies and rituals we can use to analyze the significance of the sacred numbers is unending, and suggests a new sense of meaning. All of these variations tell us that numbers are at once a statement about time and space, about synchrony and diachrony, about states of movement and motionlessness. Numbers have the capacity to analyze, and at the same time synthesize, and for this reason serve as one of the greatest of symbolic vehicles: they are singularly powerful messages because of their multidimensionality. They are at once paradigm and syntagm, metaphor and metonymn.

In Lakota cosmology as well as ritual, we find exhaustive references to the number four in both static and dynamic representations. The Four Winds or directions are frequently depicted in the static form of a cross or other design marked by four points, such as those found in quill and beadwork designs. The symbolic design is a synchronic statement about the relationship between the four constituent parts which it represents. But the parts themselves, the personalities or attributes that make up the Four Winds, are always seen as being related diachronically. For example, the Four Directions are equated with the four seasons, and as such are referred to in a sequential order beginning with the West Wind, moving clockwise to the North, East, and South. Adherence to this ritual formula is attributed to the cosmology in which the Four Directions are brothers, the son of Tate, the wind, and Ite, Face, born in the following order: North, West, East, South. Because of various circumstances, the birth order is changed so that the North and West exchange positions thus producing the proper directional sequence. Thus the symbol of the four directions—the four-pointed star or cross—static as it may be, conjures up the image of movement, a diachronous statement about the birth of the Four Winds. Also, there is an equation between the cardinal directions, or more accurately, quarters of the universe, and the four seasons which appear in real life in the same order that the four brothers are born in the myths. West equals Fall; North equals Winter; East equals Spring; and South equals Summer. Each direction then has a temporal as well as spatial dimension; the relationships are always constant, but as a whole they are in continuous and predictable paths of movement.

Looking at other symbols of the Four Winds, we can see that new modes of analysis can help unlock potential meaning. For example, in the past we would have been likely on "logical" grounds to see the members of the Four Winds, the West, North, East, and South as constituting, in semiotic terms, a paradigm. At the same time the relationships between the directions, and say colors, animals, and birds that symbolize each of the respective directions were syntagmatically related. A syntagmatic chain hypothetically would be produced by the association of, say, West Wind representing the paradigm "direction"; Fall representing the paradigm "season"; Black representing the paradigm "color" associated with the direction; Buffalo representing the "animal" symbolizing the direction, and so on. The entire series may be schematized in the following way:

Direction	Season	Color	Animal	Bird
West	Fall	Black	Blacktail Deer	Swallow
North	Winter	Red	Buffalo	Magpie
East	Spring	Yellow	Whitetail Deer	Crow
South	Summer	White	Elk	Meadowlark

The above schema may be considered the Western inclination to arrange topically and paradigmatically, that is, into things that go together. It produces a group of static categories. However, from the Lakota point of view, the schema makes more sense if we view it in the following way:

1	2	3	4
West	North	East	South
Fall	Winter	Spring	Summer
Black	Red	Yellow	White
Blacktail Deer	Buffalo	Whitetail Deer	Elk
Swallow	Magpie	Crow	Meadowlark

From this perspective, we see that all members of paradigm 1 are interchangeable; that is, in the language of semiotics, they are metaphorically related, while the relationships expressed between paradigmatic sets express metonymical relationships. The point is that in the first schema there is a tendency to see each paradigmatic set as static while in the second schema there is a sense of movement. Both schemata, of course, are two aspects of a singular analytical perspective, one based on the notion of a two-dimensional model rather than a single one. One model produces a static or synchronic representation of the number four, the second produces a dynamic or diachronic representation.

The second schema also represents what might be a mechanism for breaking the mythical code. Any reference to a singular member of a paradigmatic set is implicitly a reference to all other members of the set (by definition) as well as a reference to the relationship between all four paradigmatic sets. Hence when a medicine man sings that he is calling a "red stone friend" he is really making a reference to a totality whose aid may be sought by addressing only one of its parts. "Red stone" then is really a referential marker that signifies the North, Winter, Buffalo, etc. Any reference to one member of the set is a reference to all of them. Therefore, a prayer or song that in theory addresses specifically the swallow, a red stone, a whitetail deer, and summer has in fact made a general reference to the four directions.

Sun Dance at Pine Ridge, ca. 1920. O'Neill Photo.

We should not be so dazzled by analysis that we overlook the quality of fulfillment in sacred numbers, that in fact a recitation of the numerical components of the series *leads* somewhere. For example, in the creation story we find metaphorical references to personified gods who through their actions result in the creation of a viable universe out of a static matrix. Investing static objects with movement ultimately causes the creation of the universe as the Lakota now see it. During the process, a four-part plan unfolds in which (1) days and nights are distinguished, (2) the month is established, (3) the year and the seasons (that is, space) are established, leading up to the present "time" period, the fourth generation, which is (4) the present time.

Another symbol underscores the sense of fulfillment inherent in the number four, even though the symbol itself is a highly negative one, in the form of apocalyptic story. In it the old Lakota envision the state of affairs of the current universe as one symbolized by a buffalo literally on its last legs. In the story, the buffalo starts out with four legs and thick hair. Over time, the buffalo begins to lose its hair and ultimately three of its legs. When the buffalo is totally bald, and has lost its fourth leg, the world as we know it will come to an end. There is some sense of optimism though because the demise of the buffalo will lead to a spiritual reincarnation, and the universe will start all over again, the next time being, it is hoped, more favorable for the Lakota then the last has been.

But it is not only in myth and ritual that we see symbolic fulfillment expressed in the number four. Four is seen as a means of classifying empirical reality too. Not only does the one-legged buffalo die, but the four seasons come and go sequentially unchanged. It is also believed that the stages of one's life develop in a quadripartite way, through childhood, adolescence, adulthood, and old age. The stages of one's life also can be integrated into the total paradigmatic and syntagmatic schema so that, metaphorically speaking, upon birth one "leaves" the South, in this reincarnative system, to "arrive" in the West and pursue one's own course of living in a way that corresponds with the movement of the four seasons. Thus a lifetime is a microcosmic symbol of the annual rounds, themselves symbolic of the way the universe came into being. It makes sense in the language of Lakota to say of a person who has just died that *itokagata iyaye* 'he has gone south'.

The number four also should be seen as a means of classifying contemporary ideas relevant to Lakota culture, as well as to old traditions. This is perhaps proof that it is the system of classification that is important rather than the things that are classified, that is, it is the relationships between persons, places, and things that are deemed important rather than the persons, places, and things, themselves.

As one example of the viability of the system, we need only look at certain relationships that have been made between the directional color system, and the concept of "race." At one time, the precise colors selected to represent important directions or other religious concepts varied greatly between medicine men. There are a number of published accounts which are often explained to be contradictions in what is naively viewed as a systematic color-ordering system.[10]

Dancers saluting the kettle during the Kettle Dance at Pine Ridge, July 4, 1919. Photograph by William A. Edwards. Courtesy Heritage Center, Inc.

But it was only during the early 1970s that the color-directional system was codified into the present correspondencies of West-Black, North-Red, East-Yellow, and South-White. Currently, younger Lakota see a relationship between these colors, and a rather arbitrary classification of human "races" based on old-fashioned scientific and folk notions of "great races of mankind," a scientific position no longer acceptable. In this new use of the sacred colors, Black is equated with Black people, Red with Indians, White with Europeans, and Yellow with undifferentiated Orientals.[11]

Now whether scientifically acceptable, which it is not, or even acceptable to traditional religion, which old Lakota claim it is not, the numerical system clearly takes precedence over the objects which it seeks to classify and therefore to explain. The system is simply an elegant way of explicating a very complex system of relationships. It is conjectural whether all things in nature may be "inherently" divided into components of four. But from the Lakota viewpoint, all things in culture may be classified by their "natural" proclivity to confine, constrain, even squeeze things that are meaningful to them into units of four.

In a culture where even the most significant concepts of the universe are governed by forces like spirits that enjoy a good laugh, what is the consequence of playing what must seem to people outside Lakota culture as a frivolous game of numbers? The answer to outsiders must be that it is perhaps a persisting, habitual means of explaining the universe and adding a sense of cogency and predictability to an otherwise unknowable environment. It is a tradition no less significant than others based on other numerals. For the Western analyst, the system of classification precedes the means of classification. For the Lakota, they are one and the same.

CHAPTER 6

NAMING THE SACRED

ALTHOUGH ritual is required to actively transform profane people and things into sacred ones, the rituals are always accompanied by meaningful words in both prayer and song; ultimately the ritual process creates a new state of a person or object which is in part identified by assigning a new and sacred name to it.

THE LINGUISTIC UNIVERSE

Much of a people's universe is based on what they have to say about it, and over long evolutionary periods humans share in the need to accept a new food, animal, or custom only after they have assigned it a name. Among the Lakota, foods newly introduced by whites at the end of the nineteenth century were avoided, and were even considered inedible because of the way they looked or smelled. They were eaten only after they could be transformed into acceptable, edible foods through the ritual process of naming. One case in point is cattle, which the Lakota initially avoided because of their stench. They could not understand how the white man could eat such a filthy and odiferous animal. Over time, however, cattle were hunted as if they were buffalo, and they became partly acceptable because they had become transformed into an ersatz buffalo—a *ptegleška* 'spotted buffalo cow'.[1]

Even before the advent of cattle and a greatly modified culinary culture, the Lakota must have realized that such a strange animal as was to be called *horse* greatly expanded their linguistic universe. The *šunkawakan* 'sacred dog' required a new and specialized language to talk about its various colors, shapes, sizes, gender, abilities, and particularly the various types of tack and decoration needed to adorn it and make it fit for riding. The introduction of the horse added literally hundreds of concepts, words, and phrases, which were assigned new meanings so the Lakota could talk about this awesome new phenomenon. For example, *šung* an abbreviated form of *šunkawakan*, when used with other words, gave rise to:

Šungbloka 'stallion' from *šung* plus *bloka* 'male'
Šungwinyela 'mare' from *šung* plus *winyela* 'female'
Šungleška 'pinto' from *šung* plus *gleška* 'spotted'
Šungicakce 'curry comb' from *šung* plus *icakce* 'to comb with'
Šungicapsinte 'quirt' from *šung* plus *icapsinte* 'to whip with'
Šungicaške 'picket pin' from *šung* plus *icaške* 'to bind with'
Šungikan 'lariat, rope' from *šung* plus *ikan* 'rope'
Šunginaȟtake 'spurs' from *šung* plus *inaȟtake* 'to kick with'
Šungipaȟte 'bridle' from *šung* plus *ipaȟte* 'to tie up with'
Šungonajin 'stables' from *šung* plus *onajin* 'to stand in'

Šungakan yanka 'to be on a horse' means to ride; *šungkoyagya* 'to tie up a horse' means to rope it; and *šungluzahan* 'fast horse' is the term for race horse.

And so it must have been for the precursors of the Lakota. Lévi-Strauss has argued that the single phenomenon that has transformed humans from natural to cultural creatures was recognition of the incest taboo. At this point, he argues, humans were no longer promiscuous hordes like their animal brethren; instead they carefully and selectively organized their societies along what were later to be known as kinship systems with rigorous rules and regulations about who can marry whom, and who had jurisdiction over the raising of children.[2]

Of course, a similar argument can be made for the importance of the development of language over evolutionary times. And one can argue that incipient language preceded the establishment of *Homo sapiens*, and became critical to the formation of anatomically modern man as we know him. Stated another way, the difference between prehuman cultures and modern human culture is largely a matter of developing a system of classifying and thus distinguishing between important

objects, places, and people, all of which enhanced the like-
lihood of human survival. People are largely human because
they have the capacity to name their universe—and that includes themselves.

For several hundred years, Euro-Americans believed that
tribal peoples like the Lakota were incapable of systematically
viewing and understanding their universe in a coherent and
cohesive way. The process of classification and the task of assigning discrete terms to discrete objects based on such characteristics as morphological features (as in the case of classifying life forms) was totally in the purview of Western science.
"Primitive" peoples, it was believed, were inconsistent and
unknowledgeable about important relationships between the
various domains of their universe. But this soon proved to be
an untenable thesis. If language was an integral part of being
human, including the ability to discern causal and correlative
relationships between natural phenomena, then "primitive"
peoples should be able to express in some theoretical way
their ideas about these relationships. All peoples of the world
must have some kind of scientific view of their universe, and
these ideas must somehow be embedded in their languages.[3]

Since the mid-1950s social scientists, particularly anthropologists and linguists, have been interested in the way people
classify their social and cultural universe in their own language. This field of study, generally called ethnoscience or
ethnolinguistics, begins with the premise that all peoples are
capable of classifying the world around them in such a way
that logical relationships are underscored. Ethnoscience, of
course, was in many ways a reaction against the traditional,
and some would say outdated positions of the mid-nineteenth
century evolutionists who believed that "primitive" peoples
were incapable of rational and logical thought.[4]

Many of the examples studied by ethnoscientists were life
forms such as animals and birds which were seen to be related
hierarchically in a manner analogous to Linnaean taxonomy,
the essential method for establishing convincingly that although tribal peoples had coherent systems of classifying
their universe, frequently their conceptualizations of relation-

ships were quite different from our own. But, of course, this matters little as long as the classification process is a coherent system that makes sense to those who participate in it.

As one example of how our own system of classification differs from the Lakota, we can use the term *eagle*.

In contemporary ornithological science, there are two species of eagles known to the Lakota, the golden eagle (*Aquila chrysaetos*) and the bald eagle (*Haliaeetus leucocephalus*). Both belong to the family Accipitridae, which they share with hawks and harriers. Since eagles share more common features with hawks than with harriers, both hawks and eagles are classified by some ornithologists in the subfamily Buteoninae. Hierarchically, then, according to Linnaean principles, both species are classified:

I. Accipitridae
  1. Buteoninae
      i. *Aquila chrysaetos*
      ii. *Haliaeetus leucocephalus*[5]

It is generally agreed by both modern scientists and Lakota ornithologists that each of the two eagles may further be identified on the basis of whether they are immature or adult. Although there are differences in coloration between young and old birds, these differences do not become part of the classification system in modern science. For the Lakota, however, the relative age of the eagle is the most important diagnostic feature. Where modern science establishes two species of eagles, the Lakota establish four species, which they call generically *wanbli* 'eagle'. These are:

  1. *Anukasan* 'white on both sides'
  2. *Wanbligleška* 'spotted eagle'
  3. *Ȟ'unyan* 'aged, worn out'
  4. *Anukiyan* 'cross-breed'

These names actually refer to the coloration and condition of the eagles' feathers. The word *anuka* means 'both sides'. *Anukasan*, then, refers to a head and tail that is entirely white. *Gleška* 'spotted' refers to white flecks on a black background, and *anukiyan* to a tail that is part black part white. *Ȟ'unyan* is a tail that has been worn with age. If we look at the diagnostic features in our modern classification system and compare them with the Lakota classification system, we see the following:

English	Lakota
Eagle	*Wanbli*
Mature bald eagle	*Anukasan*
Immature bald eagle	*Wanbligleška*
Mature golden eagle	*Ȟ'unya*
Immature golden eagle	*Anukiyan*

No one remembers why *anukiyan*, the immature golden eagle, is called 'cross-breed'. Perhaps at one time there was a myth that explained why this bird has the favorite type of tail feather, a white feather with a black tip. But the word suggests that the black and white tail was somehow a result of interbreeding, perhaps between the other species, particularly the mature bald eagle and the mature golden eagle. It is quite clear in the sacred language of prayers and song texts that it is the *wanbligleška*, the spotted eagle, who serves as a messenger to Wakantanka. The bald eagle is slightly larger than the golden eagle, and it is quite possible that the Lakota observed this and associated the bird's size and strength with its religious role of messenger.

This is but one small example of how the Lakota classify their world in a systematic way. Lakota classification does not in fact coincide with the way modern science classifies the same forms, but then what is really important is that the respective systems are internally coherent and logical.

The Lakota frequently do employ the same criteria as modern science to classify natural phenomena. Certainly in the case of the eagle, the major criterion is morphology, that is, color and size. But the Lakota differ from modern science in that they simply choose different morphological criteria. Additionally, the Lakota place much more emphasis on the way living creatures behave, sometimes seeing correlations between human and animal behavior, sometimes seeing pecu-

The Grandfathers: Little Killer (left) and Little Shield. Courtesy Heritage Center, Inc.

liar relationships between animals of different species that modern science largely ignores. In the latter case, the idea of species is often treated quite differently than modern science defines it.

For example, for modern biologists species generally are determined by the ability to interbreed. Only members of the same species can reproduce successfully. Obviously the La-kota are cognizant of certain visible features of, say, animals and birds which immediately identify them as members of the same species. In purely secular terms these relationships are marked by the use of the term *owewepi* 'of the same blood' or simply 'blood relatives'. For example, brothers and sisters who have the same mothers and fathers are called *owewepi*, a term useful in distinguishing between consanguineal siblings and "half brothers and sisters" or "stepfathers and mothers." If people are really related by blood, the Lakota say they are *owewepi*.

The same term is applied to entire nonhuman species. Therefore, in secular language, all bluejays would be seen as being of the same blood—*owewepi*. But in sacred language, all animal and bird species are regarded as being on the same level with humans—that is, all species—and this would in-clude animals, birds, insects, trees, flowers, and rocks. All are considered *oyate* 'people' or 'nation'.

We might say that the Lakota employ metaphorical exten-sions between humans and animals: Nonhuman species are, in sacred language, treated as if they are human. The sum total of bird species is seen as a superfamily and is called in sacred language Zintkala Oyate 'Bird Nation'. The Bird Na-tion is then further divided into constituent species—Wanbli Oyate 'Eagle Nation', Cetan Oyate 'Hawk Nation', Hinhan Oyate 'Owl Nation', and so on.

In a vision, if one of the Hawk Nation is seen as a leader or spokesman, it will be addressed in song and prayer as Cetan Itancan 'Hawk Chief.' If medicine men have derived their power through a vision from any of these "nations" he will address them directly in his songs and prayers, and in the *hanbloglaka* he will tell how the supernatural "people" gave him instructions about the proper way to walk with the pipe. A medicine man deriving such instructions from an Eagle is said to have *wanbli wowaš'ake* 'eagle power'. Wanbli Gleška is the Chief of the Bird Nation.

Just as there are relationships between the animal nations and humans, there are relationships between the various animal nations. Certain animals and birds are believed to be companions. For example, the Yuwipi man George Plenty Wolf was instructed in his visions that the swallow was the companion of the blacktail deer; the magpie of the buffalo; the crow of the whitetail deer; and the meadowlark of the elk. In this case, the bird nations are regarded as the *akicita* 'soldiers', or the advance guard of the animal nations they accompany. Since each animal nation is also symbolic of the Four Winds, their respective bird *akicita* are frequently regarded as harbingers of each of the seasons—the swallow of fall, the magpie of winter, the crow of spring, and the meadowlark of summer.

Just as the animals and birds exhibit metaphorically the characteristics of humans, humans may also exhibit the characteristics of animals. Hence, when medicine men receive a peculiar vision they are frequently required to act out their vision in public performances, sometimes imitating the animals and birds from whom they derive their power.

All of these metaphorical extensions in the sacred language, then, serve to underscore the interdependency of humans and other species including, in the Lakota classification system, all animate and inanimate objects. Humans, then, are very much just another part of the universe—nothing less, nothing more.

THE PARADOX OF INKTOMI

The idea that each constituent of the social universe must be named, and the naming process itself, symbolize a new cosmological plane, which is not an exclusive product of modern science. The Lakota believe that humans lived a cultural preexistence in a subterranean world where they were known as

Pte Oyate 'buffalo cow people'. After the earth as we know it was formed through the intercession of Takuškanškan, the people were led up to the earth by Inktomi, and his counterpart, the wolf—*sungmahetu* 'underground dog'. The supernatural people who had been put on the earth as a result of breaking social rules dealing with proper marriage and childbearing became lonely. Consequently, one of the supernaturals, Anukite 'Double Face', sent Inktomi in the form of a wolf to seek out her people who lived below. Their successful trip from their cavernous home to the surface of the earth marks a time period in Lakota cosmology that separates a prehuman existence from a human one. Although the first man, Tokahe 'First', and the six families who accompanied Inktomi to the surface of the earth were fully anatomically human, they were devoid of the mechanisms for behaving like humans do today. What was absent then in their prior life was culture itself. And Inktomi taught it to them.[6]

Although the creation of the universe is seen by most people as a theological statement about first causes, one may look at the same stories profitably from the point of view of classification. The creation story in any culture is an attempt to put the chaotic universe that surrounds humans into some kind of order, and part of the mechanism used to accomplish this is the simple act of naming everything. In the creation of the Lakota universe, we find logical beginnings. Everything is divided into fours—the world is partly created by the separation of undifferentiated time and space into the day, night, month, and year; the four winds establish the directions, the seasons. The remainder of the world, so to speak, is off on its own waiting to be organized, classified, typologized, categorized, and named.

The creation of culture including the Lakota, then, is tantamount to the classification of nature, and that act is what makes humans a special kind of animal. But for the Lakota, humans are perhaps not so distinctly separated from the animals, birds, reptiles, and other life forms that make up their universe. The Lakota see a continuous relationship between nature and culture, and as Indians they do not see themselves as having the same privileged position as the white man affords *Homo sapiens*. If there is any difference, humans are the last arrivals to the created world, and they must do whatever they can to learn *as much* as the other life forms that preceded them. And here one of the great differences between Indians and non-Indians is underscored. Whereas Euro-American science and theology understand humans to be the sine qua non of all living things, the Lakota see humans as the most humble. For whites, the humans were the last to inhabit the earth, and are therefore a crowning glory of all that preceded them. For the Lakota, humans were last, and that makes them newest, youngest, and most ignorant. When Lakota seek knowledge about their present state of affairs, they seek it through the instructions imparted to the medicine men from animals, birds, and other animate and inanimate forms that serve as his helpers.

If we understand the term culture as the way that humans live differently from animals, then we can assign the creation of culture to the trickster, Inktomi. And it was by the act of naming that Inktomi differentiated all natural phenomena. He is given the credit for having not only named all species, but for having assigned them their distinctive colorations, configurations, and behaviors. He also is credited for having taught humans how to obtain and prepare food and how to make clothing and shelters from otherwise natural phenomena. But Inktomi himself, important as he was to the establishment of Lakota culture, remains a paradox: He who served to distinguish between all living things as well as all inanimate forms was destined never to have his own distinguishable features. Inktomi, one might say, in the process of naming the constituent elements of the entire Lakota universe, never named himself. As a matter of fact, the term Inktomi refers to only one of his many shapes and forms that he is capable of assuming, the spider, and it is a term that he never uses when he addresses himself.

In the many stories still told about him, Inktomi spends a good deal of his time changing his identity to deceive someone.[7] In the now famous stories he plays tricks on humans, animals, and birds only to find himself in compromising situations. In his quest to deceive, he winds up being deceived, an apt moral story to tell young children. Not only does he fail to have a well-defined personal identity, he has a doubtful position in a Lakota kinship system. His brother is Iya, the giant who gorges himself on humans periodically and has to be killed and roasted to make him disgorge the humans so that they can populate the earth. But there is always a crucial question that Inktomi asks his cannibal brother—Who is the eldest? This is important in terms of the naming process because relative age plays a great deal of importance in determining proper behavior, not only between brothers but between other members of the family who behave differently with each other depending on their relative age.[8]

Furthermore, Inktomi can change himself into virtually anything or anybody. In the trickster stories, he transforms himself into a man and marries his mother-in-law. He takes his mother-in-law on the warpath with him and returns with numerous children he has fathered with her. He then transforms himself into a young and handsome man so that he can marry his oldest daughter. All these behaviors are antithetical to Lakota rules of marriage, but throughout the several transgressions highlighted in the stories, the listener is always aware that Inktomi must be an imposter before he can justify committing these social transgressions.[9]

Since Inktomi does take on so many different kinds of characteristics and personalities, one wonders why he should be called Inktomi and not by a name more befitting his reckless and immoral sojourns. The answer lies in the fact that the Lakota regard the spider as the wisest of all creatures, and part of this reasoning is based on observations of real spider behavior.

According to Lakota medicine men with whom I have spoken, the spider is the most knowledgeable of creatures because he is the most ubiquitous; he lives and travels everywhere. Ellis Chips, the grandson of the well-known Yuwipi man, Horn Chips,[10] told me that spiders walk on the ground and walk underground. They can fly, and they can also swim.

They can be found anywhere even in the most remote places, and there is nowhere a person can go without being seen or heard by spiders.

Because of their ability to traverse the four important planes of Lakota cosmology—the sky, the place between the sky and the clouds, the earth, and beneath the earth—they are particularly knowledgeable about sacred things. They make homes that are indestructible, and which serve as traps for their prey. The spider web is called Inktomi *tawokaške* 'Spider's bindery'. Most important, spiders are related to the *wakinyan*, the 'thunder beings', and are therefore beseeched to intervene on behalf of humans to protect them from the wrath of the thunderers. One should therefore never kill a spider lest he be struck by lightning. If they accidentally kill one, children are instructed to say *Ho* Tunkašila *wakinyan niktepi*, "Ho, Grandfather, the thunder struck you!" The thunder is the only one who can kill the spiders without fear of retribution.

Spiders are also seen to have different kinds of personalities just as the mythological Inktomi represents himself in multitudinous forms. According to George Plenty Wolf, each of his personal helpers were all manifestations of different species of spiders as well as some of their unusual personal characteristics.

When Plenty Wolf was asked to conduct a meeting for the purpose of finding lost objects, the so-called *okile lowanpi* 'hunting sing', he said the following prayer first:

Tunkašila Inktomi omakiya ye. Taku wagnuni na iyewayin kte.

Grandfather Inktomi help me. I have lost something and I want to find it.

Only the Inktomi spirits arrived. Among them were:

Inktomi Kinyan 'Flying Spider'
Inktomi Luzahan 'Fast Spider'
Inktomi Wakagišni 'Daring Spider'
Inktomi Hunkešni 'Weak Spider'
Inktomi sabic'iya 'Spider who paints himself black'
Inktomi ognaya šica 'Spider who is hard to fool'
Inktomi mniakinyan 'Spider who flies over the water'

Wendle (sic) Smoke (left) and Peter Iron Cloud in traditional dress at Pine Ridge, ca. 1900. Wendle Smoke wears an old-time Scout head-dress and smokes a traditional long-stemmed pipe.

Inktomi ektašniyetunwan 'Spider who does not look there'
Inktomi takuni oholašni 'Spider who respects nothing'
Inktomi maka mahel mani 'Spider who walks underground'[11]

When a sacred stone, *wašicun tunkan*, was going to be named,[12] again Plenty Wolf addressed only the Inktomi spirits by beginning the prayer with Tunkašila Inktomi 'Grandfather Inktomi', thus guaranteeing that only the Inktomi spirits would come into the meeting. The stone is then named after one of the spirits present. Interestingly, Inktomi, who named everything in the universe in the mythological past except himself, arrives to bestow one of his multitudinous attributes on a heretofore unnamed stone.

Inktomi also has the power to change names. One Yuwipi man, Mark Big Road, always called on *Inktomi ognaya šica* 'Spider who is hard to fool' for help. One night the spirit came to Mark during a meeting and told the Yuwipi man that he disliked his name 'Hard to fool' and wanted to change it. He chose the name of a deceased Lakota who went by the name "Scotty," and from that time on, whenever this Inktomi arrived at the meeting, he was addressed as Scotty.

In this particular classification system one of the most important figures in Lakota cosmology, the general category Spider, is addressed as 'Grandfather Spider'. This delineates it as a separate class and ritually ensures that only the appropriate (Inktomi) spirits will avail themselves as helpers during the attenuated meetings used for "hunting" or naming. The individual Inktomi spirits, however, are named after the various attributes of the Inktomi portrayed in the many stories told about him.

What becomes apparent in Lakota is that often behavioral traits serve as the major diagnostic features of classification. In our own modern scientific approach it is morphological characteristics that serve as the basis for classification. It stands to reason, then, if behavior (including not only the anthropomorphized traits associated with animals but ethological characteristics as well) serves as a major criterion, then certain behavioral characteristics are likely to be considered more important than morphological ones. In the Lakota case, certain species which are differentiated from each other in the Linnaen system are merged in the Lakota system. In the example of the spider, different behaviors tend to be treated as if they represent different species rather than different moods or temperaments. And just as morphological traits are compared in order to create larger families of related life forms, the Lakota compare behavioral traits and in so doing create larger categories of interrelated species. As in the case of the eagle, these categories are puzzling only because we fail to understand their logic and rationale. However, once understood, these new typologies and classifications of the Lakota universe are predictable and meaningful.

Consider the case of the behavioral quality which views an animal or insect capable of traversing through various planes of Lakota cosmology. The important trait to be compared is the specie's ability to live and travel underground, on the ground, between the earth and clouds, and in the sky. Those beings which are capable of traversing all planes are perceived to be the most powerful, most pervasive and most knowledgeable. Part of their potency comes from the simple fact that they are in constant association with those other animals that are more restricted in their habitat, and they can carry their knowledge to other cosmological planes where those more constrained cannot tread. The spider emerges as one of the most ubiquitous because it is believed that he is capable of movement through all these planes.

The spider is also important because of his relationship with lightning and thunder. What is most important about this relationship is that he cannot be harmed by the lightning because they are kin. Anyone who seeks protection from being struck by lightning, then, will prevail upon the spider for help. The reason that the spider is a logical protector from lightning is that it builds a web for its home, which is seen as being impervious to destruction. Bullets, arrows, and lightning simply pass through it without destroying it. All living things that have the capacity to thwart danger in the same way are also classified together, frequently along with that which they serve to defend. Hence there is a strong relationship between thunder, lightning, spider, dragonflies, turtles, lizards, and other unlikely classificatory bedfellows because they all have the power to protect as well as to harm human beings. No matter how morphologically dissimilar these phenomena are, they share a number of mythological features and therefore are considered similar rather than different.

Hence we find a strong relationship between the whirlwind, butterfly, and dragonfly. *Wamniomni* 'whirlwind' is seen to skip across the prairie frivolously and figures prominently in Lakota mythology as the youngest brother of the Four Winds who because of the nature of his birth is given no particular direction and must live with his other brothers. *Kimimila* 'butterfly' like the whirlwind darts about incessantly, and hides among trees and flowes and bushes to be seen in its brightly colored paint only when it wants to.

Tunsweca the dragonfly also flits about quickly from branch to branch, often transparent to those who would chase it. All three have the capacity to avoid danger quickly through making abrupt motions and deceiving those who follow them. Therefore, they served as appropriate protectors of warriors who long ago set out for battle and needed the ability to deceive their enemies with their quick moves on the battlefield. The Lakota link them on the basis of these most observable behavioral qualities—quickness of flight and erratic movement through space, all diagnostic of the devil duster, butterfly and dragonfly.

Even the common "miller" moth that flies from one flame to the next, attracted by any kind of flame, is to be emulated because the Lakota of old saw this tiny creature as brave. And so they said about a warrior who was intrepid in battle, or even a reckless rider of wild horses who never seemed to be discouraged by being thrown from a horse, *Kimimila ska s'e takuni kokipapi šni* 'He is as fearless as a miller moth' (that is, a white butterfly).

It is not surprising, then, that painted, quilled and beaded designs representing these phenomena were drawn on weapons as an aid to the old warriors who sought their protection and the ability to emulate their behaviors to escape the arrows and bullets of their enemies.[13]

By the same classificatory logic, the spider has much in common with those other species that are capable of moving between the subterranean part of the world. The wolf, coyote, snake, mole, and ant, to name the most important, are all capable of burrowing into the earth and communicating with those that dwell beneath the surface of the earth. The skins of wolves, coyotes, and snakes are important protections against the unforeseen and dangerous world, and the dirt brought to the surface of the earth by moles is regarded as sacred when used in the curing ceremonies because it is untainted by humans and those who tread the earth's surface. The ant that diligently pushes tiny rocks (*tunkan*) to the top of its ant hill is revered, and the stones themselves are wrapped up in tiny medicine bags and are called upon in time of need.

Pete Catches preparing the pipe for a ceremony. Photograph taken in June, 1974, by Michael Steltenkamp, S.J. Courtesy Heritage Center, Inc.

In addition to the burrowing animals, there are animals that traverse other planes, to wit, the places above the earth and the earth's surface. This category of animals would include *t'elanuns'e* 'lizards'; *gnaška* 'frogs'; and *keya* 'turtles', because it was believed by the old Lakota that these species fell to the earth during rainstorms. But they also have other features that make them sacred. First, the lizard can disappear easily into small crevices and therefore represents not only areas above the earth and the earth's surface, but also places beneath the earth. The word *t'elanuns'e* means 'almost dead' and refers to the fact that the lizard can deceive enemies by holding itself very still. It is also regarded as capable of living to an old age which is also true of the other creatures in this category. For this reason, the umbilical cord of a newborn is placed inside a beaded bag fashioned in the shape of a lizard. This amulet is sometimes tied to the baby's cradle for good luck and is frequently kept by the mother after the child has grown.

Gnaška 'frogs' also mediate between the water and the earth, and they are seen to be hard to catch, therefore good to emulate. *Keya* 'turtles' play a prominent part in Lakota mythology and are regarded as good to imitate not only because they, too, mediate between the water and the earth's surface, but also because of their obvious shell which enables them to protect themselves from marauders without having to move fast like the lizards and frogs. Like their subterranean counterparts, these creatures are helpful to medicine men in diagnosing and curing illnesses.

Inktomi ranks supreme of all the creatures mentioned here because of his perceived mythological importance, because he is the most ubiquitous, and because in many ways he shares with the other sacred creatures the fact that they do not quite fit into the normal Lakota classification of all living and breathing things.[14] The old Lakota classified all these things into four major categories, in keeping with the sacredness of the number four. These classes were (1) *wakinyan* 'things that fly', (2) *waslohan* 'things that crawl', (3) *wahutopa* 'things that walk on four legs', and (4) *wahununpa* 'things that walk on two legs'. In theory, every breathing creature fits one of these four categories (although in reality nobody has ever tried to do it).

The first category, of course, would include the birds (and bats), and in sacred language the category refers to the thunder and lightning. The second category includes snakes. The third category is the largest because it includes not only all the mammals known to the Lakota but also amphibians and reptiles that walk on four legs. The last category is reserved for humans. Interestingly, all the categories employ the notion of locomotion for their basis, probably because the ancient world of the Lakota was perceived always to be in movement. The perfect state of the world was one in which it was constantly raining, an idea possibly held over from the times when ancestors of the modern Lakota farmed in the Great Lakes. There is only some sparse linguistic evidence that leads to understanding this earlier period of Lakota history. The most striking, perhaps, is the term for rainbow, *wigmunke* 'trap'. It was believed by the old Lakota that the rainbow stopped the continuous flow of rain from reaching the earth. The relationship between rain, thunder, and lightning with Inktomi and all of his manifestations might simply be a metaphorical one because the name for Inktomi's web is *wokaške* 'bindery', another kind of trap. On the one hand, the obvious empirical observation that spiders trap their prey in their webs goes without saying. On the other hand, the relationship between Inktomi and the Thunder-beings at a higher cosmological level could be explained better by understanding that in both "traps" the universe is more or less controlled by relatively few, and these few are related to each other.

Although the Lakota system of naming and classifying the universe is frequently a radical departure of the way modern science conceptualizes the world, it is a coherent and logical system that appropriately underscores those relationships that constitute the Lakota perception of their own history and culture.

CHAPTER 7

SHAMANS AND PRIESTS

HISTORICALLY, social scientists have adopted certain exotic words to explicate alleged universal phenomena for which there are no English equivalents, e.g., mana, taboo, totem. One such word, shaman, is derived from the Tungus *saman* 'one who is excited, moved, raised' and has come to signify a ritual specialist whose personal characteristics and ritual functions are similar to those found elsewhere in the world, but especially in Asia and North America.[1]

As is true of other exotic words originally employed to designate a specific function in a relatively limited geographic area, as new ethnographic data become available the use of the term is raised to typological status. In the case of totemism, for example, a restricted concept was erroneously expanded to universal importance.[2] I believe there is something similar to be said about the term "shaman" and its anthropological derivatives, shamanism and shamanic, becoming another candidate for the totemic illusion. Shamanism has, of course, already achieved typological status.

Ever since Evans-Pritchard distinguished between witchcraft and sorcery among the Azande,[3] anthropologists have debated the preciseness of terms needed to discuss comparative religions, especially the nature of the individuals who serve as ritual specialists. A partial list of those familiar terms which are ever in need of clarification would include—in addition to shaman and priest—magician, sorcerer, witch doctor, wizard, doctor, medicine man, juggler, and conjurer. Terms such as witch doctor and medicine man have become disreputable mainly because of their popular use and have by and large been discarded by anthropologists (despite the fact that the literal translation of terms used to designate certain kinds of ritual specialists among the Lakota is *pejuta wicaša* 'medicine man').

Some of these terms have achieved typological status. This implies that any given term would have to stand in contra-distinction to at least one other term. In recent literature, shaman has been so contrasted with priest. For example:

In the comparative analysis of religious organization one of the most useful analytical distinctions has been between the "sha-man" and the "priest." These two polar types of ceremonial practitioners are found in all parts of the world, and the differ-ence between their religious roles provides a significant index of contrasts between different types of religious systems. [Lessa and Vogt 1972, 381]

The authors contrast the two types of ritualists and con-clude that:

A "shaman" is a ceremonial practitioner whose powers come from direct contact with the supernatural, by divine stroke, rather than from inheritance or memorized ritual; a "priest" is a ceremonial practitioner who often inherits his position and who learns a body of codified and standardized ritual knowl-edge from older priests and later transmits it to successors.

Another way of looking at the difference between shamans and priests is in terms of communications between super-naturals and men. Shamans are essentially mediums, for they are the mouthpieces of spirit beings. Priests are intermediaries between people and the spirits to whom they wish to address, themselves. This is what Evans-Pritchard has in mind when, writing about the priests and prophets (shamans) of the Nuer of the Sudan, he says: "Whereas in the priest man speaks to God, in the prophet . . . God speaks to man. [P. 381]

I have taken the time to quote at length from these authors because I believe that, although at first glance the contrasts appear to be useful analytical distinctions, some of the traits mentioned for each of the two types do not contrast for the Lakota, or perhaps for any group of people. I will return to this point later when I attempt to demonstrate that, from the point of view of society, there are as many similarities between the two types as there are contrasts.

Other authors have made similar contrasts between shaman and priest. Less polar is I. M. Lewis, who defines *shaman* as a word used to denote "a variety of social roles, the lowest common denominator of which is that of inspired priest" (Lewis 1971, 49). Lewis sees a range of variation in ritual functions based on the degree of inspiration, or ecstasy, displayed by the ritual specialist. It is not clear, however, how one measures these varying degrees of such an affectual trait as inspiration; neither does the author tell us where we might place the ritual functionary who is an "uninspired" priest (nor why the inspired priest is the "lowest" common denominator).

Another author interested in ecstasy is Mircea Eliade who adopts a conventional evolutionary position in distinguishing shamanism (primitive) from priesthoods (higher religious orders). The major contrast is based on the notion that priests attend to functions in religion which are "infinitely more complex" (Eliade 1958, 103). This point of view requires one to completely ignore any semblance of cultural relativism, and like Lewis, requires acceptance of purely arbitrary traits.

A. F. C. Wallace has attempted to place all religious systems into four typologies using as his main criteria the role of the ritual specialist and the role of the layman. Based on personal traits of functionaries, and degrees of complexity of religious organization, he establishes four types of "cult" institutions. The first, the individual cult institution, has no ritual specialist; the second, the shamanic cult institution, includes specialists who act as "shamans *proper* (in Siberia), as diviners, as magicians, witch doctors, medicine men, mediums, and spiritualists, palm-readers, astrologers, and so forth" (Wallace 1966, 86; italics added). The third, the communal cult, is an institution that occasionally employs a ritual specialist, but ceremonies are primarily under the supervision of lay groups. Finally, the ecclesiastical cult institution is characterized by the presence of a professional clergy organized along the same principles as the society's sociopolitical structure. If we eliminate the two typologies which have no particular ritual specialists, we are left with a contrast between shaman and priest.

Particularly interesting is Wallace's distinction between "shaman proper" and the remainder of the typology. Presumably the shaman proper is unique, and I would guess that these distinctions correlate with the proto-Tungus variety of shamanism mentioned earlier. In any respect, before looking at what I consider to be a common denominator of the two typologies, let us look at some of the diagnostics which serve to contrast shaman and priest.

SHAMANIC TRAITS

Although "shamanism" is found worldwide, I believe the authors cited would agree that in discussing "shamans proper," one would focus on eastern Siberia and western North America, particularly in the circumpolar regions. In Siberia, between the Indigirka River and the Bering Sea, we find the Tungus, Yakut, Kamchadel, Koryak, and Chukchee. In North America, beginning with Alaskan Eskimo and working southward through British Columbia and the Northwest Coast of the United States, we find shamanic ritualism among the Haida, Tsimshian, Tlingit, Bella Bella, Bella Coola, Kwakiutl, Nootka, Quileute, Quinault, Snuqualmi, Tillamook, Alsea, Tututni, Tolowa, Yorok, and Hupa.[4]

If we were to include a particular variety of shamanism called the "shaking tent rite" (Ray 1941), we could expand our map to include literally all of Canada and the northern United States as far east as the Atlantic coast. The relationship between these tribal groups, including the Lakota, and their particular forms of ritualism is based on a number of traits which have diffused from Siberia. A prototype of shamanic traits, I believe, can be derived from two particularly good ethnographies on the Chukchee and on the Eskimo.[5]

In these societies, the shaman is primarily male (although as one travels southward in the United States one finds "shamanesses") who specialize in curing illnesses. He performs rituals upon request by clients living in his community and is

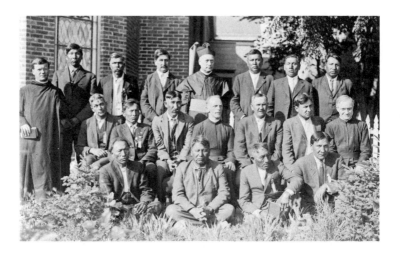

Shamans and priests. This photograph was taken in 1920 at a Sioux Indian Congress held under the auspices of Holy Rosary Mission, at Pine Ridge. Seated in the front row, left to right: Nicholas Black Elk, Peter Red Elk, Silas Fills the Pipe, and Ivan Star. Black Elk was the subject of *Black Elk Speaks*, by the poet John G. Neihardt, who visited Black Elk ten years after this photograph was taken. Courtesy Heritage Center, Inc.

paid a fee for his services. His ability to cure illness stems from his particular relationship with the supernatural. By means of "magical flight" or possession, he becomes a medium through which the intentions of his clients are transmitted to the spirit world, and through which the diagnoses and cures are made known to the real world by spirit helpers.

There is a connection between this particular ritualistic tradition and the ecology. Among the reindeer-herding Chukchee of Siberia, the ritual, held in a darkened inner room of a household, takes the form of a seance. The shaman sits in the master's place praying and singing for those crowded into the small area. His spirit helpers enter into his body and he is not only able to diagnose illnesses (which he conveys by means of ventriloquism) but also to predict the availability of reindeer during the year. At other times, the shaman "sinks" into a trance during which time he visits various spirit helpers.[6]

Among the coastal Eskimo a shaman is often required to make a magical voyage to the bottom of the sea to propitiate the Sea Goddess, Sedna, who controls the sea mammals, the most important source of subsistence for the Eskimo. The ritual likewise takes place in an inner room. Those who have committed some social error gather together with the shaman and participate in prayers and songs similar to the Chukchee ritual.[7]

Some of the personal traits of the shaman are also worth noting. A man usually chooses to become a shaman as a result of an initial mystical experience, perhaps some kind of danger or illness, which prompts him to seek counsel from another shaman. He may exact upon himself ordeals such as physical separation from the community for periods of time, e.g., the Lakota Vision Quest. These are often ordeals which he does not require his clients to perform. Because he is capable of communicating with the supernatural, he may also be linked with witchcraft.[8]

There are also numerous similarities in the performance of the shamanic rituals. Common traits include: a darkened room; use of a drum; communal singing and praying; presence of audio-visual stimuli (lights, sparks, animal sounds, voices); ventriloquism (hence the "mouthpiece of spirits"); the tying, covering, or otherwise inconvenient positioning of the shaman; and public confessions of the clients, all of which are traits associated with the Lakota Yuwipi ritual.

As we move out of the circumpolar region, however, these traits break down and give rise to others. Wallace restricts shamanic cult institutions, in addition to the above area, to the Andaman Islands, the Semang of Malaya, pygmies in Africa, and wherever there are surviving Negrito groups. These groups primarily lack the magical flight and spirit helpers of the circumpolar area.[9]

Although lacking the specific diagnostics of circumpolar shamanism, the Andaman *oko-jumu* is a magician who acquires his supernatural powers through communicating with spirits and is capable of diagnosing and curing diseases caused primarily by evil forces.[10] Similarly, the Mbuti pygmies practice no witchcraft or sorcery but believe that certain individuals have the power to do harm. They are concerned with witchcraft, however, only when they are in the villages of the Negro Bantu.[11]

Wallace does not specify the Australian aborigines as having shamanic cult institutions, but others report some striking similarities to circumpolar shamanism: seances, ventriloquism, curing illness, magical flights to the sky, and ordeals in which men isolate themselves in caves.[12]

Without resorting to a worldwide sample, it is safe to say that what has been heretofore classified as shamanism is also found in Mesoamerica (although sometimes obscured by Christian influences) and Oceania, among others.[13] With the exception of Mesoamerica, however, the term "shamanism" is not used by these authors. Moving westward from Siberia through Asia, we would expect to find a grading away of circumpolar traits and variations in ritual performance. But we do find a strong correlation between what is labeled shamanism and the kind of power that is invested in the individual curer by the society which benefits from his services; in these societies, the shaman is charged with curing illnesses whose etiologies are nonmedical by Western standards.

PRIESTLY TRAITS

As is true with shamanism, the priesthood is found worldwide, but especially among the "olympian" and "monotheistic" religions associated with the cultures of the Aztec, Maya, and Inca; among the Central African kingdoms such as Ashanti, Dahomey, and Uganda; in East Asian societies such as those kingdoms found in Burma, Indonesia, Korea, and Japan; and in the "great" religions of the world, Hindu-Buddhist, Judeo-Christian, Islamic, and Chinese monotheism.

Wallace characterizes the traits of the priesthood in his analysis of ecclesiastic cult institutions. The priest is a member of a professional clergy who devotes all, or a regularly scheduled part, of his time to his duties. The professional clergy is organized into a bureaucracy modeled after the same principles that govern the sociopolitical structure. The clergy is exclusively responsible for performing ceremonies on behalf of its community. It claims religious authority over laymen, and there is a clear-cut division of labor between the sacred (clerical) and the profane (laiety).[14]

As mentioned earlier, some state that the priest learns a standardized body of knowledge from those whom he succeeds, while others state that the priest attends to "infinitely more complex" religious functions. Generally, however, these authors are more concerned with providing details related to the characteristics of shamanism than the priesthood. The paucity of information on the priest may be owing to the fact that "there are perhaps more intriguing problems still unsolved in the questions of recruitment, roles, performances, and defining characteristics of the shamans of the world" (Lessa and Vogt 1972, 382).

But certainly there must be equally intriguing problems not yet solved for the same characteristics of the priesthood. Could it be that this concentration on shamanism is nothing more than a vestige of the age-old lure of the exotic which has encouraged anthropologists to study the religions of preliterate peoples and largely to ignore their own? One observer made this point clear:

> It is indeed surprising that . . . writers . . . should have turned their attention exclusively to the religions of present-day primitive peoples . . . about which information was the most lacking . . . rather than to the contemporaneous world religions with their vast literatures and known histories . . . Had they done so, . . . they would have seen how inadequate their theories were. Also, the religions of primitive peoples could not then have been treated . . . as something so unlike the religions of civilization. [Leslie 1960, 99]

If we then treat shamanism and the priesthood on equal footing, I find it equally intriguing to examine the earlier equation of prophet and shaman in the earliest statement, ". . . in the prophet, God speaks to man." A logical conclusion of this equation would be that Moses, Jesus Christ, and Mohammed—that is, founders of all monotheistic religions— were, by definition, shamans. A closer examination of other contemporaneous world religions would reveal a number of other traits that would tend to classify, say, some Christian sects, under shamanic cult institutions.

To summarize, typologies are constructed out of the ethnographic raw materials which produce groups of similarities that contrast with other groups of similarities. Each group must have some common denominator. In the contrast between shaman and priest, different common denominators are used but result in the same typological distinctions. For some we have "direct contact of supernaturals" versus "inheritance of codified ritual," and "medium" contrasted with "intermediary." Others find the contrast related to degrees of inspiration. One takes an evolutionary stance between "primitive" and "higher order." Another establishes his criteria on degrees of complexity, and the presence or absence of a professional body of practitioners opposed to individual curers who practice on an ad hoc basis.

In each case, the determination of the typology is based on traits or roles of the ritual specialist. But in each case the denominators are not the same; each author selects his own criteria. Furthermore, the oppositions used to differentiate between each typology are based on interpretations which in some cases might be reversed, that is, a category which distinguishes a shaman, say, mediumship, might by interpretation be a trait applied to a priest, who reiterates a recent revelation from Jesus Christ. To clarify what is meant by "medium" is not a problem with which most authors are concerned. But it seems critical to know what "medium" or any other trait really signify if they are to be useful for analytical distinction.

A number of generalized traits used to differentiate between shamans and priests can just as easily be unified to show *similarities* between the two typologies. This approach requires that the social scientist not be fettered by evolutionary notions of religious "progress" and that he subdue his own ethnocentrism. For example, the following table shows traits which are normally used to dichotomize between shaman and priest.

Shaman	Priest
Initial mystical experience	Calling
Receptacle of spiritual power	Receptacle of sacramental power
Mouthpiece of spirits	Word of God
Possession by spirit	Possession by Holy Ghost
Physical isolation from society	Religious retreat
Visions sought	Revelations sought
Exorcism of evil spirit	Exorcism of devil
Ordeal	Ordeal
Interpretation of oracles	Interpretation of Bible

Obviously there are no real differences between the traits; the only distinctions are semantic ones. I could expand this table but to follow through with this kind of methodology is futile. We simply arrive at two ways of looking at the same phenomena, one by lumping, the other by splitting. Either way, it is difficult to determine what more we know about comparative religion after we have sorted out the similar or contrasting traits of the ritual specialist. But the futility of it all begs another question. How may we look at the nature of a ritual specialist without resorting to trait comparison? Is there some underlying common denominator which enables us to look at the role of the ritual specialist in a more nearly universal manner?

SYMBOLIC ILLNESS

Earlier I stated that the two typologies are similar inasmuch as both shaman and priest are charged with curing their respective communities of symbolic illness. "Cure" was used as a metaphor to mean ritually cleanse. Before discussing symbolic illness, and as a starting point for offering another way to look at the concept of the ritual specialist, I would call attention to one anthropologist's statement that "Most primitive

Seated, Istasula (left) and Yellow Blanket, pioneer members of the Saint Mary's Society, a lay society for Roman Catholic women. Standing: the Reverend Eugene Buechel, S.J., a famous recorder of Lakota language and culture. The photograph was taken in June, 1938, at Holy Rosary Mission during a Roman Catholic Sioux Congress. Courtesy Heritage Center, Inc.

peoples are medical materialists in an extended sense, in so far as they tend to justify their ritual actions in terms of aches and pains which would afflict them should the rites be neglected" (Douglas 1966, 44).

I would add to this that the extension of "medical materialism" may be applied to "civilized" as well as "primitive" peoples, and that medical materialism itself refers to the kinds of illnesses, as I mentioned before, whose etiologies are nonmedical in the Western sense of the word. That is not to say there are not real aches and pains associated with those who seek out a Lakota medicine man, nor are there less real aches and pains for those who seek out the assistance of a Christian priest or clergyman. What both have in common is that people from all societies can distinguish between spiritual and medical aid, despite the nature of the symptoms; and in selecting spiritual aid, they consciously eliminate the need for medical aid in the Western sense of the word. After all, all societies have bona fide practitioners of medicine no matter how simple the treatment. Medicine men are capable of stopping bleeding and setting bones, even in the most primitive setting. But those are not the practitioners to whom people afflicted with symbolic illness turn.

I regard symbolic illness as a category much as Douglas regards pollution as a category which represents "matter out of place" (Douglas 1966, 44). But symbolic illness is specific inasmuch as there are real aches and pains, and these real aches and pains lead people to spiritual rather than medical help. It is the primary function of the ritual specialist to cure, that is, ritually cleanse, his patients of symbolic illness. And it is the power *to cure symbolic illness that society invests in an individual* that becomes the common denominator of shaman and priest. In looking at the ritual specialist from society's point of view, we are not primarily concerned with the characteristics and traits of the individual specialist, but rather of *the benefits which society derives from his functional role*. If there is to be a contrast made, the interesting one is that drawn between society and the individual practitioner.[15]

The primary function of the ritual specialist reflects the primary concerns of the society he serves. Thus, it is not surprising that the Chukchee patient is cured in discovering the availability of this year's reindeer, or that the Eskimo patient loses his aches and pains after Sedna has been propitiated and the sea mammals sent up to be caught on the shores. These are the anxiety-producing phenomena of worlds in which hunting and fishing are the primary means of subsistence. In "infinitely more complex" worlds of the Roman Catholic or Episcopal priest, the state of grace insured by the confessional is no less anxiety-reducing than that guaranteed by magical flight or spirit helpers of the Lakota medicine man. In both cases, the shaman or priest mediates between a constant dialectic, that between life and death, because anxiety over life and death are universal to all societies. Thus, the primary functions of the shaman and the priest, from society's point of view, are the same.

But as I have stated, the interesting contrast is between society and the individual, and here I find it useful to refer to Durkheim's dichotomy between the sacred and the profane. If the collective group, society, could mediate its own concerns over life and death, there would be no need for ritual specialists. But the data prove otherwise; every society requires some kind of *individual* intervention or mediation. Thus, it must be concluded that if society seeks a specialist to guarantee its own sacredness, society is in itself profane; and conversely, its opposite, the individual, is sacred.

The sacredness of the individual is enunciated by society, which gives him the power to do what society cannot do for itself: separate himself from the rest of the collective group. Society dictates that the ritual specialist who mediates between the dichotomy between life and death, symbolically expressed in the illness of the individual, be capable of isolating himself from society. This is done both realistically and supernaturally. Realistically, the ritual specialist embarks on vision quests and retreats because his physical separation supports his supernatural separation from his people. He alone experiences this separation when he visits the spirit world, or otherwise holds communion with the supernatural forces. Thus, physical isolation itself symbolizes magical flight and possession which are beyond the cognitive powers of the collective group. Only the ritual specialist is capable of experiencing supernatural isolation; but the group, society, can experience his absence when he is physically isolated from them, and in this collective experience society is reassured of its specialist's sacredness and power. If there are equations to be made, they are not between shaman and prophet, but rather between the individual and society in terms of mediation between the sacred and profane, that is, Sacred : Profane : : Individual : Society.

ILLNESS AS A SYMBOLIC CATEGORY

Anthropologist Mary Douglas has suggested that the destruction of books by students at the University of Illinois represents the destruction of a symbolic category: establishmentarian control.[16] Similarly, I believe that symbolic illness represents the ritual acting out of the drama of life and death. Symbolic illness also marks a larger category, that of social disorder in general, further symbolized in terms of aches and pains, or personal anxieties related to the individual's transgression of social regulations, that is, the commission of error or sin.

The transgression of social regulations can produce any number of medical symptoms, whether they be aches and pains or inexplicable feelings of being upset over "something." Real cuts and bruises can be treated by other specialists, primitive or civilized. But these are nonsymbolic disorders which call for established medicine men to ply their trade, recognizing that their respective trades sometimes overlap (the medical doctor's "bedside manner" and the shaman's herbal brew). When there is doubt regarding the exact nature of the pathology, a medical practitioner can always refer the patient to a spiritual healer and vice versa. The clear-cut division of labor may not always be that clear-cut. Witness in our own society, especially during the 1960s, the Age of Alienation, when God was proclaimed dead and psychiatry was claimed as the "new" religion. The title of the ritual specialist changed, but his functional role did not. The recognition that certain illnesses emanated from society itself was particularly well manifested in the 1960s when drug abuse reached monumental proportions. The myth of the local pusher selling hard drugs in the school yard was dispelled and replaced with the addict's conviction that "Society is the *real* pusher." Durkheim could have said no better.

But whether symbolic illness takes the form of drug abuse, aches and pains, or anxiety over error or sin, the diagnostic powers often attributed to "shamans" or "priests," "primitive" or "civilized," have nothing to do with the association between "symptom" and "treatment." In treating symbolic illness, the ritual specialist can only cure illness that emanates from within his society, not illness that originates from without. Thus, the Lakota *yuwipi* man sends his patient who suffers from diabetes or heart trouble to the Public Health Hospital because his society has declared that these are illnesses which have come from the white man. If the patient is successfully treated, the *yuwipi* man is credited with the power to diagnose exotic illness. If the patient dies, it is the fault of the public health authorities who represent the other society. Patients never die from "Indian sickness"; the *yuwipi* man is always successful.

Symbolic illness serves, then, as the marker for the category which subsumes all forms of social disorder. The rituals which people dare not ignore for fear of social disintegration are those rituals which are capable of destroying the category which symbolic illness represents. The individual practitioner, made sacred by his ability to detach himself from the social organism, is invested with the power to resynthesize society by ritually destroying the category. Destruction of the category, then, symbolizes the potential for the continued existence of the society. Thus:

Sacred : Profane :: Individual : Society
Illness : Health :: Death : Life.

That the specific nature of various ritual specialists should change from one society to another presents another kind of problem, an age-old one which asks what are the reasons for cultural variation. We should not be surprised that there is a correlation between the "priest" and the local sociopolitical organization. The same correlation exists between the "shaman" and his society's organization. Ritualism only reflects society's integrative processes at another functional level. To ask why there is a difference between a Tungus shaman and a Catholic priest is to ask why each society has a different kind of political system, economic system, environmental niche, or language.

To understand cultural variation, we should not hasten to create spurious typologies unless we seek only to treat "primitive" religions, as Evans-Pritchard has stated, "as something so unlike the religions of civilization." Which, of course, they are not.

RITUAL SPECIALISTS

Now that the various types of mediators between the common people and the supernaturals have been placed into a larger context, we turn to the manner in which the Lakota classify their own ritual specialists, who refer to themselves *wakanic'-ilapi* 'to consider oneself sacred' or *wakan iglawapi* 'to count oneself sacred'.

The generic term for males who act as such mediums is *wicaša wakan* 'sacred man'; women are called *winyan wakan* 'sacred woman'. Aside from gender difference, other terms are used to indicate specific ways in which men and women perform their sacred duties, and the sources from which they derive their power. *Wicaša wakan* may cure various illnesses, somatic and psychosomatic. They may find lost or stolen articles, or simply advise common people about family matters, money, jobs, school, and other exigencies confronted by people growing up in a modern reservation community. Some *wicaša wakan* are better than others in treating certain kinds of sickness, thus they may be subclassified according to their fields of specialization, not unlike modern medicine divides itself into specializations.

The source of power is particularly important in the Lakota classification system. Medicine men and women, as the two terms are glossed by the Lakota when speaking English, are inspired by virtually any kind of animal or bird that appears to them in visions to instruct them in the proper use of power. However, pragmatically, a relatively few species actually appear in visions. Most important are the bear, buffalo, deer, elk, and eagle, and each is seen as a specialist in types of curing or other ritual knowledge. Historically the bear has always been seen as a specialist in treating wounds sustained on the warpath or in hunting accidents. The buffalo is seen a having power over female disorders. Deer and elk are inextricably linked with the ability to control affairs of the heart, and frequently aphrodisiacs are concocted from parts of their bodies.[17] Mythical deer are rampant in many Plains Indian myths where women seduce a lost warrior and then turn into a deer driving the man crazy. The eagle is powerful in many general ways and, of course, is the chief messenger between the medicine man, the common people, and Wakantanka.

The public demonstration of the source of power also figures prominently in the classification of ritual specialists. This enactment is called *wakan kaga* 'sacred performance' (or 'imitation'), a term which may be applied not only to the performance but to the performer. Thus, medicine men who derive power from the bear may be referred to or addressed in a number of ways—*mato wapiye* 'bear curer', or *mato kaga* 'bear performer'.

There is still another classification of medicine men and women which corresponds closely to our notion of wizard and witch, that is, people who have derived power for the sole purpose of doing harm to others. In Lakota, men are *wicaȟmunga* 'wizard', and woman are *wiȟmunga* 'witch'. The term *ȟmunga* means 'buzzing, or making a whizzing sound' and probably comes from the belief that a person's will, behavior, or life can be influenced or controlled over long distances by transmitting thoughts over sound waves. Unfortunately we know little about the origin of this term, but it has become synonymous with a person who exercises control over another, sometimes for pay from a client, which results in the patient becoming ill, depressed, or dying.

Finally, another type of classification is exclusive to males called *winkte* 'would-be woman'. It refers to the custom of certain men dressing and behaving like women.

Based on these characteristics, specializations, public performance, and gender, all Lakota medicine men and women are classified from the most general to the most specific.

MEDICINE MAN

The generic term *wicaša wakan* 'sacred man' or, in English, 'medicine man' encompasses four major types of sacred persons based on the kinds of criteria discussed above: (1) *wapiyapi* 'curers"; (2) *wakan kaga* 'performers'; (3) *wicaȟmunga* 'wizards'; and (4) *winkte* 'transvestites'.

The *wapiyapi* are those sacred men who most closely conform to the characteristics of "shaman" as it is used in its conventional meaning. As a subclass of medicine men, the *wapiyapi* (also known as simply *wapiye* 'a person who makes over, renews'), or as *wapiye wicaša* 'curing man' may be divided into subclasses that reflect the source of power of spirit helper, such as *mato wapiye* 'bear curer' (but conventionally "bear doctor" in English). Another subclass is the well-known Yuwipi *wicaša* 'Yuwipi man', who, despite similarities in rituals with other *wapiye,* is regarded as different from the other *wapiyapi* and whose essential diagnostic feature (seances, binding the yuwipi man in a blanket, and so forth) conforms to the Siberian "proper" form of shamanism discussed earlier. Still a third subclass is *hohu iyapa* 'to hold a bone in the mouth' or conventionally "bone doctor" or "bone sucker" in English. This is an older type of medicine man who was believed to cure patients by placing a bone in his mouth and sucking out of the patient's body some material object regarded as the cause of the illness. Because the *hohu iyapa* frequently made a sucking noise as he attempted to extract a foreign object from the patient, the act was called *yagopa* 'to make a sucking noise'. One Lakota described the curing ritual:

> If someone has a pain in his chest—no matter what part of his body—the *wapiye* puts this portion of the flesh in his mouth and sucks at it, thus extracting the cause of the pain from the patient's back. After sucking out the matter, he spits out blood or whatever might have been the cause of pain.
>
> The *wapiye* then tells the patient's mother what caused the pain and predicts whether or not her son will live. Each time these *wapiyapi* are called the people believe in whatever they do. These *wapiyapi* also find hawks, woodpeckers, buffalos, rattlesnakes, and bears in their patients' backs.
>
> When a patient is being doctored, the *wapiye* sometimes kicks the ground, and one can hear a pleasing sound emanating from the patient's back . . . The people truly believe that it is a voice and stand outside the lodge listening. It is the healing that causes whatever is in the patient's back to be heard.
>
> If the *wapiye* spends a lot of time sucking at the flesh, and nothing is extracted, he talks with whatever mysterious power is in the patient. From within, a voice cries out, and often he can then begin to use those powers which he received in his vision to cure the patient.
>
> Long ago there was a most powerful man that doctored. People placed a bowl of water in front of him and he vomited in it. And from out of his mouth came snakes, and they began swimming around in the bowl or water. He opened his mouth again and the snakes gently returned. He told the people that it was the snakes that had caused the patient's suffering. They believed him and from then on considered him *wakan*.[18]

The fourth kind of *wapiye* is the *pejuta wicaša* 'medicine man', who cures his patients by means of sacred herbs. These herbs can be found only by the *pejuta wicaša* and instructions for their preparation and use are received in a vision. Although herbal teas and brews, as well as the ability to wrap wounds and set bones are his main stock in trade, rarely does any *pejuta wicaša* perform his curing without praying to the supernaturals who represent the source of his power. Before administering an herb to a patient, the *pejuta wicaša* prays in the following way:

Wakantanka unšimala ye.
Kuje kin le asniwayin kte.
Pejuta kin le wak'u kte.
Ho hece omakiya yo.

Wakantanka, please pity me.
I will make this sick person recover.
I will give to him this medicine.
So help me![19]

Although differing somewhat from other *wapiye* counterparts, it was still necessary for the *pejuta wicaša* to pray and sing over his patients to ensure that the spirit helpers would aid in his recovery.

Another class of *wicaša wakan* were those who performed the sacred feats, *wakan kaga*. Some of them cured people, some of them changed their own behavior radically after having received visions of the thunder and lightning, others had control over people's behaviors. *Wakan kaga* is a confusing class of *wicaša wakan* because the term refers to both the performer and the performance. Also, somewhat misleading is the fact that members of this class who actually cure are also called *wapiye*. Yet I believe it stands as a class separate from the *wapiye* because many of the *wakan kaga* simply do not cure at all. Rather they simply act out their wakan visions in public. The most famous curing member of the *wakan kaga* is the *heyoka kaga* 'clown performers'. The gloss 'contrary' has often been applied to these people in the anthropological literature because it was believed that if a person dreamed of thunder or lightning, or any symbols of the two, they must spend at least part of their life acting in an anti-natural manner. They dress warmly in summer, and go naked in winter. They speak backwards. In their famous performance, the *heyoka* dance around a kettle of boiling water in which a dog is cooked and splash themselves, claiming that the water is cold.[20]

Historically, the *heyoka kaga* was much more complicated

Saint Elizabeth's Catholic Church, Oglala. Courtesy Heritage Center, Inc.

than we find it today. Those ancestors of the Lakota living in Minnesota believed that there were four types of *heyoka*. One was a tall man with two faces. He carried a bow on which a lightning symbol was painted, and a dewclaw rattle. The second was a little old man with a cocked hat and large ears who carried a yellow bow. The third was a man who carried a flute around his neck. The fourth was invisible but manifested itself as a wind that caused ripples on the water.[21]

Here *heyoka* is elevated to a supernatural state equal to that of other Lakota gods. If the *heyoka kaga* performed properly, they gained the power to make the wind blow and the rain fall. The old people believed that the *pajola* or little hills that rise on the prairie were the homes of *heyoka* and called them *heyokati* 'Heyoka's lodge.' Today, many of the features of the four types of *heyoka* appear as spirits who are beckoned by the Yuwipi man in order to help him cure his patients, and many of the manifestations of *heyoka* are accounted for in the meetings in the darkened room, particularly the little man with a cocked hat and a bow.

Another subclass of *wakan kaga* is the *heȟaka kaga* or "*heȟakela*" 'elk performers' or simply, 'elk people'. These men have dreamed of a man who turns himself into a female elk (*unpan*) and instructs the dreamer what medicines to use. Usually, a *heȟakela* has four visions, twice of a man, and twice of an elk. Those who have dreamed thusly make a mask out of rawhide with branches fastened to represent the horns of an elk. They also make a *cangleška* 'hoop' covered with buffalo hair with a bunch of sage tied to it, and a staff with eagle feathers affixed to the upper end. During the *heȟaka kaga*, the performer purifies the accoutrements in sage smoke. He paints his entire body yellow, and paints black stripes across his chest and upper legs. He then paints a face on the mask and purifies it. He grabs at the smoke with his hands and rubs them over his eyes. His mask has no eyeholes in it, but if he is truly *wakan* it is believed that he can see things clearly once the mask has been put on.

Some of the people who have gathered take various objects such as small stones, or nail clippings, and shake them in their hands as the masked *heȟakela* passes among them. When his procession among them is finished, the people throw the objects down. The *heȟakela* then begins to vomit. If he vomits any of the things that the others have held in their hands, he is considered *wakan*.[22]

A man who has dreamed of a man twice and a buffalo twice is eligible to perform the *tatanka kaga* 'buffalo performance' and conduct a ceremony for a girl who has menstruated for the first time. He dresses in the full skin of a buffalo bull including the mask complete with horns. During the *išnati awicalowanpi* 'they sing over her menses', he prays:

Wakantanka unšimala yo.
Wicincala tatanka ouncage wak'u kte lo.
Tokata winunȟcala ihunni kte wacin yelo.
Tatanka ouncage wak'u kte lo.

Wakantanka pity me.
I give this girl the likeness of a buffalo.
I want her to live to be an old woman.
So I give her the likeness of a buffalo.

After the ceremony the girl is officially considered a woman, and the relationship between women, as mothers of the Lakota nation, is symbolically equated with the buffalo, the primary source of sustenance.[23]

Another subclass of *wakan kaga* is the *sungmanitu* (also *sungmahetu*) *kaga* 'wolf performance' conducted in conjunction with going on the war path. Like the other *wakan kaga*, only a man who has dreamed twice of a man and twice of a wolf is eligible to perform this ceremony. He wears a wolfskin mask, and wolf fur covers his body. Through an opening in the mask, a *šiyotanka* 'whistle' is inserted which he pipes on repetitiously as they do in the Sun Dance (ti-ti-ti, etc.). In his right hand he carries a rope which he manipulates to resemble the slithering movements of a snake (called *zuzeca kaga* 'snake performance'). In the old days, warriors about to embark against the enemy employed the *sungmanitu kaga* to ascertain the whereabouts of the enemy. They brought him a pipe as an invitation to foresee where the enemies were camped. This presentation of the pipe was called *iwašipi* 'to retain with'. The meaning of this term is that the *sungmanitu kaga*, if he accepted the pipe and smoked it to the cardinal directions, would agree to perform the ceremony. He smoked the pipe and then held it close to the wolfskins making up his costume. He then said to the warriors who brought the pipe:

Blihici'iya waunšipelo.
Tanyan slolyewacin yo!

We have entered into this pact courageously.
Take care to understand what I say!

The actual ceremony began at night. The *sungmanitu kaga* told the warriors to sit in a line with their horse behind them. No one was allowed to talk. He then walked up and down the line, blowing on his whistle and howling like a wolf. By so doing, he could make the real wolves howl about the enemies and thus inform him about their whereabouts. The act of making the wolves howl was called *houya* 'to summon a voice'. As wolves begin to howl, the *sungmanitu kaga* continued to walk up and down the line of warriors singing:

Wakanyan mawani ye
Wakangli yewaye.

Sacredly I walk.
I send the lightning.

These words had been received in a vision and demonstrated the power of those spirits who had invested the *sungmanitu kaga* with the power to foretell the consequences of a war party. It was the responsibility of the *sungmanitu kaga* to interpret the howls that he heard. He then told the warriors to follow his instruction. If they did, they would kill many enemies. If they failed to follow his instructions, they would be killed.[24]

The last example of the *wakan kaga* deals with those men who have dreamed twice of a man and twice of a bear—the *mato kaga* 'bear performance'. In front of an entire assemblage of persons who had similar dreams, the bear performer dresses himself in a bear robe and pretends to attack people, fiercely growling and frightening the children. These performances are given when wounded men have returned from the warpath with wounds. The doctoring is also auspicious for fractured bones.

A curing session requires four evenings, and all of the *mato kaga* are present. One who is considered the chief of the bear doctors paints his body red, adding black stripes running perpendicularly across his eyes. He carries a bag made from bearskin containing herbal medicines and ointments. The doctoring is conducted in the patient's tent, during which time he is given medicine to drink, and an ointment is applied with the tail of a blacktail deer or with an eagle feather. Bear grease is rubbed around the swelling of a wound. The *mato kaga* paints the patient's body red, and he is led or carried outside the tipi. A procession is led by two women carrying pipes. The patient follows them and, in turn, is followed by the *mato kaga*, his helpers, and the remainder of the *mato ihanblapi* 'bear dreamers'. As they walk, the members sing

Ate hiyu ye
Tuwa aiyaȟpemaye
Ina hiyu ye
Tuwa aiyaȟpemaye.

Father, please come here.
Someone made me fall over.
Mother, please come here.
Someone made me fall over.

The singing continues until the procession returns to the patient's tipi.[25]

Not as much is known about the evil-doers classed as *wicaȟmunga* 'wizards'. They are capable of making a person ill or depressed, but they are never identified. As is true in other societies, the *wicaȟmunga* represent a class of people to blame for misfortune. They explain otherwise inexplicable events such as accidents, murder, the sudden death of children, and catastrophe. Although the *wicaȟmunga* is never named, another medicine man can predict that certain incidents are caused by these evil-doers and can reverse the harm or misfortune that the *wicaȟmunga* have caused through proper prayers and ceremonies.

The final class of *wicaša wakan* is the *winkte,* variously translated as transvestite, hermaphrodite, homosexual, or more appropriately "would-be woman." Anthropologists have noted this kind of behavior among all peoples of the world and refer to the institution as the *berdache,* a French corruption of the Arabic word *bardaj* meaning 'slave'.[26] It should be noted, however, that among the Lakota, *winktes* were never slaves and, in fact, enjoyed a decided amount of prestige and high status. They were regarded as extremely sacred people who followed their particular lifestyle as a result of instructions received in visions, usually from Anukite 'Double Woman' or from visions of menstruating women. Their vow to live a life modeled after the roles of women was not entirely mandatory as in the case of the *heyoka kaga,* where antinatural behavior was required after having dreamed of lightning or thunder. In some visions, the dreamer might be offered a choice of affecting male or female behavior. In a rather typical vision, the dreamer was offered a burden strap or an arrow and asked to choose. The burden strap symbolized the role of women; the arrow, that of men.[27]

It is not clear why males chose to imitate female behavior,

nor has it ever been determined just what percentage of the male population participated in a feminine lifestyle, but the most reasonable estimate is that it was a very small number. Furthermore, there has always been some controversy over the sexual nature of *winktes* and whether or not they had intimate relations with men. It is known, however, that in other tribes the berdache was, in fact, homosexual.

Some authors conclude that *winktes* were "sissies" and "mama's boys," but this is inconsistent with Lakota ideology. *Winktes* were indeed considered the most sacred and played important roles in Lakota culture. They frequently did (and do) take care of the old and feeble, and looked after orphaned children. Although it is claimed that men chose the *winkte* role to avoid danger, *winktes* in fact often went on war parties. *Winktes* were also regarded as good hunters although they usually hunted alone for small game and did not participate in the larger communal buffalo hunts. One psychiatrist explained the berdache as an institution that permitted some to cross-dress to prevent unsuspecting heterosexuals from being "recruited" as homosexuals, but this is clearly a twentieth-century idea unsupported in Lakota ideology.

The *winktes* frequently served as go-betweens (usually) between their female cross-cousins and an intended male paramour. The naming of children by *winktes* was considered prestigious, and many famous Lakota names were bestowed this way despite the fanciful notion that Indian parents named their children after the first natural phenomenon they saw immediately after the birth of the child. Frequently, *winktes* were also asked to counsel over matters important to the tribe as intelligent critics of tribal policy. The institution was exclusively male, and there was never a female counterpart among the Lakota, although it does exist in other tribes.

MEDICINE WOMEN

The generic term for medicine woman is *winyan wakan* 'sacred woman', which in turn represents three major subclasses of female ritual specialists (the fourth, a hypothetical counter-

Joint meeting of Saint Mary's and Saint Joseph societies with the Reverend Eugene Buechel, S.J. (standing, left), presiding, ca. 1938. The man seated in the center at the desk, facing the windows through which light is streaming, is Henry White Calf, who was a catechist at Loafer Camp through the 1940s and was a prominent singer at celebrations. Courtesy Heritage Center, Inc.

part of the medicine man subclass *winkte* does not exist among women). These subclasses parallel those of the male specialists consisting of (1) *wapiyapi* 'curers', (2) *wakan kaga* 'performers', and (3) *wiȟmunga* 'witches'.[28]

The *wapiyapi* conform to the anthropological convention "shamaness" and comprise two subclasses, *wapiye winyan* 'curing woman' (also called *wapiye wakan*) and *pejuta winyela* 'medicine women'. Curing women are rare, but medicine women are prevalent and are charged with identifying, procuring and preparing various kinds of herbs to cure almost any ailment considered a "Lakota" illness including kidney disease, liver disease, gall stones, gynecological disorders, urinary problems, and venereal disease. The right to collect *pejuta* is given to a woman either in a vision or by a medicine man. An elaborate ritual accompanies the search for appropriate plants, and special songs are sung and prayers are made prior to leaving the house to collect such plants.[29]

Herbal brews in the form of tea are usually given to the patient, but occasionally it is the medicine woman who drinks the tea and then spits the medicine on the part of the body affected and massages it into the skin.

Wapiye wakan frequently are the wives of *wicaša wakan* and assist their husbands in various kinds of curing ceremonies such as Yuwipi. These sacred women, as long as they are past menopause, are also entrusted with overseeing sacred objects used in the ceremonies. A number of keepers of the White Buffalo Calf Pipe at Green Grass, South Dakota, including the present one, have been women.

Frequently women, including common women who have had no visions, may accompany a medicine man to a sacred hill where they will leave offerings for the spirits. This may be the result of a vow (*woiglakapi*) or an entreaty to the benevolent spirits who live in the West to help a relative who is sick, or a loved one who has left the reservation to go into the military or to school. The woman will decide how many tobacco offerings to make (*canli wapaȟte*), and may also include yard goods of cotton cloth. Once the woman has reached the summit of the sacred hill, the medicine man and woman face each other and she displays the offerings while the medicine man prays in the following way:

> Wakantanka makatakiya wanmanyanka yo. Nihukuya unšiwayin kte lo. Winyan kin le tokata blokecokanyan tanyan ni ihunni kinhan šina luta kin le wašte canli wapaȟte wikcemna oniciyake k'un he le e yelo. Okikcu wo, Wakantanka. Ake tokata sutaya mni kte wacin yelo.
>
> Wakantanka, look toward the earth at me. Here below you I will do this bidding. This woman was able to make it through

the summer all right, so here is the red blanket and ten tobacco offerings that she pledged to you. Take them, Wakantanka. In the future I want to walk strongly again.[30]

The offerings are then placed on sticks in the ground and the blanket torn into strips so that no one will be tempted to steal it and use it for some other purpose.

Of the *wakan kaga*, women participated only in the *heyoka kaga* but this was in the distant past and no known examples of female *heyoka* exist at Pine Ridge.[31] Similarly, as in the case of the men, the *wiȟmunga* 'witch' was a woman capable of inflicting sickness or hysteria on others, but they were never publicly known or confronted. Like the men, they served as the object of accusation and blame; but no one ever admitted to being a witch, and no one was ever named as one.

To summarize, the way the Lakota classified their ritual specialist was based on a number of role behaviors that were initiated through visions and differentiated on the basis of each sacred person's source of power and specific instructions from the spirit helpers. These supernatural mandates frequently were enacted at public ceremonies which gave credibility to the efficacy of the ritual specialists. Some confusion arises in the classification process because the same medicine men and women often are known by more than one name. These referential and descriptive names depend on the ritual occasion, or the particular segment of a ritual process beginning with one or more visions, enactment or performance of that vision, and finally, in those cases in which ritual specialists are endowed with the ability to cure, the doctoring ritual itself.

Various terms for ritual or ceremony are coupled with the source of the ritual specialist's power to form descriptive classificatory terms for forms of religious performance. In private performances such as Yuwipi, the men who conduct these short-term rituals are referred to as Yuwipi *wicaša* or *wapiye*. In public performances, most of which are mandated by the vision itself, a step necessary in legitimizing the medicine man's or woman's specific powers, the sacred persons are classified by a number of factors. Most of these substitutional

Table 2. Sources of Power

Perfor-mance	Source of power	Feast	Sing	Perfor-mance	Curing
Heyoka kaga	wakinyan ihanblapi	Heyoka wozepi	—	Heyoka kaga	—
Mato kaga	Mato ihanblapi	Mato wohanpi	Mato lowanpi	Mato kagapi	Mato wapiye
Heȟaka kaga	Heȟaka ihanblapi	Heȟaka wohanpi	—	Heȟaka kaga	Heȟaka wapiye, or Heȟakela

names are found among the *wakan kaga*. To provide an example of how the nomenclature changes, let me contrast three types of *wakan kaga*: the *heyoka kaga* 'clown performance', the *mato kaga* 'bear performance' and the *heȟaka kaga* 'elk performance'. There are five potential means of classifying these two enactments: (1) source of power, (2) presence or absence of feast, (3) presence or absence of song as a major medium of communication with the supernatural, (4) the nature of the performance including time and place, and (5) whether curing is associated with the enactment.

In Table 2 we see that the source of power for the *heyoka* is a dream of *wakinyan* (lightning, thunder or symbols of them). The feast is called *Heyoka wozepi* which means 'the Heyoka ladle out', referring to the act of reaching into a boiling kettle for choice morsels of dog. The ceremony is never referred to as a *lowanpi* 'sing', and the *heyoka* do not assume the term *wapiye*.

In *mato kagapi*, each of the processes is classified as *mato*. Hence, *mato ihanble* (the singular form), *mato kaga*, and *mato wapiye* may all refer to the same person during different ritual episodes. The *heȟaka kaga* has characteristics of both the *heyoka* and *mato*.

Finally, the relationship between the various classes and

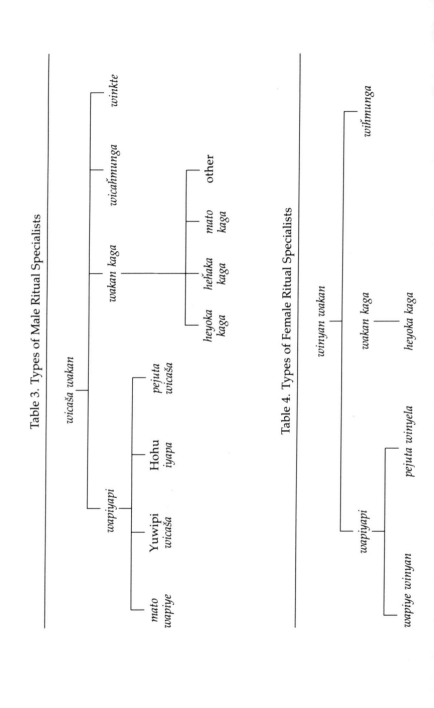

Table 3. Types of Male Ritual Specialists

Table 4. Types of Female Ritual Specialists

subclasses of medicine men and women may be examined from a more formal perspective.

Table 3 is a diagram of the hierarchical relationships between *wicaša wakan*. Table 4 provides the same information for *winyan wakan*.

This, then, represents the way the Lakota classify those sacred men and women who are entrusted with mediating between the common people and the supernaturals. One must always be cautious in attempting to interpret ideas from one culture into the neat pigeon holes of one's own. The Lakota normally do not view sacred persons in terms of dominance or hierarchy. These tables, however, are meant to serve as an heuristic device which most closely resembles the way the Lakota people understand relationships between sacred persons and sacred rituals.

APPENDICES

PHONOLOGICAL KEY

LAKOTA has eight vowels, five oral and three nasal:
  a Low, oral, approximately as in father. Written *a*.
  a Low, nasal, approximately as in calm. Written *an*.
  e Mid, front, oral, approximately as in they. Written *e*.
  i High, front, oral, approximately as in machine. Written *i*.
  i High, front, nasal, approximately as in seen. Written *in*.
  o Mid, back, oral, approximately as in open. Written *o*.
  u High, back, oral, approximately as in boot. Written *u*.
  u High, back, nasal, approximately as in boom. Written *un*.

Twenty-eight consonants, of which twenty-one represent seven consonantal triads (*p, t, k, c, z, ž,* and *x*), each of which is comprised of a voiced, aspirated, and glottalized member. The remaining seven consonants are *w, y, l, m, n, h,* and *?*.
  p Bilabial, voiced as in boy. Written *p* when word initial, *b* when first position in consonant cluster.
  p' Bilabial, aspirated as in pin. Written *p*.
  p' Bilabial, glottalized. No English equivalent. Written *p'*.
  t Alveolar, voiced, as in dim. Written *t*.
  t' Alveolar, aspirated, as in tin. Written *t*.
  t' Alveolar, glottalized. No English equivalent. Written *t'*.
  k Velar, voiced as in got. Written *k* when word initial, *g* when first position in consonant cluster.
  k' Velar, aspirated, as in kick. Written *k*.
  k' Velar, glottalized. No English equivalent. Written *k'*.
  c Alveopalatal, voiced, as in jaw. Written *c*.
  c' Alveopalatal, aspirated, as in church. Written *c*.
  c' Alveopalatal, glottalized. No English equivalent. Written *c'*.

z Alveolar, voiced, grooved, as in zip. Written z.

s Alveolar, aspirated, grooved, as in sip. Written s.

s' Alveolar, glottalized, grooved. No English equivalent. Written s'.

ž Alveopalatal, voiced, grooved, as in azure. Written j.

š Alveopalatal, aspirated, grooved, as in shake. Written š.

š' Alveopalatal, glottalized, grooved. No English equivalent. Written š'.

γ Velar, voiced, as in Spanish cigaro. Written g.

x Velar, aspirated, as in German nach. Written ħ.

x' Velar, glottalized. No English equivalent. Written ħ'.

w Bilabial, voiced, as in water. Written w.

y Alveopalatal, voiced, as in yes. Written y.

l Alveolar, voiced, as in link. Written l.

m Bilabial, voiced, as in mink. Written m.

n Alveolar, voiced, as in not. Written n.

h Glottal, voiceless, as in hat. Written h.

? Glottal, voiceless. Written as '.

APPENDIX B

GLOSSARY

THE following glossary contains words and phrases discussed in the previous chapters with the exception of those terms contained in songs and prayers which are part of everyday Lakota grammar and do not refer particularly to sacred language.

aglata   To answer, to respond, to echo, as when females accompany male singer.

ahiyaya   To pass around a pipe; to sing a song.

akicita   Soldier, marshal; in sacred language, a representative or messenger of a supernatural being or power.

akiš'a   To yelp, a style of singing.

anpetu wi   Sun; lit., 'day' *wi*.

anukasan   Mature bald eagle; lit., 'white on both sides'.

Anukite   Double Face ('Face on both sides') who in Lakota cosmology had an adulterous affair (as Ite) with the Sun and was sent to the earth.

anukiya   Immature golden eagle; lit., 'cross-breed'.

apa   To strike with the hand; to drum.

ate   Father; father's brother; mother's sister's husband.

can   Wood; stick; tree.

cancan   Shaking.

cancega   Drum.

cangleška   Hoop such as that worn as a hair ornament or carried in the *heňaka kaga* (q.v.).

cangleška wakan   Sacred hoop; a representation of a circle inscribed with a cross symbolizing the total universe.

caje   Name.

cankahotun   Guitar.

canku   Road, way.

canli   Generic term for tobacco.

canli wapaȟte   Tobacco offering; a pinch of tobacco placed in an inch-square piece of cloth and tied with others to a string; used for offerings, and to delineate the sacred area on the Vision Quest and in the *yuwipi lowanpi* (q.v.).

canotida   Dakota variant of *canotila* (q.v.).

canotila   Forest spirits; lit., 'they live in a tree'.

canyukize   Violin.

caš   Attenuated form of *caje* 'name'.

caštun   To name; a naming ceremony, lit., 'to give birth to a name'.

catkatahan   Left (direction).

catkatahan ukiye   To come from the left, said when the wind blows from the east.

cega   Earthen pot.

ceȟohomni wacipi   Kettle or "pot" dance.

cekiya   To pray; lit., 'to cry for'.

cetan itancan   Hawk chief, the head of the hawk nation, or hawk species.

cetan oyate   Hawk nation; hawk species; all hawks.

ceya   To cry.

cincala   Baby.

econpi   Spelling variation of *ecunpi* 'doings, ceremonies', also *woecun*.

etanhan   From.

Eya   Attenuated form of *wiyoȟpeyata* 'west'.

eya   To say.

gnaš   Attenuated form of *tatang gnaškiyan* (q.v.).

gnaška   Generic term for frog.

ha   Skin; hide.

hanbloglaka   Vision talk; discourse between medicine men and the supernaturals; also, a speech given at the beginning of a ritual which legitimates the ritual specialist's right and ability to conduct the ceremony.

hanhepi wi   Moon; lit., 'night' *wi*.

ȟ'anhi   To be slow.

hanska   Long.

hanwi   Sacred word for moon; according to Walker, a type of *wakan kolaya;* one of the sixteen aspects of Wakantanka.

heȟaka   Bull elk.

heȟaka ihanblapi   Elk dreamers.

heȟaka kaga   Elk performance.

heȟaka wohanpi   Elk feast.

heȟakela   A member of the *heȟaka kaga* (q.v.).

Heyoka   A Lakota god pictured variously as a giant or a dwarf.

heyoka kaga   A clown performance in which members act in an antinatural way.

heyokati   The lodge of Heyoka (q.v.).

heyoka wozepi   The *heyoka* ladle out, a ritual; dancing around the kettle, thrusting one's hands into the boiling water, and ladling out choice morsels of dog are part of the ritual.

hihan oyate   Owl nation; owl species; all owls.

hinanpa   To enter; lit., 'to come into sight', 'to appear from behind something'.

hiyanpa   Corruption of *hinanpa* (q.v.).

ȟlaȟla   Bells.

ȟmunga   To buzz, hum (witchcraft is believed to be transported over sound waves).

ho   Voice.

hocoka   The area inside the camp circle of tipis; in sacred language, any ritual space; also, metaphorically, safe, unified, Indian.

hocoka wanji ogna iyotake cin   The one sitting in the camp circle, a metaphor for the person conducting a ritual.

hocoka wooglaka olowan   A declaration of intent from the sacred place song, sung by the singers while the *yuwipi wicaša* (q.v.) delivers his vision talk.

hohu iyapa   To suck with a bone; lit., 'to suck with a bone held in the mouth'; to draw out a source of pain through a bone tube; a person who performs this ceremony.

hoišta   A wooden match, lit., 'fish eye'.

hoiyoȟpeya   To tire the voice with singing.

ȟ'oka   A group of male singers; an Omaha word.

hokapsanpsan To whine.

hokawinħ The area outside the camp circle of tipis; meta-phorically, danger, disorganization, enemies.

hotanin To raise one's voice in song; to make one's voice heard in song.

hotanka Loud-voiced.

hotun To give rise to voice; to produce a sound (birth of a voice).

"Ho Tunkašila, wakinyan niktepi" 'Ho Grandfather, the thunder struck you'! lit., '. . . killed you'; said when one accidentally kills a spider.

houkiye To receive or learn a song in a vision; to cause a song to come.

hoyeya To sing; to send a voice.

ħpe Radical element 'to fall off'.

hukuciyela Down below.

Hunkpapa 'End of circle'; a division of the Teton.

hunonp Variation of *hununpa* (q.v.).

hunonpakan Variant spelling of *hununpakan* (q.v.).

hununpa Sacred language for human beings; lit., 'two leg-geds'; also, *wahununpa;* according to Walker, a type of *wakan kuya;* one of Wakantanka's sixteen aspects.

hununpakan Sacred word for *hununpa* (q.v.).

ħ'unyan Mature golden eagle; lit., 'worn out'.

hutopa 'Four-legged', a sacred word for all animals.

icabu Drumstick.

icu To take.

ihanblapi Dreamers; persons who have had visions.

ijena Mixed up, as apples and oranges.

ikce wicaša Old-time man, original Indian, "real" Indian.

ikpage Arrow notch.

ina Mother; mother's sister; father's brother's wife.

inakiyapi olowan Quitting song, sung at the end of the *yuwipi* ritual as the last song.

Ink Attenuated form of Inktomi (q.v.).

Inktomi Spider, the trickster and bringer of culture to the Lakota, who named all things; he is the subject of a cycle of tales that serve as morality stories for young children.

Inktomi ektašniye etunwan   Inktomi who looks nowhere, a personal helper.

Inktomi hunkešni   Weak Inktomi, a personal helper.

Inktomi kinyan   Flying Inktomi, a personal helper.

Inktomi lowanpi   Inktomi sing, a special ritual in which only Inktomi spirits are summoned by a *yuwipi* man.

Inktomi luzahan   Fast Inktomi, a personal helper.

Inktomi maka mahel mani   Inktomi who walks underground, a personal helper.

Inktomi mniakinyan   Inktomi who flies over the water, a personal helper.

Inktomi ognaya šice   Inktomi who is hard to fool, a personal helper.

Inktomi sabic'iye   Inktomi who paints himself black, a personal helper.

Inktomi takuni oholašni   Inktomi who respects nothing, a personal helper.

Inktomi tawokaške   Spider's web; lit., 'Spider's bindery'.

Inktomi wakagišni   Daring Inktomi, a personal helper.

inyan   Rock; according to Walker, a type of *wakan ankatu;* one of Wakantanka's sixteen aspects.

inyankan   Sacred word for rock.

Ite   Face; also, the wife of Tate in Lakota cosmology.

itokagata   South; lit., 'facing the place of creation'.

itokagata iyaye   To go south; metaphorically, to die.

iwašipi   To retain; to make a contract; to negotiate; to seal a bond by smoking the pipe.

iwaštegla   Easy, casual, gentle; when referring to dance, it means medium tempo.

iya   To speak (*iye*, 'he speaks').

Iya   The brother of Inktomi, and offspring of *wakinyan* and *inyan;* he is a giant and has a voracious appetite for human flesh.

iye   To speak.

iyeska   Medium, interpreter; mixed-blood, "half-blood"; lit., 'to speak white'; in secular life the children of whites and Indians; in sacred language, a medicine man or woman.

iyeya   To cause to go away.

iyeyaye   To go away suddenly.

iyoȟpeya   To cast out, as a fisherman's line.

iyoja   Amplified.

iyonihan   Barely audible.

jiyahan   Lowly, softly, as in singing a song.

jo   To whistle.

johotun   To whistle up a tune.

jolowan   To whistle a tune.

kabubu   To drum; also, the sound of clapping hands.

kaga   To make, create; also, a ritual, ceremony, performance, or imitation, as in *heyoka kaga,* 'clown performance' or 'clown imitation'.

kaijena   To drum out of time.

kan   Old; when suffixed to common words, renders them sacred.

kašna   To miss a beat, as in drumming.

kat'inze   To drum in steady beats.

keya   Generic term for turtle.

kico   To cry out.

kimimela   Generic term for butterfly.

kiza   To squeak, as a mouse.

kola   Friend; comrade. Medicine men address their spirit helpers as *kola.*

kolatakuya   To have a relationship of friend; the relationship between a medicine man and his spirit helpers.

kpankpanyela   Countless; used in drumming to express tremolo or "thunder drumming."

kuta   Low.

la   A morpheme; a radical element conveying the idea of intention, regard, demand, asking, consideration; also a diminutive suffix. When added to common words makes them proper names.

Lakol wicoȟ'an   The Indian way; the Indian religion.

Lakota   The native word for Teton, Indian, "western Sioux"; the term for the language spoken by them.

locin   To be hungry.

logute   Hollow of the flank of a man or animal.

loȟe   Flabby part of the cheeks or throat.
loigni   To hunt food.
lolicupi   Rations.
loliȟ'an   To prepare food.
lolo   Soft, tender, moist, flabby, fleshy.
lolobya   To boil until tender.
lolopetun   To buy groceries.
lolopiye   Bag for storing meat.
lote   Throat.
lotku   Flesh under the chin, the "double" chin.
lowan   To sing.
lowanpi   A sing, a ritual, particularly one dominated by singing.
lowans'a wicaša   Male singer.
lowitaya   Fresh, raw, as meat.
loyake   Fresh (as opposed to dried) meat.
maka   Earth; according to Walker, a type of *wakan ankatu;* one of Wakantanka's sixteen aspects.
maka ina   Mother earth; in Lakota cosmology, the source of all growing things.
makakagapi   Mellowed earth; lit., 'they make it from earth'; the earthen altar found in the *yuwipi* ritual, usually made from earth found around mole burrows.
makakan   Sacred word for earth.
maške   Friend, chum; a term used by females for other females.
masopiye   Store.
mato ihanblapi   Bear dreamers.
mato kaga   Bear performance.
mato lowanpi   Bear ritual.
mato wapiye   Bear doctor.
mato wohanpi   Bear feast.
maza   Iron; metal.
mazacanku   Railroad; train; lit., 'iron road'.
mazaska   Money.
maza wakan   Gun; lit., 'sacred iron'.
mila hanska   American; lit., 'long knife'.
mitak' oyas'in   A contraction of *mitakuye oyas'in* 'all my rela-

tions', a formulaic utterance that concludes a number of ritual acts, particularly in the sweat lodge and in the *yuwipi* ritual.

mniwakan   Whiskey; lit., 'sacred water'.

nagi   An aspect of "soul"; attenuated form of *wanagi;* according to Walker, a type of *wakanlapi;* one of Wakantanka's sixteen aspects.

nagila   "Ghost-like"; according to Walker, a type of *wakanlapi;* one of Wakantanka's sixteen aspects.

nagoya   To scratch, i.e., record, a song.

naȟlaȟla   To jingle bells with the feet.

napopela   Motorcycle.

ni   Breath, life; one of the four aspects of "soul"; evidence that an essence exists.

nide   Sacred word for water.

niya   Attenuated form of *woniya* 'breath, life'; according to Walker, a type of *wakanlapi;* one of Wakantanka's sixteen aspects.

num   Attenuated form of *nunpa* 'two'.

nunpa   Two.

nup   Attenuated form of *nunpa* 'two'.

oceti   Fireplace, stove; figuratively, a kin group, such as a lineage.

Oceti Šakowin   The Seven Fireplaces, the major political division of the Lakota and their antecedents.

Oglala   To scatter one's own; proper name for the largest division of the Teton.

oȟ'ankoya   Quickly.

oinikage   A sweat lodge.

okaga   Attenuated form of *itokagata* 'south'.

okile lowanpi   Hunting sing or searching ritual, conducted for the purpose of finding a lost or stolen article.

olowan   Song.

olowan kaga   To make a song, to compose a song.

olowan kin ho   Melody; lit., 'song's voice'.

olowan oyuspe   To catch a song; to learn a song.

olowan unspeic'iye   To teach oneself a song; to learn a song in a vision.

olowan unspekiya   To teach a song.

opagi   To fill a pipe with tobacco.

opagipi olowan   Filling the pipe song, usually the first song sung in a curing ceremony such as *yuwipi;* sometimes a translated 'opening song'.

ouncage   Likeness, generation.

oyate   People, nation; in sacred language, species.

oyuspe   To catch.

pan   To whine, cry; a style of singing.

patujela   A sidecar (on a railroad track).

pawankiye   To push the voice upward, the part of a song called the "second."

paza   Sacred word for wood.

peji   Grass.

Pejimignaka Wacipi   The Grass Tucked in the Belt Dance; the Grass Dance; also known as the Omaha Dance.

pejito aicamna   "It is snowing on green grass"; said when an unexpected snowstorm arrives after spring growth.

pejuta   Medicine, from *peji* 'grass' and *huta* 'root'.

pejuta wicaša   Medicine man, a man who treats patients with herbal medicines.

pejuta winyela   Medicine woman, a woman who specializes in herbal medicines.

petawata   Fire boat, i.e., riverboat.

pispiza   Prairie dog.

piyalowan   To repeat a song.

piya wiconi   Rebirth; lit., 'to live again?', live again.

piza   To squeal, as a prairie dog.

psanpsan   Swaying back and forth, as a swing.

pte   Buffalo cow.

ptecela   Short.

ptegleška   Domestic cow; lit., 'spotted buffalo cow'.

Ptehincalasanwin   White Buffalo Calf Woman, who in Lakota cosmology brought the sacred pipe and seven sacred ceremonies to the Lakota; also known as Woȟpe, Falling (Star).

pte oyate   Buffalo-cow nation, a sacred term for humans.

ša   Red.

Šaglaša   British, perhaps from some reference to the red coat, but the etymology is not clear.

šakowin   Seven.

sam iyeic'iye   To do more than required; to continue dancing after the song has stopped; to continue to drum after others have finished.

šawicaša   Sacred word for Indian; lit., 'red man'.

semni   Teenager(s).

šicun   An aspect of "soul" that is immortal; according to Walker, a type of *wakanlapi;* one of Wakantanka's sixteen aspects.

sinte   Tail; the coda of a dance song.

sinteȟla   Rattlesnake.

šiyo   Prairie chicken.

šiyotanka   Whistle, flageolet.

ska   White.

škan   Sacred word for *takuškanškan* (q.v.); according to Walker, a type of *wakan ankatu;* one of Wakantanka's sixteen aspects.

škanškan   Reduplication of *škan* (q.v.).

skawicaša   Sacred word for white man; lit., 'white man'.

šni   Negative enclitic, 'not'.

šungakanyanka   To ride a horse.

šungbloka   Stallion.

šungicakce   Currycomb.

šungicapsinte   Quirt.

šungicaške   Picket pin.

šungikan   Lariat.

šunginaȟtake   Spurs.

šungipaȟte   Bridle.

šungkoyagya   To rope a horse.

šungleška   Pinto.

šungluzahan   Race horse.

šungmahetu   Underground dog, i.e., wolf.

šungmanitu   Wolf.

šungmanitu kaga   The wolf performance.

šungonajin   Horse barn, stable.

šungwinyela   Mare.

šunka   Dog.

šunka pa aokawingapi olowan   Retreat from the dog head song, a segment of the kettle dance performed by the spirits in the *yuwipi* ritual.

šunkawakan   Horse; lit., 'sacred dog'.

ta   Attenuated form of the suffix *yata* 'toward'.

taȟca   Deer.

taȟcašunkala   Lamb, a missionary interpretation.

taku   Something.

takuškanškan   Something that moves; a force that approximates the notion of a creative life force, the energy behind things that move. In Lakota cosmology, a god who directs the creation of the earth and makes the wind blow.

taku wakan   Something sacred; collectively, the sacred, all things sacred; according to Walker, a division of Wakantanka comprising the *wakan kuya* and *wakanlapi.*

talo   Meat.

tanka   Large, great, big.

tankinkinyan   Important.

takoja   Grandchild; grandchildren.

tanyan kinapewaye   "I sent it home out well," a statement made in a *yuwipi* song meaning that the objective of the ritual was accomplished.

tatang gnaškiyan   Crazed, enraged buffalo, a legendary beast that attacks humans and that when killed contains a large, frothy bolus in its stomach.

tatanka   Buffalo bull; according to Walker, a type of *wakan kuya;* one of Wakantanka's sixteen aspects.

tatanka kaga   Buffalo performance.

tate   Wind; in Lakota cosmology, the father of the four winds (Tate); according to Walker, a type of *wakan kolaya;* one of Wakantanka's sixteen aspects.

tatekan   Sacred word for wind.

tate tob   A variant of *tobtob* (q.v.); according to Walker, a type of *wakan kuya;* one of Wakantanka's sixteen aspects.

tatetopakiya olowan   Four winds song; lit., 'song toward the four winds', which invites the spirits to enter a sacred area, such as the *yuwipi* ritual.

t'elanuns'e   Generic term for lizard.

t'inze   Firm, tight.

to   Blue; green.

tob   Attenuated form of *topa* 'four'.

tobtob   In sacred language the sixteen aspects of and a synonym for Wakantanka; lit., 'four times four'.

tokahe   First; the first man.

ton   Variant spelling of *tun*.

topa   Four.

tun   To be born, to give rise to, to produce; one of the four aspects of "soul"; potentiality.

tunkan   A small stone, especially the kind used for a *wašicun tunkan* (q.v.).

tunkašila   Grandfather; also used in formally addressing Wakantanka (as "Ho Tunkašila Wakantanka") and a medicine man.

Tunkašila Inktomi   Grandfather Inktomi, a form of address to the Inktomi helpers to ensure that only they will come to a ritual; the chief Inktomi; the embodiment of all Inktomi attributes.

tunkašila ukiye   "The grandfathers are coming," a sacred phrase meaning that a storm is coming.

tunsweca   Generic term for dragonfly.

tuntun   Reduplication of *tun* (q.v.).

tuntunšni   Absence of potentiality (see *tun*).

ukiye   To cause to come.

Unk   Attenuated variant of Inktomi (q.v.).

unpan   Female elk.

unšike   Pitiable.

unšila   To consider pitiable.

unspe   To know; to have learned something.

unspeic'iye   To learn; lit., 'to teach oneself'.

unspekiya   To teach.

waapapi   Things struck with the hands; drums; the ethnomusicologist's "membranophones."

wacilowan   Any kind of dance song.

wacipi   Generic term for dance.

wagmu   Gourd.

wagmuha   Rattle.

waȟtelašni   To consider·as evil; to dislike.

wahununpa   Beings that walk on two legs, human beings; a class of things that breathe; a variant of *hununpa*.

wahutopa   Beings that walk on four legs, animals; a class of things that breathe.

wakan   Sacred, holy, mysterious, awesome.

wakan ankatu   Superior *wakan;* according to Walker, one of two subdivisions of *wakan kin,* the other being *wakan kolaya* (q.v.); in turn this subdivision comprises *wi, škan, maka,* and *inyan.*

wakangli   Sacred word for lightning.

wakanheja   Children.

wakanheja kin wakanpelo   "Children are sacred," a saying.

wakanic'ilapi   Medicine men and women; lit., 'they consider themselves sacred'.

wakaniglawapi   Medicine men and women, lit., 'they count themselves among the sacred'.

wakaniye   Sacred language employed by medicine men in philosophical discussions about religion.

wakan kaga   Sacred performance, performer; a class of public performance in which visions are enacted.

wakan kin   The Sacred; according to Walker, one of two subdivisions of Wakantanka, the other being *taku wakan* (q.v.). *Wakan kin* is subdivided into *wakan akatu* and *wakan kolaya* (q.v.).

wakan kolaya   Kindred *wakan;* according to Walker, one of two subdivisions of *wakan kin* (q.v.); in turn this subdivision comprises *hanwi, tate, woȟpe,* and *wakinyan.*

wakan kuya   Subordinate *wakan;* according to Walker, one of two subdivisions of *taku wakan* (q.v.); in turn, this subdivision comprises *tatanka, hununpa, tatetob,* and *yumni.*

wakanla   To consider or regard as sacred.

wakanlapi   *Wakan*-like; according to Walker, one of two subdivisions of *taku wakan* (q.v.); in turn, this comprises *nagi, niya, nagila,* and *šicun.*

wakan oyate   Sacred nation; the sum total of all animals, birds, human beings and inanimate objects that help a medicine man or medicine woman.

Wakantanka   Variously translated as Great Spirit, Great Mystery, Most Sacred, and, by Christians, God. Wakantanka is a single appellation for sixteen supernatural aspects also called *tobtob* (q.v.).

Wakan Tanka   Variant spelling of Wakantanka.

Wa-kan-tan-ka   Variant spelling of Wakantanka.

Wakantanka Taȟcašunkala Cincala   Missionary interpretation, Lamb of God.

"Wakantanka unšimala ye"   "Wakantanka pity me, a formulaic phrase heard in prayers and songs.

wakan wacipi   Sacred word for sacred dance, also known in the literature as "mystery dance."

wakan wicoȟ'han   Sacred word for sacred rituals, ceremonies.

wakanyan   Sacredly.

wakasotešni   Sacred word for indestructible things; lit., 'impossible to deplete'; the white man's world.

wakinyan   Thunder beings; the thunderbird, symbolized by lightning and thunder; a Lakota god who brings forth rain and rids the world of filth; an avatar of the west wind; along with *inyan*, the rock, the parent of Inktomi and Iya; birds; a class of things that fly; according to Walker, a type of *wakan kolaya*, one of Wakantanka's sixteen aspects.

wakinyan agli   "Thunder beings are coming home," a sacred phrase meaning that a storm is coming.

wakinyan etunwanpi   "Thunder beings are glaring"; a sacred term for lightning.

wakinyan hotunpi   "Thunder-beings are sounding" or "making a noise"; a sacred term for thunder.

wakinyan ihanblapi   Thunder-being dreamers.

wakinyan oyate   Thunder-being nation; the total number of helpers from the west represented by lightning and thunder who often manifest themselves as giant human beings riding horses and whose faces are covered with black hoods.

wakinyan ukiye   "Thunder beings are coming," a sacred phrase meaning that a storm is coming.

wakinyan wayaka   Thunder-being slaves; people who have been killed by lightning who appear in visions being driven by the *wakinyan oyate* on leashes of lightning.

Wakonda   Omaha Indian equivalent of Wakantanka.

wamakaškan   Animals; lit., 'those who move about the earth'.

wamakaškan oyate   The animal nation, the sum total of all animals in the universe.

wamniomni   Whirlwind, dust devil; the youngest brother of the four winds.

wanagi   Ghost, an aspect of soul which remains near the earth after a person's death; a medicine man's helper; a shade.

wanagi kiglapi   "The spirits depart," the segment of the *yuwipi* ritual in which the spirits leave to go home.

wanagi tacanku   Ghost road, a term given to the Milky Way, which is viewed as campfires of the departed.

wanbli   Generic term for eagle.

wanbligleška   Immature bald eagle, lit., 'spotted eagle'; the messenger of Wakantanka who carries prayers of medicine men and common people upward.

wanbli oyate   Eagle nation, eagle species, all eagles.

wanbli wowaš'ake   Eagle power, a term indicating that a medicine man derives his supernatural powers from the eagle.

wankata   High.

wankatuya   Up above.

wanunyanpi   Offering, particularly offering of colored cloth used in the *yuwipi* ritual, the sun dance, and the vision quest, left on hills for the spirits.

wapiyapi   Plural form of *wapiye* (q.v.).

wapiye   Curer, a person who renews a patient; doctor.

wapiye olowan   Curing song, sung when a patient is being doctored by a medicine man.

wapiye wakan   Sacred curer, another name for a *wapiye winyan* (q.v.).

wapiye wicaša   Curing man, one who cures patients by supernatural means.

wapiye winyan   Curing woman, one who cures by supernatural means.

wapoštan   Hat.

wašicu   Variant of *wašicun* (q.v.).

wašicun   Generic term for white man.

wašicun tunkan   Sacred word for sacred stones, particularly a small, translucent, hemispherical stone found near an anthill that is placed in a small buckskin bag and invested with a protective spirit helper.

wašin   Bacon.

waslohan   Things that crawl; snakes; a class of things that breathe.

wayabupi   Tuba; trombone.

wayajopi   Things played by blowing; the ethnomusicologist's "aerophones."

wayuȟlaȟlapi   Things rattled with the hands; rattles; the ethnomusicologist's "idiophones."

wayukize   Things played on strings; lit., 'things that are made to squeak'; the ethnomusicologist's "chordophones."

wazi   Pine tree.

waziyata   North; lit., 'the place of pines'.

wi   Sun, moon; *anpetu wi* (daylight *wi*) is the sun; *hanhepi wi* (dark or shadowy *wi*) is the moon; according to Walker, a type of *wakan ankatu;* one of Wakantanka's sixteen aspects.

wicaglata   Responders; female singers.

wicaȟmunga   Wizard, a male evil doer.

wicaho   Voice.

wicaho hukuciyela   Low tones, notes.

wicaho oegnake   Scale; a series of notes.

wicaho oyuspe   Tape or wire recorder.

wicaho wankatuya   High tones, notes.

wicakan   Old people; the older generation; elders.

wicakicopi olowan   Calling song; lit., 'they call them'; another term for *tatetopakiya olowan* (q.v.) inviting the spirits to attend the ritual.

wicanagi   Generic term for ghosts, frequently translated as soul.

wicanagi gluhapi   Ghost keeping, a ceremony that frees a bound spirit approximately one year after a person has died.

wicapaȟtepi   "They tie them," referring to the segment of the *yuwipi* ritual in which the *yuwipi* man is wrapped in a blanket and bound.

wicape wacipi   Fork or Spear Dance, the final dance of the Kettle Dance, in which choice morsels of dog are speared from the kettle by the dancers.

wicaša   Man.

wicaša wakan   Medicine man; lit., 'sacred man'. A generic term for all men who mediate between common people and supernaturals.

wicayujujupi   "Untying," the segment of the *yuwipi* ritual in which the *yuwipi* man is untied by the spirits.

wicayutecakiyapi   Rehabilitation; lit., 'they make them new'.

wicite   Face, particularly the face drawn on the *makakagapi* by the *yuwipi* man that represents his patient.

wicoȟ'an   Deed, act, ceremony, ritual, way.

wicoȟ'an wakan   Sacred ceremonies.

wigmunke   Rainbow; lit., 'trap (that holds back the rain)'.

wiȟmunga   Witch; female evildoer.

wikan   Sacred word for sun.

winkte   Male transvestite; lit., 'would-be woman'.

winyan   Woman.

winyan wakan   Generic term for sacred woman, medicine woman.

witunšni   Sacred word for liar.

wiwanyang wacipi   Sun Dance.

wiyohiyanpata   East; lit., 'the sun comes in and arrives'.

wiyoȟpeyata   West; lit., 'the sun falls off (the earth).

wocaje   Name, kind, class, type; songs sung with meaningful texts.

wocekiye   Prayer.

wocekiye olowan   Prayer song, a class of songs sung in the sweat lodge and *yuwipi* ritual.

woecun   Doings, happening, celebration, ceremony.

wohanpi   Feast.

woȟpe   Falling star, the daughter of the sun and moon who in Lakota cosmology becomes the White Buffalo Calf Woman; according to Walker, a type of *wakan kolaya*, one of Wakantanka's sixteen aspects.

woiglakapi   Vow, pledge.

wosna   To blow out a candle.

wounspe   Lesson; teaching.

wowahtani   Evil, badness; missionary translation of "sin."

wowakan   Sacredness.

wowaš'ake   Power, strength.

wowicala   Belief.

yabu   To growl while singing.

yagopa   To make a sucking noise as in the *hohu iyapa* (q.v.).

yahla   To make the voice rattle.

yahmun   To hum.

yahogita   To become hoarse from singing.

yahtaka   To bite.

yahwa   To bore (cause boredom) by speaking.

yaignuni   To confuse by interrupting a conversation.

yaiha   To make laughter by talking.

yainila   To silence one by speaking.

yaiyowaza   To trail the voice, a type of female singing.

yajo   To play a wind instrument; to sing like a bird; to whistle through the lips.

yajoho   The sound of a whistle, flageolet.

yaka   To tell, mean.

yala hwo?   "Are you going to ask for things?" Said to those who want to make offerings in a ritual.

yanpa   Attenuated form of *wiyohiyanpata* 'east'.

yaotanin   To make public in speech or song.

yapizapi   Mouth organ.

yaptan   To change the tune, song.

yašna   To sing incorrectly; to blunder in song.

yaštan   To finish speaking, end the song.

yata   To chew.

yata   Suffix 'toward'.

yata   Attenuated form of *waziyata* 'north'.

yatkan   To drink.

yatokca   To alter, modify, change a song.

yatun   To sing out; to compose.

yawankicu   To begin or lead a song.

yazilya   To sing slowly, drawl.

yeya   To cause to go; to send.

yucancan To shake with the hand, to rattle.

yuȟlaȟla To rattle, to make a rattling sound.

yuilepi Modern word for a match; lit., 'to make something blaze by hand'.

yumni Attenuated form of *wamniomi* (q.v.); according to Walker, a type of *wakan kuya;* one of Wakantanka's sixteen aspects.

yupesto To sharpen, used to describe a sharp attack in singing.

yuš'a To make a sound like that of rubbing one's finger around the rim of a glass; used in describing sustenato in singing.

yušna To extinguish a light.

yusupi Tremolo drumming; lit., 'to make the sound of hail with the hands'.

yutokanl To put in another place (far away).

yuwakan To render sacred, to bless.

yuwipi Lit., to roll up like a ball of yarn.

Yuwipi lowanpi A curing ritual; a meeting in a darkened room in which the medicine man is wrapped and bound.

Yuwipi olowan *Yuwipi* song; a generic classification for all songs sung in the *yuwipi* ritual.

Yuwipi wicaša A man who performs the *yuwipi* ritual.

zintkala oyate Bird nation; bird species; all species of birds.

zuzeca kaga Snake performance, particularly in the *sungmanitu kaga* (q.v.).

NOTES

Introduction

1. See particularly Hymes (1965, 1970) and Hymes, ed. (1964). Gumperz's work on linguistic communities (1970) which is analogous to Hymes's notion of speech community. A number of authors working in American Indian communities are identified with the ethnography of speaking, or somehow employ native language theory in their research. Among the most outstanding works, in my opinion, are those of Basso (1970, 1976, 1979), Gill (1981), Tedlock (1972), Tedlock and Tedlock (1975), and Witherspoon (1977), although this list is certainly not exhaustive. Hymes's own fieldwork continues to elucidate the ongoing problems and their solutions in sociolinguistic as well as ethnopoetics, and in this regard his analysis of North Pacific coast poems (1965) is a milestone.

2. Most of the Lakota-speakers I interviewed are from the Pine Ridge Reservation, in South Dakota, where I have done fieldwork for thirty-six years. The Oglala Sioux Tribe is the official and legal name of the Lakota of Pine Ridge despite the fact that "Sioux" is considered derogatory. The term Lakota has become increasingly popular as a substitute, and there is some indication that "Sioux" will be officially dropped in the near future. For example, in 1983 the Oglala Sioux Community College changed its name to Oglala Lakota College, and the name of the newspaper serving all Lakota reservations is called appropriately the *Lakota Times*.

3. In particular, see my *Oglala Religion* (1977). Chapter 6 devotes several pages to the process of becoming a medicine man (pp. 59–63).

4. For a synthesis of ritual language, see Malefijt (1968, 204–8). Eliade discusses what he terms "secret language" and "animal language" with respect to shamanism, suggesting that even where such languages are not found "traces of it are to be found in incomprehensible refrains that are repeated during seances" (1964, 96–99). But of course there is no evidence of this. Further, in writing about the Okipa ceremony, Bowers tells us:

The songs, chants, and rituals were conducted by men who by virtue of their inheritance and purchase had acquired (a) right, but the words were unintelligible to the population at large, being, according to tradition, in an ancient Nuptadi dialect. Only the legitimate officers understood their meaning, and that information was never divulged to another except when purchase was being made into the ceremony. The few phrases recognized, such as "Corn Mother" and "Thunder Father," were insufficient to understand the substance of the rites. [Bowers 1950, 111]

Radin (1957, 329) stated that among the Oglala the theological system is "definitely and consciously confined to the priests and is clothed in ceremonial language known only to them." Radin's evaluation was based largely on the earlier work of James R. Walker, which he highly regarded but recognized as containing "inconsistencies and contradictions" (p. 333). Reichard (1950, 533–34) also considered ceremonial language which she regarded as too pretentious to include in her Navajo research "for it involves first the careful presentation of the ordinary language; it is impossible to judge what is extraordinary when we do not even know what is ordinary." Nevertheless she included fourteen common Navajo terms and their ceremonial equivalents. Finally, in some rituals the incomprehensibility of sacred language is partly owing to certain paralinguistic features, such as word distortion or singing phrases that are normally spoken but in such a way as to distinguish the textual presentation from true song. On this latter point of paralinguistics, see Halliday et al. 1970, 156–57.

    5. In writing about North American sodalities, Driver (1961, 424) states that "Most of the rituals are chanted in unison by the entire company, and some contain archaic words, phrases, and even entire sentences which no member can translate." Unfortunately, like others, Driver provides no data for such a bold speculation and one wonders what these archaic terms might be.

    6. For example, see Nida (1966).

    7. Number symbolism has been discussed in the past by many scholars. See, for example, Brinton (1894), Buckland (1895), and Crawley (1897), among others.

    8. Newman (1964) has discussed the exclusivity and high status assigned to speakers of ritual language among the Zuni.

Chapter 1

    1. However, Lévy-Bruhl continues to inspire a number of anthropologists such as Douglas (1966, 1970) and Needham (1972). See also

my modification of Lévy-Bruhl's notion of "appurtenances" in chapter 2.

2. Although not an article on linguistics as such, Marla N. Powers (1980) employs a Van Gennepian framework to demonstrate *inter alia* the relationship between female reproduction and Lakota terms for stages of an individual's sexual development.

3. This is not to say that some vocables (as I prefer to call them) do not have some semantic range. However, Halpern (1976) goes too far when she ascribes all vocables to archaic language. This is also not to say that vocables lack structure. On this latter point see Frisbie (1980), Hymes (1965), and Powers (1979).

4. The term "Sioux," although once popular, is recognized as derogatory. It is a French corruption of the Ojibwa term for the Dakota whom they called "little snakes." On this corruption see Densmore (1918) and Powers (1977).

5. In Lakota, *hununpa* 'two-legged' and *hutopa* 'four-legged'.

6. See in particular Walker (1917, 1980, and 1982). Walker's material also served as a basis for discussion in Radin's work on religion and philosophy (Radin 1957, 1937). For a discussion of Walker's life and general contributions to anthropology, see DeMallie's introductions to Walker (1980, 1982).

7. The editors have retained Walker's original orthography where *on = un*, *x = š*, and *r = ȟ*. The phrase *mni wakanta najin kin* should be *mni wakanya najin kin* if the translation is to hold. However, it could also be *mni wankata najin kin* 'water standing above', i.e., 'rain'. Later the phrase beginning *cuwita tanmahel ...* should end *... owakita kin lena e kayeš ko iyecetu šni kin*. Walker was not fluent in Lakota and frequently separated words erroneously.

8. For a description of a Yuwipi, and a translation of an entire *hanbloglaka* recorded by the late Oglala medicine man, George Plenty Wolf, see Powers (1982).

9. With respect to the fact that the meadowlark speaks the "truth," see Beckwith (1930), as well as Lévi-Strauss's lengthy discussion and analysis of the meaning of the meadowlark in several American Indian myths (1978, chapter 2).

10. For an explanation of the cyclical visit and the original and translation of a brief but related myth see Marla N. Powers (1982).

11. For an analysis of these terms see Powers (1977).

12. It should be noted here that the initial phoneme of *kan* as it appears in these terms is aspirated (/k'/) also refers to old things, e.g., *wicakan* 'old people'.

Chapter 2

1. This chapter is based on a paper presented at the meeting of the Society for Ethnomusicology held in Philadelphia in 1978. The

paper was subsequently published in 1980 as "Oglala Song Terminology," in Charlotte Heth, ed., *Selected Reports in Ethnomusicology*
vol. 3, no. 2, pp. 23–41, 1980. It appears here with permission and in
a slightly revised form.

2. Since this was written, musical ethnotheory has been the subject of several excellent works by Feld on the Kaluli (1982 inter alia)
and by Zemp (1978) on the 'Are'Are. These deal with the manner in
which these people verbalize and theorize about their own musical
systems.

3. Implicitly, one could construct an ethnotheory of Oglala
speech, but that is beyond the scope of this book.

4. The sound of the flageolet is said to have mystical origins. It is
associated with the elk, believed to exercise great sexual control over
females. On the myth of the origin of the courting flute see Blish and
Amos Bad Heart Bull (1967). On the relationship between flageolet
songs and love songs see Powers (1980). Standing Bear (1933) gives a
delightful account of the courtship practices of the Oglala when he
was young.

5. One could perhaps argue then that the Oglala are as capable of
classifying the musical instruments of the world as are ethnomusicologists, at least at this level of taxonomy.

Chapter 3

1. Yuwipi is not the only kind of ritual held in a darkened room.
However, the term has become popular at Pine Ridge and other reservations as a generic term for similar rituals classified by the Lakota
as *lowanpi* 'sings' or 'rituals'. For a clarification of nomenclature related to rituals see Powers (1982, "An Anthropological View").

2. There are a number of similar structural features in both Yuwipi
and the Sweat Lodge. For example, both rituals are conducted in
darkness, and it is anticipated that spirits will enter and commune
with the adepts in each of these rituals. Curing may also be done in
the Sweat Lodge, and as recently as 1984, at least one medicine man
at Pine Ridge has conducted a complete curing ritual in the Sweat
Lodge. Finally, songs learned in the Vision Quest are appropriate for
both rituals.

3. *Segue* is a term used in musical theater to indicate a form of
musical presentation in which a performer sings two (or more) songs
in succession without rest between them.

4. There are no texts in the first rendition, which is sung with
vocables only.

5. In the myth, the North Wind is born first but relinquishes his
birthright to the West Wind. For a lengthy description of the an-
thropomorphic relationship between the winds, see Walker (1917).
For an analysis of the Four Winds see Powers (1977).

6. When speaking English, Lakota prefer "doctoring" over "curing." Local white people also use the same expression.

7. The term "pot dance" is also used. When I was a boy I had the good fortune to participate in a Kettle Dance at Oglala, South Dakota, in the summer of 1949. I saw the dance at celebrations through the 1950s. It was also performed at the Gallup Inter-tribal Ceremonials by Lakota performers from Pine Ridge, but lately it seems to have been discontinued. The dance itself is secular in nature, having been diffused from the Pawnee via the Omaha during the mid-nineteenth century as part of the Grass Dance complex. Parts of the Lakota version of the dance, however, were regarded as sacred, and still are. Wallis (1947) provides an exhaustive ethnography of *Heyoka* rituals in which the Kettle Dance figures prominently.

8. These little people are described as being about three feet tall and they wear breech cloths and mocassins. They have long hair, their bodies are daubed with clay, and they carry small bows and arrows. Old Lakota cosmology constantly refers to little people and to giants. For example the *canotila* (also *canotidan*) of earlier myths are forest spirits of diminutive proportions. Similarly, the *Heyoka* "god" appears as a giant among the Dakota (Eastman 1962, Riggs 1869). The Lakota provide no native exegesis for the presence of either, but for an interesting philosophical discussion of diminution and exaggeration, see Lévi-Strauss (1966, 22–27).

9. Like their human counterparts, the spirits of animals and birds are also miniature. Frequently their diminutive tracks are discovered on the mellowed earthen altar.

Chapter 4

1. In particular, see the works of Rev. Eugene Buechel, S.J., who translated Bible stories (1924), wrote a grammar (1939), and collected materials later published posthumously as a dictionary (1970) and an anthology of myths (1978).

2. Durkheim (1915), Evans-Pritchard (1965), and Leach (1954).

3. Mauss compared *wakan* to *mana*, calling them both a "power-milieu" (1972, 115–16). Durkheim regarded *wakan* as the "Sioux" counterpart of totemism (1915, 224fn). He stated that the *wakan* "comes and goes through the world, and sacred things are points upon which it alights" (pp. 228–29), a point later reiterated by Lévi-Strauss who compares Dakota metaphysics with Bergsonian philosophy (Lévi-Strauss 1963c, 98).

4. In Tedlock and Tedlock (1975). Here the authors draw upon the published works of Joseph Epes Brown on Black Elk (1954) and Walker's interviews with Sword, Finger, One Star, and Thomas Tyon (Walker 1917). Brown, Walker, and John G. Neihardt (1961) have become the foremost interpreters of Oglala religion. Black Elk has

become famous mainly through the works of Neihardt and Brown, resulting in a rash of literature which transcends all academic disciplinary lines. Black Elk in particular has become famous in the United States and in Europe largely owing to these interpretations. Ironically, if one were to look for native shamanic heroes, that is, those religious leaders regarded highly by the Lakota themselves, Black Elk would not rank very high. Among older traditionalists, the medicine man Horn Chips is unequivocally attributed with saving and promulgating Lakota religion when it was being challenged by the white man. Among the younger generation, Frank Fools Crow is unquestionably the leading Oglala medicine man. Most Oglala, however, do not see medicine men in any historical light. They are to be revered and followed only as long as they demonstrate their power through healing and their ability to mediate between Indian and white cultures.

5. By "proper" I mean a ritual lasting for one to two hours in which the medicine man is wrapped up in a quilt and tied.

6. These are rarely conducted now for fear that a medicine man successful in finding lost articles may in fact turn up stolen property and have to deal with the local police. This would be particularly embarrassing if the thief turned out to be a relative of the medicine man, who would be obliged to protect his relative.

7. These stones are frequently worn or carried by believers and may be addressed in prayer during times of danger or distress. See the chapter on "Sacred Stones" in Powers (1982).

8. The term "ritual status" was first used by Radcliffe-Brown (1952) enabling him to "scientifically" explain transformations not in terms of sacred or profane but simply in terms of change in an individual's or object's status.

9. Stephen R. Riggs offers an alternate explanation, one which is quite controversial, and to my knowledge, one that has never been adequately argued. He states:

> It has been a debated question whether the *Wa-kán-tan-ka* is the ancient and true God, from whose worship the Dakotas have elapsed, or a recent creation to fill up their list of divinities. The latter seems to be the true idea. The name itself is proof of this. It is not a primitive, but a derived form. [Riggs 1869, 72]

He then goes on to compare Wakantanka with other forms such as *sunkawakan* 'horse' and *mazawakan* 'gun', suggesting that all innovations brought by the white man were simply designated *wakan*, including the white man's god which was simply referred to as Wakantanka, because, as Riggs (1869, 73) says, "what is more natural than that they should give expression to the corresponding greatness of the white man's god, in comparison with their own *wakan*, by calling him the *Great Wakan?*" Whatever the history, contemporary Lakota refer to Wakantanka as the superior diety, one comparable to Creator God.

10. This may have happened even if it was inspired by Christianity. The point is that today traditional Lakota regard *Wakantanka* as the primary supernatural.

11. Another overlooked meaning of Wakantanka is that of Wallis, who rather casually translates it as "most *wakan*" (Wallis 1919, 323). Although his work deals with Wahpetun from Minnesota who fled to Canada after the 1862 massacre, much of his information on the Sun Dance and other aspects of Wahpetun obtain well for the Lakota. Wallis, an excellent ethnographer, has been sadly neglected by most Siouanists. His prose is lucid, and his analogies frequently are filled with surprises. To wit, in speaking of sacred stones he writes in a footnote that "The Indians use the stone for power. So do the white men; of it they build the houses that last the longest" (p. 325). Since Wallis does not attribute this footnote to any of his respondents, one must conclude that this is his own sentiment.

12. After Walker (1917). See also DeMallie and Lavenda 1977, 155–56 and Powers 1977, 170–71.

Chapter 5

1. Much of this chapter is inspired by the works of de Saussure (1959); Douglas (1966, 1970); Leach (1976) and Lévi-Strauss (1963b, 1966, 1981). Elsewhere (Powers 1977) I have provided a detailed analysis of the use of sacred numbers as a means of structuring Oglala reality, and I have written a more technical account of the effect of numerical systems on the central nervous system (Powers 1986).

2. On numerically based configurations and the relationship between numbers and geometric shapes, see the article by Mansfield on sacred mandalas (1981) as well as my comment (Powers 1981).

3. On the sacredness of the number three, see the witty and amusing article by Dundes (1968).

4. The relationship between numerical systems and the structuring of reality is a major theme of the French sociological tradition, particularly Durkheim and Mauss's work on primitive classification (1963). One chapter titled "Zuni, Sioux" makes the point that both tribes divided the world in such a way that it is analogous to the manner in which they structure their society into clans, and that these divisions are underscored by numbers, colors, animal, and bird symbols. When they speak of "Sioux" however (as is true with Durkheim and Lévi-Strauss in other works) they are rarely speaking about the Dakota and Lakota. In one instance in the above-cited

work, the authors even go so far as to make the claim that the Dakota do not classify their world into quarters, which of course is an error. Instead they see a resemblance between Dakota and Chinese classificatory systems.

5. The most frequently cited reference to the number four in Lakota thought is a small section called "The Number Four" by Thomas Tyon in Walker (1977).

6. For the extent to which the number seven persists over time as a significant organizing principle of political organization, see Powers (1977).

7. Black Elk gives a vivid symbolic analysis of the sacred circle through Brown (1954) and Neihardt (1961).

8. On the concept of soul in North America see the work of Hultkranze (1953). Lévy-Bruhl also discusses the concept of four souls (1966).

9. Amiotte has recently written an interesting account of concept of soul (1982), but I think he confuses the "fourth" soul with some speculations of Walker calling it *nagila* instead of *tun*. Lévi-Strauss also uses Walker as a source for some speculations on the number four (1978:350). Eliade (1964) calls upon the earlier works of the missionary Pond (1867) for a discussion of ideas about reincarnation found among Dakota medicine men.

10. For example, both Dorsey (1894) and Fletcher (1884) describe color symbolism differently from the one described here. There is no reason to believe, however, that color systems themselves are static.

11. To demonstrate how numerical systems can be manipulated, one needs only to refer to a speech made by a leader of the American Indian Movement (AIM). In an address before a Puerto Rican assembly at Madison Square Garden in 1974, AIM leader Russell Means described the Lakota color symbolism to his audience. He then added "And you know what you get when you mix red, black, white, and yellow together—BROWN!" The crowd responded with ecstatic approval.

Chapter 6

1. On this point of symbolic transformations related to newly introduced foods, see Powers and Powers 1984.

2. Cf. Lévi-Strauss (1949).

3. The idea of "getting into peoples' heads" through understanding their language was paramount in the teachings and research of Franz Boas, founder of American anthropology. Boas insisted that his students learn the languages of the tribes they studied, devise orthographies for them, and teach their native respondents how to

read and write their own languages. Native texts were later collected and analyzed, but a number of them have never been published.

4. Lévy-Bruhl's "pre–logical mentality" is a case in point. However, *ethno* when prefixed to acceptable scientific disciplines (ethnolinguistics, ethnopharmacology, etc.) really belies the continuation of the belief that "their" science is somehow different if not inferior to "ours."

5. See Peterson (1969) and Johnsgard (1979) for slightly differing approaches to classifying the eagle.

6. For the Lakota creation stories, see Walker (1917); for an analysis of these stories, see Powers (1977).

7. Although no systematic collection of Inktomi stories exists that is on par with, say, the Winnebago stories collected by Radin (1956), the most popular may be found in other collections, most notably those of Beckwith (1930), Deloria (1932), and Walker (1917).

8. For stories of Iya, see Walker (1917). Inktomi and Iya continue to be the subjects of contemporary Lakota oral narratives, and lately have served as source material for comical bilingual readers published by several reservation schools and community colleges.

9. Both these stories are found in Deloria (1932).

10. I have discussed the importance of Horn Chips in Powers (1982).

11. For use of Inktomi spirits in the Yuwipi ritual, see Powers (1982).

12. A named stone is given to an adept and serves as a personal helper. When in danger or distress, the Lakota calls upon the spirit of such a stone for help.

13. See Wissler (1905, 1907).

14. The seminal work here is by Mary Douglas (1966) who views certain anomalous phenomena as constituting separate classes. Sacred animals are frequently those that do not fit in with a people's normal categories. The spider serves as an exemplary case; it flies, swims, and walks on six legs, thus making it impossible to classify along traditional Lakota lines.

Chapter 7

1. The Tungus are a tribe of aboriginal people of Siberia. For more on the nature of Siberian shamanism, see Eliade (1964) and Lewis (1971).

2. Emile Durkheim (1915) in particular is frequently cited as the person responsible for raising the totemic concept to universal status. For another view, see Lévi-Strauss (1963c).

3. E. E. Evans-Pritchard was a famous British anthropologist

whose fieldwork was among the Azande (1937) and Nuer of Africa. In his terms, witchcraft is something inherited, while sorcery is something learned. These distinctions, however, do not apply to the Lakota.

4. Underhill (1965).

5. For the Chukchee, see Bogoras (1904); for the Eskimo, see Rasmussen (1929).

6. See Bogoras (1904).

7. Rasmussen (1929).

8. Wallace (1966).

9. Ibid.

10. The Andaman Islanders, who live off the coast of India, were studied by the famous British anthropologist A. R. Radcliffe-Brown (1964, 176).

11. Turnbull (1961, 228).

12. Elkin (1964, 295–307).

13. For Mesoamerica see Metzger and Williams (1963); and Shweder (1972). For Africa, Forde (1954). For Oceania, Malinowski (1961), Fortune (1932), and Firth (1936).

14. See Wallace (1966, 87–88 and 100–101).

15. One of the best treatments of this subject is Lévi-Strauss (1963b).

16. Douglas (1970, xv–xvi).

17. On this matter and other courtship practices, see Powers (1980).

18. This is my free translation of Story 109 from the Bushotter Texts written by George Bushotter, a Lakota. The collection of stories is on file at the National Anthropological Archives, Smithsonian Institution. The act of vomiting various animate and inanimate objects is a common feature of *wakan kaga*.

19. Narrated by Mrs. Little Cloud on April 7, 1915, and again by Calico on May 27, 1915, both Oglalas, to the Reverend Eugene Buechel, S.J., at Pine Ridge (Buechel 1915–1919).

20. A detailed description of *heyoka kaga* can be found in Wallis (1947). The *wakan kaga* are synonymous with "dream cults" discussed in Wissler (1912).

21. See Neill (1872).

22. Narrated by Red Feather, an Oglala, to Buechel on March 31, 1915, at Pine Ridge. (Buechel 1915–1919).

23. This ceremony is described by Densmore (1918) and Walker (1917). On symbolism related to menstruation and reproduction, see M. N. Powers (1980). The prayer was narrated by Red Feather to Buechel on April 10, 1915 (my translation) (Buechel 1915–19).

24. Narrated by Red Feather to Buechel, April 20, 1915 (Buechel 1915–19).

25. Narrated by Red Feather to Buechel, April 10, 1915 (Buechel

1915–19). It was customary to donate horses, robes, and other commodities to those who performed curing ceremonies. The term *wiši* *k'u* 'to give "payment"' refers to this exchange of service and goods. However, the term *wiši* has many connotations including contract, bargain, negotiation, bond, and fee.

26. The best works on berdache are by Callender and Kochems (1983), Forgey (1975), and Thayer (1980). A number of people responded to Callender and Kochems. See my response, and that of Åke Hultkranze for the etymology of *berdache* in the same issue.

27. On Lakota myths about *winktes*, see Hassrick (1964) and M. N. Powers (1980, 1986).

28. Feraca (1963) provides interesting backgrounds of medicine women with whom he worked at Pine Ridge.

29. For a discussion of the preparation and use of these herbal medicines, see M. N. Powers (1982).

30. This is my translation of a prayer narrated by Red Feather to Buechel, September 17, 1915 (Buechel 1915–19).

31. Wallis (1947) also has a detailed account of female *heyoka*.

BIBLIOGRAPHY

Amiotte, Arthur
1982 "Our Other Selves: The Lakota Dream Experience." *Parabola* 7(2):26–32.
Basso, Keith
1970 "To Give Up on Words: Silence in the Western Apache Culture." *Southwestern Journal of Anthropology* 26:213–30.
1976 "'Wise Words' of the Apache: Metaphor and Semantic Theory." In Basso and Selby (1976).
1979 *Portraits of "The Whiteman."* Cambridge: Cambridge University Press.
———, and Henry A. Selby, eds.
1976 *Meaning in Anthropology.* Albuquerque: University of New Mexico Press.
Beckwith, Martha W.
1930 "Mythology of the Oglala Dakota." *Journal of American Folklore* 43:339–442.
Blish, Helen H., and Amos Bad Heart Bull
1967 *A Pictographic History of the Oglala Sioux.* Lincoln: University of Nebraska Press.
Boas, Franz
1940 *Race, Language, and Culture.* New York: Free Press.
Bogoras, Waldemar
1904 "The Chukchee." In Franz Boas, ed., *The Jessup North Pacific Expedition.* Memoirs of the American Museum of Natural History, vol. 11, parts 2, 3. Leiden: E. J. Brill.
Bowers, Alfred W.
1950 *Mandan Social and Ceremonial Organization.* Chicago: University of Chicago Press.
Brinton, Daniel G.
1894 "The Origin of Sacred Numbers." *American Anthropologist* 7:168–73.
Brown, Joseph Epes
1954 *The Sacred Pipe.* Norman: University of Oklahoma Press.

Buckland, A. W.
1895   "Four as a Sacred Number." *Journal of the Anthropological Institute* 25:96–102.
Buechel, Rev. Eugene, S.J.
1915–19   *Diarium.* Copy of ledger in the archives of the Heritage Center, Inc., Holy Rosary Mission, Pine Ridge, S. D.
1924   *Bible History in Teton Sioux.* New York: Benziger Brothers.
1939   *Grammar of Lakota.* St. Louis: John S. Swift.
1970   *Lakota-English Dictionary.* Edited by Paul Manhart, S.J. Pine Ridge: Red Cloud Indian School.
1978   *Lakota Tales and Texts.* Edited by Paul Manhart, S.J. Pine Ridge: Red Cloud Indian School.
Burke, Kenneth
1961   *The Rhetoric of Religion.* Berkeley: University of California Press.
Callender, Charles, and Lee M. Kochems
1983   "The North American Berdache." *Current Anthropology* 24(4):443–70.
Cazeneuve, Jean
1972   *Lucien Lévy-Bruhl.* New York: Harper and Row. Original 1963. Colorado University Lakhota Project, Boulder.
Colorado University, Lakhota Project, Boulder
1976   *Beginning Lakhota.* Department of Linguistics, University of Colorado, Boulder.
Crawley, E. S.
1897   "The Origin and Development of Number Symbolism." *Popular Science Monthly* 51:524–34.
Deloria, Ella C.
1932   *Dakota Texts.* New York: G. E. Stechert.
DeMallie, Raymond J., and Robert J. Lavenda
1977   "*Wakan:* Plains Siouan Concepts of Power." In Raymond D. Fogelson and Richard N. Adams, eds., *The Anthropology of Power: Ethnographic Studies from Asia, Oceania, and the New World.* New York: Academic Press.
Densmore, Frances
1918   *Teton Sioux Music.* Bulletin of the Bureau of American Ethnology, no. 61. Washington, D.C.
Dorsey, J. Owen
1894   "A Study of Siouan Cults." Smithsonian Institution, Bureau of American Ethnology, *Annual Report 14,* pp. 351–544.
Douglas, Mary
1966   *Purity and Danger.* London: Routledge and Kegan Paul.
1970   *Natural Symbols.* New York: Pantheon Books.

Driver, Harold E.
1961   *Indians of North America.* Chicago: University of Chicago Press.

Dundes, Alan
1968   "The Number Three in American Culture." In Alan Dundes, ed., *Every Man His Way.* Englewood Cliffs, N.J.: Prentice-Hall.

Durkheim, Émile
1915   *The Elementary Forms of the Religious Life.* London: George Allen & Unwin. Original 1912.
———, and Marcel Mauss
1963   *Primitive Classification.* Translated and introduced by Rodney Needham. Chicago: University of Chicago Press. Original 1903.

Eastman, Mary
1962   *Dahcotah; or, Life and Legends of the Sioux Around Fort Snelling.* Minneapolis: Ross & Haines. Original 1849.

Eliade, Mircea
1958   *Rites and Symbols of Initiation.* New York: Harper Torchbooks.
1964   *Shamanism: Archaic Techniques of Ecstasy.* Princeton, N.J.: Princeton University Press.

Elkin, A. P.
1964   *The Australian Aborigines.* New York: Anchor Books. Original 1938.

Evans-Pritchard, E. E.
1937   *Witchcraft, Oracles and Magic Among the Azande.* Oxford: Clarendon Press.
1965   *Theories of Primitive Religion.* London: Oxford University Press.

Feld, Steven
1982   *Sound and Sentiment: Birds, Weeping, Poetics, and Song in Kaluli Expression.* Philadelphia: University of Pennsylvania Press.

Feraca, Stephen E.
1963   *Wakinyan: Contemporary Teton Dakota Religion.* Studies in Plains Anthropology and History, no. 2. Browning, Mont.: Museum of the Plains Indian.

Firth, Raymond
1936   *We, the Tikopia.* London: George Allen and Unwin.

Fishman, Joshua A.
1970   *Readings in the Sociology of Language.* The Hague: Mouton.

Fletcher, Alice C.
1884   "The Elk Mystery or Festival of the Ogallala Sioux." Pea-

body Museum of American Archaeology and Ethnology. *Annual Reports* 3(3, 4).

Forde, Daryll
1954   *African Worlds*. London: Oxford University Press.

Forgey, Donald G.
1975   "The Institution of Berdache Among the North American Plains Indians." *Journal of Sex Research* 11(1):1–15.

Fortune, Reo F.
1932   *Sorcerers of Dobu*. New York: E. P. Dutton.

Fowler, Loretta
1979   Review of William K. Powers *Oglala Religion*. *American Ethnologist* 6:404–406.

Frake, Charles O.
1964   *Notes on Queries in Ethnography*. Special publication, *American Anthropologist* 66(3), part 2:132–45.

Frisbie, Charlotte J.
1980   "Vocables in Navajo Ceremonial Music." *Ethnomusicology* 24(3):347–92.

Gill, Sam D.
1981   *Sacred Words: A Study of Navajo Religion and Prayer*. Westport, Conn.: Greenwood Press.

Grobsmith, Elizabeth S.
1981   *Lakota of the Rosebud*. New York: Holt, Rinehart and Winston.

Gumperz, John J.
1970   "Type of Linguistic Communities." In Fishman (1970). Originally published in *Anthropological Linguistics* 4:28–40 (1962).

Halliday, M. A. K., Angus McIntosh, and Peter Strevens
1970   "The Users and Uses of Language." In Fishman (1970). Originally published in M. A. K. Halliday, Angus McIntosh, and Peter Strevens, *The Linguistic Sciences and Language*. London: Longman, 1964.

Halpern, Ida
1976   "On the Interpretation of 'Meaningless-Nonsense Syllables' in the Music of the Pacific Northwest Indians." *Ethnomusicology* 20(2):253–71.

Hassrick, Royal B.
1964   *The Sioux*. Norman: University of Oklahoma Press.

Herskovits, Melville J.
1948   *Man and His Works*. New York: Alfred A. Knopf.

Heth, Charlotte, ed.
1980   *Selected Reports in Ethnomusicology*. Vol. 3, no. 2. Los Angeles: University of California.

Hultkranze, Äke
1953 *Conceptions of the Soul Among North American Indians.* Statens Etnografiska Museum Monograph Series. Stockholm.
Hymes, Dell
1965 "Some North Pacific Coast Poems: A Problem in Anthropological Philology." *American Anthropologist* 67(2): 316–41.
1970 "The Ethnography of Speaking." In Fishman (1970). Originally published in T. Galdwin and William C. Sturtevant, eds., *Anthropology and Human Behavior.* Washington, D.C.: Anthropological Society of Washington, 1962.
———, ed.
1964 *Language in Culture and Society.* New York: Harper and Row.
Johnsgard, Paul A.
1979 *Birds of the Great Plains.* Lincoln: University of Nebraska Press.
Langer, Susanne K.
1942 *Philosophy in a New Key.* Cambridge: Harvard University Press.
Leach, Edmund
1954 *Political Systems of Highland Burma.* Boston: Beacon Press.
1976 *Culture and Communication.* London: Cambridge University Press.
Leslie, Charles
1960 *Anthropology of Folk Religion* ed. New York: Vintage Books.
Lessa, William A., and Evon Z. Vogt
1972 *Reader in Comparative Religion: An Anthropological Approach.* 3d ed. New York: Harper and Row. Original 1958.
Lévi-Strauss, Claude
1949 *The Elementary Structures of Kinship.* Boston: Beacon Press.
1962 "Social Structure." In Sol Tax, ed., *Anthropology Today.* Chicago: University of Chicago Press.
1963a "The Structural Study of Myth." In Lévi-Strauss (1963b).
1963b *Structural Anthropology.* New York: Anchor Books.
1963c *Totemism.* Boston: Beacon Press.
1966 *The Savage Mind.* Chicago: University of Chicago Press. Original 1962.
1978 *The Origin of Table Manners.* New York: Harper and Row. Original 1968.
1981 *The Naked Man.* New York: Harper and Row. Original 1971.
Lévy-Bruhl, Lucien
1966 *The Soul of the Primitive.* Chicago: Henry Regnery. Original 1928.

Lewis, I. M.
1971   *Ecstatic Religion.* Baltimore, Md.: Penguin Books.
Malefijt, Annemarie de Waal
1968   *Religion and Culture.* New York: Macmillan.
Malinowski, Bronislaw
1961   *Argonauts of the Western Pacific.* New York: E. P. Dutton. Original 1922.
Mansfield, Victor N.
1981   "Mandalas and Mesoamerican Pecked Circles." *Current Anthropology* 22(3):269–84.
Mauss, Marcel
1972   *A General Theory of Magic.* New York: W. W. Norton. Original 1950.
Melody, Michael Edward
1977   "Maka's Story." *Journal of American Folklore* 90(356):149–67.
Merriam, Alan P.
1964   *The Anthropology of Music.* Evanston, Ill.: Northwestern University Press.
Metzger, Duane, and Gerald Williams
1963   "Tenejapa Medicine I: The Curer." *Southwest Journal of Anthropology* 19:216–34.
Needham, Rodney
1972   *Belief, Language and Experience.* Chicago: University of Chicago Press.
Neihardt, John G.
1961   *Black Elk Speaks.* Lincoln: University of Nebraska Press.
Neill, Edward D.
1872   "Dakota Land and Dakota Life." *Collections of the Minnesota Historical Society* 1:254–94.
Nettl, Bruno
1956   *Music in Primitive Culture.* Cambridge, Mass.: Harvard University Press.
Newman, Stanley
1964   "Vocabulary Levels: Zuni Sacred and Slang Usage." In Hymes (1964).
Nida, Eugene A.
1966   "Principles of Translation as Exemplified by Bible Translating." In Reuben A. Brower, ed., *On Translation.* New York: Oxford University Press.
Ogden, C. K., and I. A. Richards
1923   *The Meaning of Meaning.* New York: Harcourt, Brace & World.

Peterson, Roger Tory
1969   *Field Guide to Western Birds.* Boston: Houghton Mifflin.
Pond, Gideon H.
1867   "Dakota Superstitions." *Collection of the Minnesota Histori-cal Society* 2:36–62.
Powers, Marla N.
1980   "Menstruation and Reproduction: An Oglala Case." *Signs* 6(1):54–65.
1986   *Oglala Women: Myth, Ritual and Reality.* Chicago: Univer-sity of Chicago Press.
Powers, William K.
1970   "Songs of the Red Man." Discographic review essay. *Ethno-musicology* 14(2):358–69.
1977   *Oglala Religion.* Lincoln: University of Nebraska Press.
1979   "The Structure and Function of the Vocable." MS in au-thor's collection.
1980a   "Oglala Song Terminology." *Selected Reports in Ethno-musicology* 3(2):23–42.
1980b   "The Art of Courtship Among the Oglala." *American In-dian Art Magazine* 5(2):40–47.
1981   "On Mandalas and Native American World Views." Reply to Mansfield. *Current Anthropology* 22(4):443.
1982   *Yuwipi: Vision and Experience in Oglala Ritual.* Lincoln: Uni-versity of Nebraska Press.
1986   "Counting Your Blessings: Sacred Numbers and the Struc-ture of Reality." *Zygon.*
———, and Marla N. Powers
1984   "Metaphysical Aspects of an Oglala Food System." In Mary Douglas, ed., *Food in the Social Order.* New York: Rus-sell Sage.
1986   "Putting On the Dog." *Natural History Magazine* 95(2):6–16.
Radcliffe-Brown, A. R.
1952   *Structure and Function in Primitive Society.* New York: Free Press.
1964   *The Andaman Islanders.* New York: Free Press. Original 1922.
Radin, Paul
1937   *Primitive Religion.* New York: Viking Press.
1956   *The Trickster: A Study in American Indian Mythology.* New York: Philosophical Library.
1957   *Primitive Man as Philosopher.* New York: Dover Books. Origi-nal 1927.
Rasmussen, Knud
1929   "Intellectual Culture of the Iglulik Eskimos." In *Report of*

the Fifth Thule Expedition, 1921–24, vol. 2, no. 1. Copenhagen: Gyldendalske Boghandel, Nordisk Forlag.

Ray, Verne F.
1941   "Historic Backgrounds of the Conjuring Complex in the Plateau and the Plains." In Leslie Spier, ed., *Language, Culture, and Personality: Essays in Memory of Edward Sapir.* Menasha, Wis.: American Anthropological Association.

Red Cloud Indian School
N.d.   *Ehanni Ohunkankan.* Holy Rosary Mission, Pine Ridge, S.Dak.

Reichard, Gladys A.
1950   *Navaho Religion: A Study of Symbolism.* Princeton, N.J.: Princeton University Press.

Riggs, Stephen Return
1869   *Tah-koo Wah-kan; or, The Gospel Among the Dakotas.* Boston: Congregational Sabbath-School and Publishing Society.
1893   *Dakota Grammar, Texts, and Ethnography.* Contributions to North American Ethnology. Department of the Interior, U.S. Geographical and Geological Survey of the Rocky Mountain Region. Washington, D.C.: U.S. Government Printing Office.

Sapir, Edward
1966   *Culture, Language, and Personality: Selected Essays.* Edited by David G. Mandelbaum. Berkeley: University of California Press.

de Saussure, Ferdinand
1959   *Course in General Linguistics.* New York: McGraw-Hill. Original 1906–11.

Shweder, Richard A.
1972   "Aspects of Cognition in Zinacanteco Shamans: Experimental Results." In William A. Lessa and Evon Z. Vogt, eds., *Reader in Comparative Religion: An Anthropological Approach.* New York: Harper and Row.

Standing Bear, Luther
1933   *Land of the Spotted Eagle.* Boston: Houghton Mifflin.

Steinmetz, Rev. Paul, S.J.
1969   "Explanation of the Sacred Pipe as a Prayer Instrument." *Pine Ridge Research Bulletin* 10:20–25.

Swanton, John
1911   "Siouan." In *Handbook of North American Indian Languages.* Bulletin of the Bureau of American Ethnology, no. 40, pt. 1. Washington, D.C.

Tedlock, Dennis, trans.
1972   *Finding the Center: Narrative Poetry of the Zuni Indians.* New York: Dial Press.
————, and Barbara Tedlock
1975   *Teachings from the American Earth.* New York: Liveright.
Thayer, James Steel
1980   "The Berdache of the Northern Plains: A Socioreligious Perspective." *Journal of Anthropological Research* 36(3): 287–93.
Turnbull, Colin
1961   *The Forest People.* New York: Clarion Books.
Turner, Victor
1969   *The Ritual Process.* Chicago: Aldine.
Underhill, Ruth M.
1965   *Red Man's Religion.* Chicago: University of Chicago Press.
Van Gennep, Arnold
1908–14 *Religion, moeurs et legendes: Essais d'ethnographie et linguistique.* 5 vols. Paris: Mercure de France.
1960   *The Rites of Passage.* Chicago: University of Chicago Press. Original 1908.
Walker, J. R.
1917   "The Sun Dance and Other Ceremonies of the Oglala Division of the Teton Dakota." *Anthropological Papers of the American Museum of Natural History* 16, part 2:51–221.
1980   *Lakota Belief and Ritual.* Edited by Raymond J. DeMallie and Elaine A. Jahner. Lincoln: University of Nebraska Press.
1982   *Lakota Society.* Edited by Raymond J. DeMallie. Lincoln: University of Nebraska Press.
Wallace, Anthony F. C.
1966   *Religion: An Anthropological View.* New York: Random House.
Wallis, W. D.
1919   "The Sun Dance of the Canadian Dakota." *Anthropological Papers of the American Museum of Natural History* 16, part 4:317–80.
1947   "The Canadian Dakota." *Anthropological Papers of the American Museum of Natural History* 41, part 1:1–225.
Wissler, Clark
1905   "The Whirlwind and the Elk in the Mythology of the Dakota." *Journal of American Folk-lore* 18:257–68.
1907   "Some Protective Designs of the Dakota." *Anthropological Papers of the American Museum of Natural History* 1, part 2:21–53.

1912   "Societies and Ceremonial Associations in the Oglala Di-
        vision of Teton Dakota." *Anthropological Papers of the Ameri-
        can Museum of Natural History* 11, part 1.
Witherspoon, Gary
1977   *Language and Art in the Navajo Universe.* Ann Arbor: Uni-
        versity of Michigan Press.
Zemp, Hugo
1978   "'Are'are Classification of Musical Types and Instru-
        ments." *Ethnomusicology* 22(1): 37–67.
1979   "Aspects of 'Are'are Musical Theory." *Ethnomusicology*
        23(1): 5–48.

INDEX